THE POLITICS OF SPIRITUALITY

THE POLITICS OF SPIRITUALITY

A Study of a Renewal Process in an English Diocese

MICHAEL P. HORNSBY-SMITH
JOHN FULTON
MARGARET NORRIS

CLARENDON PRESS · OXFORD
1995

Oxford University Press, Walton Street, Oxford OX2 6DP
Oxford New York
Athens Auckland Bangkok Bombay
Calcutta Cape Town Dar es Salaam Delhi
Florence Hong Kong Istanbul Karachi
Kuala Lumpur Madras Madrid Melbourne
Mexico City Nairobi Paris Singapore
Taipei Tokyo Toronto
and associated companies in
Berlin Ibadan

Oxford is a trade mark of Oxford University Press

Published in the United States
by Oxford University Press Inc., New York

© M. P. Hornsby-Smith, John Fulton, Margaret I. Norris, 1995

British Library Cataloguing in Publication Data
Data available

Library of Congress Cataloging in Publication Data
Hornsby-Smith, Michael P.
The politics of spirituality : a study of a renewal process in an
English diocese / Michael P. Hornsby-Smith, John Fulton, Margaret
Norris.
Includes bibliographical references.
1. Catholic Church—Great Britain—History—20th century—Case
studies. 2. Spiritual formation—Catholic Church—Case studies.
3. Laity—Catholic Church—History—20th century—Case studies.
4. Sociology, Christian (Catholic)—History—20th century—Case
studies. 5. Modernism—Catholic Church—England—Case studies.
I. Fulton, John, Dr. II. Norris, Margaret, 1926- . III. Title.
BX1493.2.H 282'.41'09048—dc20 94–46384 IN PROCESS
ISBN 0–19–827776–8

1 3 5 7 9 10 8 6 4 2

Typeset by Graphicraft Typesetters Ltd., Hong Kong
Printed in Great Britain
on acid-free paper by
Biddles Ltd., Guildford and King's Lynn

With love and affection
to all the people of Downlands.

Preface

you will learn the truth
and the truth will make you free
(John 8 : 32)

In the summer of 1988 a group of social scientists in the Surrey University Religious Research Group decided to undertake an investigation of the RENEW programme which was due to commence in the Roman Catholic Diocese of Downlands in the coming October. RENEW was an American programme for parish renewal and Downlands was the first diocese in England to adopt it. As social scientists we felt a certain obligation to study this major pastoral innovation on our own patch. The three of us who pursued this study for nearly six years have all been involved, in one way or another, in the religious life and activities of this diocese. But nobody asked us to undertake the study and, apart from a small grant from an anonymous donor (to whom we extend our grateful thanks), which facilitated some interviewing in the course of our research, our study was unfunded and without sponsorship. It has been a piece of opportunistic research undertaken because, as social scientists, we believe that it is our responsibility to investigate major social processes in the society in which we live, work, and worship.

Without substantial resources we were inevitably limited in the range and types of research we could undertake. We were not, for example, in a position to set up a large survey programme. What we could do was undertake a considerable amount of participant observation in our own parishes and at deanery and diocesan events. This inevitably led us to concentrate on the processes which had led to the decision to adopt RENEW in the first place, describe the 2½-year 'process', report on the experiences of a wide range of Catholics in the diocese, and offer an account of the whole exercise of organizational renewal and revitalization.

What started out as a study of a specific pastoral innovation, however, led us in time to see our research as one example of a much wider range of attempts to revitalize religion, not only in the contemporary world, but also historically. Thus, the final outcome of our study was an attempt to conceptualize initiatives to promote different types of spiritualities. Two dimensions, in particular, emerged as having crucial importance. First, we began to see that who controls spirituality is an important consideration for its emergence and growth, or decline. Secondly, the cultural nature of the spirituality is important but extremely complex. We finally interpreted this in terms of the extent to which it aimed to address the challenges of modernity or appeal to traditional sentiments. We believe this conceptualization to be conducive to a comparative and historical analysis of spiritualities.

In the course of our research we interviewed a large number of informants. Practically none of them asked for anonymity and only occasionally were we asked to be discreet about attributing personal judgements. We owe a debt of gratitude to all those people who trusted us. However, towards the end of our research and after a number of senior clergy had protested at what they regarded as the 'negative' bias in some of our early conference papers, we decided that we would have to safeguard the identity of our informants. Thus we have used pseudonyms throughout for the diocese, bishop, priests, parishes, and laity. We have similarly changed the names of public documents, such as the diocesan and parish newsletters. Social researchers could check the use we have made of taped interviews which we have dated in the text.

We would like to thank Bishop Patrick, all four members of the diocesan RENEW team, three members of the International RE-NEW Office, and all our other respondents for so generously giving us their time and for describing their experiences and evaluations of RENEW. We are also grateful to respondents in four Scottish and one South African diocese for sending us their evaluations of RE-NEW in their own dioceses, and to those in a number of English dioceses who had considered RENEW in the mid-1980s but had decided not to adopt it. Professor James R. Kelly, from Fordham University, kindly sent us a copy of his study of RENEW in the United States. Michael Hornsby-Smith is grateful to Professor Jay Dolan for a grant which enabled him to undertake library research at the Cushwa Center, Notre Dame University in 1990.

Our grateful thanks are due to all those, too numerous to list and to most of whom we have in any case promised anonymity, without whose co-operation we could not have completed this study. In particular we wish to acknowledge the help of those people who responded so helpfully to our requests for data or who commented on various drafts.

We are much indebted to Tim Barton of Oxford University Press who encouraged our project and showed considerable tolerance and understanding when our promised deadlines twice had to be post-poned. We very much appreciated his gentle assistance and support.

Finally, each of us has benefited from the love and support of our spouses: Lennie, Anne, and Ted. To them we owe more than we can express.

M. P. H-S.

J. F.

M. N.

University of Surrey
21 May 1994

Contents

List of Figures

List of Tables

Abbreviations

CAFOD	Catholic Fund for Overseas Development
CIIR	Catholic Institute for International Relations
CNHC	Churches' National Housing Coalition
DCEC	Downlands Christian Education Centre
DPC	Diocesan Pastoral Council
DT	*Downlands Times*
NLC	National Liaison Committee of Diocesan Justice and Peace Groups
NOR	National Office of RENEW (Archdiocese of Newark)
PPC	Parish Pastoral Council
PSG	Parish Strategy Group
RCIA	Rite of Christian Initiation of Adults
YCW	Young Christian Workers

1

Research Design and Perspectives

1.1 Introduction

This book is concerned with the ways in which the renewal of
spiritualities are promoted and controlled within the Roman Catholic Church. It approaches the topic both historically and empirically.
The empirical data have been drawn from a study, over more than
five years from late 1988, of a specific renewal 'process', RENEW,
in the Diocese of Downlands in England. RENEW is a diocesan-
wide, parish-based pastoral programme which was originally developed in the United States. It has been described as a 'sponsored
process of revitalization' in mainstream Catholicism, sponsored, that
is, by the diocesan bishop and his senior clerical advisers. Thus
while this book is in one sense a case study of this process in an
English diocese in the late twentieth century, its wider concern is
with processes of renewal in the Roman Catholic Church a quarter
of a century after the Second Vatican Council (1962–5), and about
the clerical control of cultures of spirituality within Catholicism
throughout its twenty centuries' history.

The search for renewal at the level of the diocese can be seen in
a wider context as a response to the plea of the Second Vatican
Council. In calling the Council, Pope John XXIII had aimed to 'let
some fresh air into the Church' and for an *aggiornamento* or 'bringing up to date' in the changing world of the second half of the
twentieth century. Bishop Butler described this process for the Church
as a whole as:

a recovery of the original gospel, its spirit and purposes, and an adaptation
of it which will be at once faithful to the same gospel as originally given,
and suited to 'the changed conditions of the times'. It is obvious that the
primary condition of such adaptation must be that it remains within limits
laid down by the objective essence of the Christian faith and Church; while
the—sole—secondary condition will be its appropriateness to the needs of
the Church and her mission in history. (Butler, 1981: 18)

Shortly after the Council opened in October 1962, the assembled
bishops issued a message in which their aims were clearly set out:

In this assembly, under the guidance of the Holy Spirit, we wish to inquire how we ought to renew ourselves, so that we may be found increasingly faithful to the gospel of Christ. We shall take pains so to present to the men of this age God's truth in its integrity and purity that they may understand it and gladly assent to it.   (Abbott, 1966: 3–4)

They continued to proclaim a concern 'to serve our brothers' and especially the 'lowly, poor, and weak' and insisted that 'the Church . . . was not born to dominate but to serve' (Abbott, 1966: 4–5).

RENEW grew out of the response of the Archdiocese of Newark in the United States in the mid-1970s to this call from the Second Vatican Council. It originated in the attempt by two priests working independently in the spirit of the Council 'to facilitate the implementation of RCIA (the Rite of Christian Initiation of Adults) in the diocese and . . . to implement parish pastoral councils, as specified in the Code of Canon Law'. Quite independently they came to the same conclusion that before new structures or new rites could be added, it was necessary to have a renewed people and a renewed parish (Creegan, 1993: 136). It was said that RENEW took seriously the major themes of the Vatican Council's teaching about faith-sharing communities, a renewed liturgy in which lay people were actively participant, collaborative ministries between priests and lay people, and a concern for justice issues in the world.

Vatican II's ecclesiology, which views the Church as a people of God, is the ecclesiology which RENEW promotes. The people of God is specified as a community of disciples who hear the Good News, are changed by it (formed and converted), respond to it with specific action; celebrate the story and the action in sacrament, life and mission. Those 'disciples' serve in the Church and the world according to the gifts they have received from the Spirit.   (NOR 1988: 61)

The diocese in which we studied the RENEW 'process' runs from the south-western boundaries of Greater London to the English Channel coast in the south. Much of it is within easy commuting range of London but the south-coast towns have higher than average proportions of retired people. The largest town in the diocese is Southlands with a population of around 250,000. There are a number of medium sized towns, such as the cathedral town of Riverton and the town of Middleton, close to a major international airport, but the diocese also contains large rural areas. In 1988 there were around 54,000 weekly Mass attenders in the diocese which had a population of 2½ million people. The average Mass attendance in each parish in 1988 was 446 and no fewer than twenty-three of the 121 parishes had under 200 Mass attenders.

While there were pockets of poverty and deprivation and increasing numbers of homeless people in the diocese, and unemployment rates had risen more than the national average in the recession of the early 1990s, there were disproportionately large numbers in professional and managerial occupations and the diocese was in one of the most affluent areas in the country. Housing costs were high, especially in the London commuter belt.

In the mid-1980s the diocesan bishop was faced by evidence of Mass attendance rates which had declined by one-quarter in the previous twenty years, the implications of this for continuing financial support, and an ageing clerical work-force nearly one-third smaller than in the mid-1960s. Indeed on the last point, the first bishop of the diocese had written with alarm in the *Diocesan Directory*, as long ago as 1969, that 'with a developing diocese a huge shadow looms large over our heads—the shortage of priests' (1969: 13). Furthermore, a series of consultations in the diocese over the previous decade had indicated a strong demand from lay people for some form of adult religious education.

In this situation the importation of RENEW, which aimed to revitalize the religious faith and involvement of the people at the local or parish level, appeared to be one of the options available to the bishop. Those advocating such a step pointed to the advantages of 'not reinventing the wheel', and benefiting from the developments and improvements made to the programme on the basis of previous and cumulative experience. In this way the local Church would be saved the time and resource costs required to develop an appropriate pastoral programme from scratch, from the identification of the main goals to the selection of methods and the mobilization of support within the Church. Such an option would avoid divisive conflicts within the Church and perceived problems would be more speedily addressed.

Between its origin in Newark in 1976 and the summer of 1990, RENEW had been taken up by 139 dioceses world-wide. A further forty-six were scheduled to commence it during 1990–2. It could, therefore, be legitimately regarded as a significant attempt by the Church leadership to revitalize parish life and commitment. A particular feature of RENEW was its non-threatening approach. It was quite explicitly not an élite training programme but aimed to 'start from where people are' in the hope of leading them gently, over a significant period of time, to a deeper understanding of their faith and knowledge of scripture, an ability to share that faith more easily with others, a revitalized local religious community life focused round the parish, and a greater commitment to putting that faith into action through a deeper social concern. Rather more ambiguously, RENEW was concerned with the 'empowerment' of lay people.

1.2   Outline of RENEW

According to the team responsible for developing it: RENEW is a spiritual process to help parishioners develop a closer relationship with Christ, to make an adult commitment to Jesus as central in their lives and to open them to the power of the Holy Spirit so that they become more authentic witnesses.   (NOR 1988: 3)

The aims of RENEW were varyingly described in the programme's literature as 'teaching and witnessing to the Word of God', 'developing vibrant faith communities', and 'establishing justice formation and action' (Martin, 1982: iv).

The RENEW literature strongly emphasized the notion of 'process' over the 2½ years of the programme and it invited inactive members to participate in the gradual process of conversion, not only of individuals, but also of the parish community. To avoid confusion we decided to treat the processual aspect of RENEW, its claim to promote a renewal *process*, as a hypothesis to be tested. We decided to use the term *programme* to refer to the specified and standardized sequence of events, materials, and themes provided for each of the six weeks in each of the five specified 'seasons' of RENEW in the autumn/fall and during Lent.

The themes of the seasons were intended 'to follow a basic conversion process, calling parishioners to a new and deeper conversion of heart' (1988: 3). These were in a fixed sequence: (1) the Lord's call, (2) our response to the Lord's call, (3) empowerment by the Spirit, (4) discipleship, and (5) evangelization. Material from the scriptures and an extensive body of supporting literature expanded on the theme of each season which was meant to be reflected on, prayed about, and discussed, especially in small 'faith-sharing' groups where participants were encouraged each week to commit themselves to some form of religiously motivated 'action-response'.

The whole RENEW programme was highly structured and organized. At the centre of it was the International RENEW office in Plainfield, New Jersey, which provided extensive literature and a small team of experts who travelled around the world to facilitate it. Following the completion of the RENEW programme in the Diocese of Downlands in 1988–90, one of the local senior parish priests, Mgr. Bob Reilly, who had shifted from an initial position of scepticism to one of enthusiasm as a result of his experiences of

RENEW in his own parish, was invited to join the International RENEW team. At the time of writing he was designated as Director of RENEW in Europe, and a number of dioceses in Ireland and continental Europe were seriously considering the programme.

At the diocesan level there was a local RENEW co-ordinating team appointed by the bishop, responsible for adapting the Newark materials for the local circumstances and culture. The diocesan team was also responsible for the training of parish core teams and group leaders. In each parish there was a core group of three or four people, led by the parish RENEW co-ordinator who was supposed to be a lay person. This group had the task of setting up the initial organization and recruiting leaders for the ten operational committees recommended. Some of these undertook their work mainly before a RENEW season commenced and their task was to mobilize parishioners and ensure their maximum involvement and commitment during each six-week season. They included sign-up, telephone, prayer network, home visiting, and publicity committees. Other committees were responsible for various activities during the seasons such as the Sunday liturgy, take-home (literature distribution to housebound parishioners), large group and small group committees. There was also an evaluation committee which assessed progress during each season and reported to both the parish core group and the diocesan co-ordinating team at the end of each season.

The tasks and duties expected of the core group and of each committee were specified in great detail in a series of RENEW publications. These tasks can be briefly summarized as follows. The full parish team, which normally comprised the convenors of all the parish committees, was to meet as required and provide mutual support and prayer. Before a parish decided whether or not to participate in RENEW, the *parish core group* was required to attend an 'overnight' training session to 'expand their leadership to see that effective people are responsible for the ten tasks needed for a full parish experience' (NOR 1988: 7). The main responsibility of this core group was to co-ordinate the entire RENEW programme 'by praying personally and as a team, meeting regularly to plan, and communicating frequently' with the clergy and parishioners (Martin, 1982: 5).

The *sign-up* committee had the task of encouraging regular Mass attenders to commit themselves to participate in the RENEW programme in a variety of ways (daily prayer and scripture reading, participating in a weekly small group, etc.) by signing up on specially designed cards in advance of each season. A visiting speaker was normally engaged to explain the RENEW 'process' and invite

maximum participation from every member of the parish. The task
of the *telephone* committee was to supplement this commitment by
telephoning other and nominal members of the parish, while that of
the *home visiting* committee was to make 'contact with people who
are no longer associated with the life of the parish. In addition, it
opens a door for those who have been alienated for some reason or
other (for example, over marital problems) to return to a parish in
the process of renewal' (Martin, 1982: 6). In these three ways it was
hoped to maximize participation before the commencement of each
season.

In the meantime the *prayer network* was seen as 'the powerhouse
of RENEW' and its responsibility 'is to get as many people as
possible praying for the spiritual renewal of their parish, to pray
personally and as a team and to help others to pray by constantly
reminding all who are involved in RENEW of the primary importance of prayer' (Martin, 1982: 5). In the Diocese of Downlands, for
example, everyone was invited to say the following prayer daily and
a special version was sung at Sunday Mass throughout the whole
period of RENEW:

> God our Father, we thank you
> for sending your only Son
> to call us to your kingdom.
> Set us on fire
> like his first disciples
> with the power of your Holy Spirit
> and use us
> as you used them
> to RENEW the face of the earth,
> through Jesus Christ our Lord.
> Amen.

This prayer expressed several of the RENEW themes: the Lord's call
and the response of members, empowerment by the Spirit and discipleship, and the call to action in order to renew the everyday
world.

During the RENEW seasons it was the responsibility of the *Sunday
liturgy* committee to ensure that, by careful planning, the liturgies
were inspiring and related to each weekly theme. Their task included
everything from ensuring a proper welcome and greeting for parishioners as they arrived at church, to music, readers, and the theme
of the homily (Martin, 1982: 5). It might also involve other groups
(for example, children or youth) in special dance, mime, or dramatical
presentations of the main theme, as well as the commissioning of
appropriate poster designs, and so on.

The responsibility of the *take-home* committee was to reach outwards into people's homes with specially designed leaflets or pamphlets. Such materials were sometimes distributed through local schools. Special care was urged to ensure that meaningful ways were found of reaching single people, the house-bound, and others who, for one reason or another, were not fully integrated into the everyday life of the parish (Martin, 1982: 5).

The official guidelines suggested that 'the *large group* committee provides an opportunity for special experiences of reflections on the RENEW themes . . . [It] should be creative in selecting and preparing . . . Bible services, simulated activities, field trips, audio-visual presentations, lectures combined with follow-up discussions, dramatic presentations, [and] group projects' (Martin, 1982: 6). It was also recommended that consideration be given to providing social activities and celebrations (possibly involving displays of parish activities) which involved large numbers of people who might not be closely integrated into the everyday life of the parish.

Throughout the whole RENEW programme a *publicity* committee had the task of making 'people aware of the facts about RENEW and its continuing progress. It provides the parish and the broader community with frequent articles, stories, press releases, photographs, posters', and so on (Martin, 1982: 6–7). There was also an *evaluation* committee whose task it was, by keeping in touch with all the other committees, to 'insure that the program is remaining true to its purpose . . . [and] to indicate where change and adaptation is needed or to reinforce what seems to be working well' (Martin, 1982: 7). We will comment later on the ways in which the RENEW concept of evaluation differs from that used by social scientists.

At the heart of the RENEW programme were the small groups of 10–12 parishioners who had signed up before each season to meet weekly for reading and reflection on recommended texts from scripture and related literature, for prayer, discussion, and 'faith-sharing'. 'It is through the small groups that the significance of RENEW will be most deeply felt . . . Through the small groups a sense of faith community will become a tangible reality in people's lives. The responsibilities of the *small group* committee include praying individually and as a team, selecting and training group leaders, selecting and distributing materials, assigning groups and developing a sense of pastoring' (Martin, 1982: 6).

A brief comment on the RENEW small groups is appropriate here. First of all the handbook for leaders gave detailed guidance on how to encourage 'faith-sharing' without being threatening and how to handle different 'emotional styles' of group members. They were to 'avoid teaching, sermonizing, or using spiritual jargon unfamiliar to group members' but to 'allow the members to rest comfortably in the presence of their God' (Martin, 1982: 51). Secondly, each small group member was provided with a booklet for each season. This provided detailed points for prayer, discussion, and reflection for each of the six weekly themes during the RENEW season. Meetings were expected to last at most 1½ hours in order not to be too intimidating to new or inexperienced members. The RENEW literature suggested that each meeting should be tightly structured around nine elements, each lasting a recommended length of time: opening prayer; greetings and action-response sharing; focus; life experience; listening to the Word of God; sharing the Word; prayer; action-response during the following week; and concluding announcements and prayer.

The above outline gives something of the ideological flavour of the RENEW process which claimed to be non-threatening and non-judgemental, to start where people are at and with their everyday experiences, their understandings of their religious faith and sense of what it meant to them and the way they lived their lives. In a set of 'Pastoral Reflections on RENEW' it was suggested that the story of the disciples on the road to Emmaus (Luke 24: 13–35) was

a paradigm for every renewal effort ... The first task of RENEW is to help people tell their stories to each other so that they may find God in their everyday experiences. They must learn how to open up their lives to others, even strangers, for in our tradition as far back as Abraham, many have met God in the person of a stranger.

Continuing the Emmaus story it was suggested that

RENEW helps people get in touch with the Scriptures, to juxtapose their ordinary experience to our faith tradition ... RENEW helps people to celebrate ... become more reflective about their experiences. It teaches people how to pray so they can have a change of heart, a conversion ... RENEW helps people witness to their faith, to reach out to others, to be on mission. (NOR 1988: 21)

To the social scientist these claims are, at least in principle, open to empirical investigation.

Further reflections in the RENEW literature stress such themes as 'healthy persons share their stories with others, and a healthy parish respects and values its individual members and their stories'; that 'the RENEW process takes place in community, not in one's privatized world', and the call to service and mission (NOR 1988: 22–5). It was concluded that as a process of spiritual renewal RENEW leads people through a conversion cycle in which they are called, formed, and sent. People are called out of their isolation into the community of the Church where they are formed as disciples and sent forth to spread the Gospel. (NOR 1988: 26)

It would seem from the above account that RENEW claimed to promote a modern form of spirituality, in the sense that it aimed to start from people's individual experiences but in a community context and with a strong emphasis on scripture. To that extent it purported to promote a this-worldly and action-oriented form of spirituality rather than a more traditional form of regimented devotionalism with a strong emphasis on a passive learning role and the didactic teaching of doctrinal beliefs. We will return to these claims later when we offer an interpretation of the spirituality espoused by RENEW in terms of the typology of spiritualities which we will develop in Chapter 2.

Finally, the *Leadership Book* for RENEW (Martin, 1982) provided detailed guidelines for each of the ten committees for each of the five seasons. It is clear from the outlines given above that the whole RENEW programme was highly structured from the top down; parishioners throughout a whole diocese were expected to follow the predetermined sequence of themes week by week in each of the five seasons. It is not surprising, therefore, that one commentator has remarked that 'the national [Newark] RENEW office supplies dioceses with step-by-step program instructions that must rival a modern general's war plans' (Kelly, 1987: 197). Nevertheless, the reality of the experiences of the RENEW process within the parishes did not always conform closely to the aspirations in the guidebooks. We shall discuss the actual experience of RENEW in the Diocese of Downlands later in this book.

1.3   Research Perspectives

We conceived our investigation to be a case study of the process leading up to the adoption and implementation of the RENEW programme from the autumn/fall of 1988 to the autumn/fall of 1990, and of the period immediately following its completion in the Diocese of Downlands in southern England. Within the diocese special attention will be paid to a case study in one particular parish, St Matthew's, though we have some comparable data from a number of other parishes. We are not claiming that our research diocese is necessarily typical of all those dioceses throughout the world which have implemented the RENEW programme, or that our main research parish is necessarily typical of all the parishes in the Diocese of Downlands. Our concern is, rather, to investigate the processes taking place in one particular case in order to seek greater understanding of the ways in which cultures of spirituality are determined and controlled. By referring comparatively to a number of historical and recent instances of religious revival, we aim to throw some light on the broader issues of institutional control of spirituality within the Roman Catholic Church.

Some critics have suggested that there are problems of both reliability and validity with case studies and that it is not possible to generalize from their findings. Stoecker (1991), on the other hand, has argued persuasively the special contribution of the case study as a research project which attempts 'to explain wholistically [*sic*] the dynamics of a certain historical period of a particular social unit' (1991: 97–8). It is not so much a method as a 'design feature' or 'a research frame with structural and historical boundaries, an integral theory component, an involved rather than a distanced researcher, and multiple methods which include collaborative methods' (1991: 108). In pursuing the goal of 'theorising idiosyncracy' (1991: 102), it is able to transcend both the weaknesses of 'extensive' forms of research by employing both quantitative and qualitative methods, and also overcome the dualism between inductive and deductive theory.

We have already noted that the structural boundaries of our investigation are those of the research diocese which celebrated the silver jubilee of its formation during the RENEW programme. Since this programme was imported from the Archdiocese of Newark in the United States, reference will also be made to the origins and development of RENEW and some of the considerations which led to its selection as a pastoral programme by certain dioceses in Scotland and its rejection by other dioceses in England. Historically, our study is bounded by the events and decision-making processes which led up to the adoption of the RENEW programme in the research diocese, and by early 1994, more than three years after the end of the fifth and final RENEW season, by which time all the parishes in the diocese were required to have presented to the bishop their 'Parish Plan for Mission'. Comparatively we have attempted to locate RENEW in a matrix of types of renewal movements throughout the history of the Church since New Testament times.

The second component in Stoecker's definition of a case study is an integral theory component. In a previous study of RENEW in the United States, Kelly suggested that RENEW is an example of a religious revitalization movement which occurs during times of transition . . . RENEW illustrates the possibility of religious revivals that affirm institutional allegiance even without offering convincing solutions to institutional dilemmas . . . so that the primary religious functions for the average believer can be affirmed and exercised, namely, the rousing of religious affections around the central faith symbols. (*c*1986: 262–3)

Ebaugh (1991) has recently suggested that post-Vatican II developments in the Roman Catholic Church can be regarded as part of an institutional revitalization movement. Such a movement, which presupposes broad mass support (Fields, 1991), is necessary 'when institutional bonds begin to snap' (McLoughlin, 1978: 13) and 'the cultural system has had to be revitalized in order to overcome jarring disjunctions between norms and experience, old beliefs and new realities, dying patterns and emerging patterns of behavior' (1978: 10). The post-conciliar period has been such a time with, for example, extensive opposition to the official teaching on contraception and, as a result and particularly among the young, opposition to claims of religious authority by the Church leadership. Old certainties and regularities have been lost or reinterpreted, and older patterns of devotion have been lost.

According to McLoughlin (1978: 214), profound cultural transformations 'are not only fruitful but necessary if a culture is to survive the traumas of social change . . . The conversion of great numbers of people from an old to a new world view . . . is a natural and necessary aspect of social change' (1978: 8). Such a process involves 'ideological reorientation' (for example, from a hierarchical model of the Church to a 'people of God' model), 'the internalization of (new) values' (such as a growing awareness of justice imperatives), and 'institutional restructuring' (such as the greater participation of lay people in the life of the Church). McLoughlin concludes his essay on the five 'great awakenings' in England and the United States over the past four centuries with the following observation which has considerable empirical relevance for the analysis of RENEW:

The reason an awakening takes a generation or more to work itself out is that it must grow with the young; it must escape the enculturation of the old ways. It is not worthwhile to ask who the prophet of this awakening is or to search for new ideological blueprints in the works of the learned. Revitalization is growing up around us in our children, who are both more innocent and more knowing than their parents and grandparents. It is their world that has yet to be reborn. (1978: 216)

Such reflections aroused our interest in the extent to which the young were to be involved in the RENEW process in the research diocese and hence the implications for future revitalization.

The model of a revitalization movement which McLoughlin followed was originally applied by Wallace (1956) to situations of total cultural upheaval and decay. Wallace defined a revitalization movement as 'a deliberate, organized, conscious effort by members of a society to construct a more satisfying culture'. Revitalization was, therefore, seen as 'a special kind of culture change'. People involved must regard their culture as a system which was unsatisfactory and in need of fundamental transformation, specifying new relationships as well as . . . new traits' (1956: 265). The culture change was not one of slow adaptation but rather an abrupt shift into a new cultural Gestalt. In a revitalization movement, people came together in an effort to change not only their own 'mazeways' (that is the mental images they had of themselves, their society, and its culture), but also to change the whole cultural system in order to reduce the levels of individual stress or cultural distortion which were apparent under the old system. For Wallace, revitalization consisted of six functional tasks or stages: maze-way reformulation, communication, organization, adaptation (in the face of resistance), cultural transformation, and routinization. Finally, Wallace considered that religious revitalization movements were usually conceived in the hallucinatory visions of prophetic figures.

While Wallace's conceptualization of a revitalization movement is a helpful starting-point, there are a number of ways in which RENEW differed significantly from the movements he describes. We shall discuss later the extent to which the 'entrepreneurial leadership' of RENEW consciously aimed to regenerate the religious culture of the Catholics in the Diocese of Downlands in ways which amounted to a form of spiritual reconversion for individuals, but were also intended to be transformative in terms of the social implications for society at large. By such fundamental changes it was hoped to confront the evidence of individual stress (arising not only from the pace of social change and reconstruction in the post-war years but also from the seemingly anomic religious situation following the reforms of the Second Vatican Council) and cultural shifts apparent in British (and indeed western industrial) society generally. However, it is clear that RENEW was not conceived by a prophet subject to hallucinatory visions but rather by clerical officers in the Church bureaucracy (both in the research diocese itself and in Newark at its genesis) who were increasingly concerned at the growing evidence of institutional decline and lassitude. From the pastoral statistics summarized in Table 1.1 it can be seen that in the twenty years from 1968 to 1988, Mass attendances in the Diocese of Downlands were down by one-quarter and the number of diocesan priests working actively was down by 30 per cent.

A second reason for qualifying the concept of revitalization in any analysis of RENEW is that it typically refers to social movements which originated among relatively powerless groups in opposition to groups with established power. We have already indicated that RENEW originated among the clerical bureaucracy alarmed by the indications of institutional decline. RENEW might, however, be regarded as an example of a sponsored revitalization or renewal movement initiated from the top down. Renewal movements are characterized as 'intense, collective episodes of tension-management activity' (Hannigan, 1991: 319, quoting Rose, 1982: 17). RENEW certainly encouraged the intensive involvement of all Catholics in the diocese over a period of 2½ years and it emerged in direct response to both the evidence of institutional decline and expressions of lay needs for adult religious formation.

The effectiveness of a social movement depends in part on the level of material and human resources devoted to its pursuit. In a comprehensive review of resource mobilization theory and focusing on 'the process by which a group secures collective control over the resources needed for collective action', Jenkins (1983: 532) has argued the need for a multi-factored approach which takes into account resources, organization, opportunities, and discontents. Resources may include both 'tangible' assets, such as money, facilities, and the means of communication, and 'intangible' assets, such as specialized organizing and administrative skills, the specialized contributions of supporters, and the legitimacy of the movement. The literature also sensitizes us to look for social control devices (such as the application of large amounts of resources) which function to diffuse criticism or radical dissent.

In this present study, such an approach is helpful in the attempt to explain (*a*) how RENEW came to be adopted in the Diocese of Downlands (Chapter 3), (*b*) the process of mobilizing both the priests and laity in the diocese to participate in the programme (Chapter 4), (*c*) the organization of RENEW at both the diocesan and parish levels, and (*d*) the outcomes of the RENEW 'process', its successes and failures (Chapters 5–8). It will be shown that the clerical leadership in the diocese had a near monopoly of tangible resources and very considerable levels of intangible resources, which enabled it to incorporate both the priests and lay activists into a programme which was legitimated as an appropriate response to the inchoate

TABLE 1.1 *Pastoral Statistics in the Diocese of Downlands (1967/8–92)*

Statistic	1967/8	1985	1986	1987	1988	1989	1990	1991	1992
Mass attendance ('000s)	70.5	56.6	56.6	54.9	53.9	52.2	51.4	51.3	51.0
Converts/receptions	347	231	219	192	225	215	244	214	252
Baptisms	3,612	2,457	2,369	2,493	2,538	2,567	2,546	2,704	2,618
Active diocesan priests	212*	151	154	149	149	144	141	145	145

Source: Annual Diocesan Directories, 1969–94.
* Estimated.

discontents within the diocese, expressed in terms of a general need for a comprehensive programme of adult religious education and formation.

In order to pursue these tasks, it is helpful to recognize some of the accumulated findings from resource mobilization studies and, in particular, note that there are a number of identifiable institutional dilemmas which have to be addressed by an entrepreneurial leadership (McCarthy and Zald, 1977). In the first place, was RENEW an 'institutional change movement' or a 'movement of personal change'? Arguably it attempted to be both and promote both a renewed individual spirituality on the part of a wider range of adherents and a revitalized diocesan Church with more vibrant parishes and local communities. But here, according to Jenkins, there is a problem:

Institutional change movements tend to conform to the basic resource mobilization model: rational actions oriented towards clearly defined, fixed goals with centralized organizational control over resources and clearly demarcated outcomes that can be evaluated in terms of tangible gains . . . The problem arises . . . in applying this model to movements of personal change in which expressive actions are intertwined with rational-instrumental action. In such movements, goals tend to arise out of interaction; centralized control is tied to a charismatic leader or is weak; outcomes are diffuse. (1983: 529)

As we shall see, our own data suggest that the outcomes of RENEW were indeed diffuse.

We were alerted by the findings from the literature on resource mobilization in social movements to look for evidence of the ways in which the organization of RENEW resolved the dilemma between a centralized diocesan bureaucracy and a decentralized informal parish model. Jenkins reports the finding that 'personal change movements tend to adopt decentralized structures and exclusive membership rules while institutional change movements are typically centralized and inclusive' (1983: 539). In the research diocese it will be shown that some sort of intermediate situation was adopted with 'centralized structures with semi-autonomous locals [for example, parishes]' (1983: 540). The strategic dilemma appeared to remain, however, between having centralized structures and strong leadership in order to achieve movements' goals but at the cost of weak membership participation, or decentralized structures with an emphasis on strong membership participation (for example, in terms of parochial involvement) but at the cost of weak goal achievement (such as concrete evidence of social concern) (1983: 541). Different organizational structures appear to be effective for the achievement of different tasks. Thus Jenkins reports the finding that

Bureaucratic structures provide technical expertise and coordination essential in institutional change efforts but are less effective at mobilizing 'grass roots' participation. Decentralized structures maximize personal transformation, thereby mobilizing 'grass roots' participation and insuring group maintenance but often at the cost of strategic effectiveness. (1983: 542)

Another finding relates to the matter of membership commitment. Jenkins reports that:

free riding is probably widespread in natural settings and, while organizing efforts can reduce its frequency, personal calculations of costs and rewards are significant considerations . . . The major task in mobilization . . . is to generate solidarity and moral commitments to the broad collectivities [such as the Church, diocese and parish] in whose name movements act. (1983: 537–8)

A third finding is that the mobilizing potential of a group (such as a parish) is likely to be dependent largely on the level of pre-existing group organization. Thus,

by providing prior solidarities and moral commitments, these identities and networks provide a basis for operation of collective incentives . . . Conversely, groups with weak identities, few intragroup networks, and strong ties to outsiders are less likely to mobilize. (1983: 538)

Such considerations provide a basis for a comparative analysis of different parishes and for intra-parish variations in involvement. Both between and within parishes, the differential recruitment of individuals can be expected to reflect the extent to which they were already 'enmeshed in interpersonal networks', were active parishioners, 'support social change' and were ideologically committed to it, and were 'structurally available for participation' (1983: 538).

Finally, in a discussion of the politics of social movements, Jenkins distinguishes four outcomes of the activities of social movements: full success; co-optation (acceptance of participants but no benefits; for example, rhetoric about lay participation without substantial change of practice); pre-emption (benefits but no acceptance; for example, parish councils with advisory functions only); and failure (1983: 543). The evaluation of the outcomes of RENEW, however, is hindered by a certain fuzziness in the specification of its goals. Two goals, in particular, will be considered in this present study: the increasing involvement and participation of lay people in the parishes and in the diocese, and a clear indication of the transfer of a generalized 'social concern' into concrete ameliorative endeavours and political action to address the causes of perceived social injustices.

At an early stage in our study it seemed to us that there were certain elements in the RENEW programme that appeared to have been inspired by the community development movement of the 1960s and 1970s. Community development originated as a means of involving members of a geographical community in endeavours for their mutual benefit (Hill, 1972). In order to attract wide community support, projects were apt to be described in terms which lacked clear definition, a situation which sometimes led to misunderstandings and conflict (Moynihan, 1969). Community development was intended to be democratic and to demonstrate confidence in all participants (Biddle and Biddle, 1965). In practice, however, it often became authoritarian (Rein and Miller, 1967; Armstrong, 1971), for example when the sponsors of change despaired of achieving it because of the complexity of the problems being addressed and the passivity of the powerless (Guskin, 1971).

Community development projects frequently referred to the concept of 'process' (Cary, 1970) which was defined as a series of changes which had not been predetermined by powerful agencies but had resulted from participant decisions. Projects often used small group work to promote individual growth and social change. Action research was developed to cope with the evaluation of unpredictable changes, which made conventional evaluation difficult (Scriven, 1967; Suchman, 1967; Lees, 1973). Commitment to the goals of the project was a strong feature of community development and participants were often resistant to evaluation and particularly to theoretical analysis (Rose and Hanmer, 1975).

It seemed to us that RENEW might have been developed by people trained and educated at a time when community development projects were popular. Like the latter, RENEW aimed actively to involve members of the geographical parish community, stressing participation both as a goal and as a means of effecting change, and frequently emphasizing the term 'process'. Some evidence of theoretical ambiguity and contradiction in the available documentation were noted at the outset, for example, between the promotion of lay participation and 'empowerment', on the one hand, and the top-down and highly structured nature of the programme, on the other. Work in small groups was a major feature of the programme. It appeared to acknowledge its roots in community development by the use of in-built evaluative research, apparently drawing on the notions of action research. The explanation of evaluation in the RENEW literature was also theoretically congruent, but the way in which it was to be executed caused us concern from the outset. As was often the case with community development projects, spontaneous comments from respondents to questionnaires indicated that some participants thought it was either impossible or improper to attempt to evaluate some aspects of the programme.

Motives for community development were usually political. Where small groups were used as a means to implement development, the promotion of personal growth in group work sometimes also had therapeutic consequences for individuals. The intense dynamics of small group work sometimes produced manifestations of religious experience (Gurvitch, 1971; Norris, 1979). In RENEW, although the motivation was manifestly religious, we wished to explore to what extent the programme might have both political and therapeutic consequences, facilitating both social change and change in individuals. As in community development, it was predicted that if changes did occur, they might not always be in the directions anticipated or welcomed by the sponsors (Miller and Rein, 1975; Lees, 1973; Edginton, 1974).

Because of the similarities between RENEW and community development projects, it was also predicted that some of the problems which led to disillusionment with community development, despite the enthusiastic commitment of participants, might also become apparent in the RENEW programme. Stress for individuals, as well as personalized conflict, was likely to result from committed participation in a programme which contained considerable ambiguities.

With these various theoretical perspectives in mind at an early stage in our research, we came to regard our research problem as the explanation of the process by which RENEW came to be adopted in the Diocese of Downlands, the goals of its advocates and the manner in which they mobilized resources to promote it in all the parishes, indications of resistance to it, and the evaluation of its outcomes. It seemed that RENEW was judged by the diocesan bishop and his senior advisers as the best available response to the evidence of institutional decline, recent transformations of religious authority, especially in the area of personal morality (Hornsby-Smith, 1991), and repeatedly expressed requests from lay people in the diocese for programmes of adult religious education.

In this study we address the related issues of cultures of spirituality and structures of authority and control. We suggest that the concept of 'spirituality' has both structural and cultural dimensions. *It refers to both the religious culture in the generic sense, that is the particular way of understanding and thinking, feeling and acting out the religious quest for salvation, and the structural or organizational framework which controls its various manifestations and interacts with its cultural content.*

In this sense, spirituality inevitably has a political dimension since questions of organizational control are intrinsic. This was illustrated in a recent editorial in *The Month* (Feb. 1992: 44–5) entitled 'The Politics of Holiness' which drew attention to possible 'political wrangling' and 'sectarian manipulation' accompanying the recent beatification of the founder of Opus Dei. That a power dimension has operated throughout the history of the Christian Church is also apparent in Sheldrake's recent study of *Spirituality and History*. As he well observes:

It does not seem unfair to reflect upon the Christian tradition in terms of those who seek to control, produce and then dispense spirituality and those who are made into the recipients of spiritual bequests that originate with others. This is an issue of power; who has it, how it is used (whether consciously or not), and what the effects are, in different contexts, on those who are, at different times, a spiritually dependent underclass. (1991: 215)

Apart from the political dimension, we also aimed to study the implicit religious culture of RENEW 'in dialogue with different ecclesiologies', as one of our colleagues observed. For this purpose we wished to observe the extent to which an institutional model of the Church was challenged by alternative models of the Church as community, sacrament, herald, and servant (Dulles, 1976). We were also interested in RENEW's implicit theology of the laity: of instrumental ministry, ecclesial presence to the world, of world transformation, of ecclesial restructuring, of self-discovery, or of being integrally Church, living as a community for the service of the world (Doohan, 1984). It was with such diverse considerations in mind that we undertook our study of RENEW.

Finally, it is proper that we should record some of the issues which concerned us early in our study a short time before the commencement of RENEW in October 1988. Three matters in particular suggested themselves as worthy of attention: the lack of clarity about (and salience of) the specification of the goals of the RENEW programme and the likely implications of this for the 'evaluation' process; the danger of goal displacement with an apparent obsession with the *means* (committees and structures, materials and specified procedures) rather than with clearly identified *ends* or aims of the RENEW process; and the inadequacy of the specification of the resource implications of RENEW either at the diocesan level or at the parish level. Subsequently we hypothesized at the global level that RENEW might be both 'a sophisticated economic enterprise marketed by religious entrepreneurs' and an unintended form of

'religious cultural colonialism'; at the diocesan level we hypothesized that 'the decision to initiate RENEW was pre-empted by the
bishop and that agreement to participate by nearly all the parishes
in the diocese was only obtained *post facto* and hardly on the basis
of informed consent'; at the parish level we planned to investigate
'changes brought about in priest–parishioner relationships, the levels
and kinds of interaction between parishioners themselves, in personal religious consciousness and in the amount and types of religious activity' (Hornsby-Smith, Fulton, and Norris, 1991: 102–4).

1.4   *Methodological Issues*

The final two elements in Stoecker's definition of a case study are
'an involved rather than a distanced researcher and multiple methods
which include collaborative methods' (1991: 108). Our case study
was primarily of the Diocese of Downlands though we also collected a limited amount of comparative data from informants in
other dioceses. Within the diocese we used a wide variety of methods
or 'triangulation'. According to Denzin, 'triangulation of method,
investigator, theory, and data remain the soundest strategy of theory
construction' (1970: 300).

First of all we collected data at the international, diocesan, and
parish levels. At the international level one of us interviewed the
Director of the International RENEW Office in Plainfield, New Jersey,
as well as two other members of the international team, and we
undertook very substantial content analysis of documentary materials and the voluminous RENEW literature. At the diocesan level
we interviewed the bishop and all the members of the RENEW
team and a number of other informants in the Diocese of Downlands.
We also carried out a considerable amount of observation and
participant observation from late 1987 through to the spring of
1993. At the parish level we carried out a major case study of one
parish, St Matthew's, using a variety of methods: surveys of small
group members and parishioners, participant observation, and interviews with both participants and non-participants. In addition
we were able to obtain the collaboration of parish priests and/or
evaluators in six other parishes who agreed to use our survey instrument. As we shall see, the results from these other parishes strongly
corroborated the findings from our main case study of St Matthew's.

Thus we used a variety of research methods, including participant observation, questionnaire surveys, focused interviews, and content analysis of documents at three different levels. All three of us

contributed to this rich variety of data collection methods. We noted in the previous section that we found several different theoretical perspectives (revitalization movements, resource mobilization, power and social control, and community development and action research) helpful in attempting to interpret RENEW comparatively and historically. We can, therefore, reasonably claim to have met the canons for triangulation proposed by Denzin (1970: 297–313). At the same time we recognize that the importance of collecting a variety of types of data is 'the attempt to relate them so as to counteract the threats to validity identified in each'. The purpose of combining theories and methods is to add 'breadth or depth to our analysis', to give a more rounded analysis in terms of both structural constraints and interpretive action, and 'to incorporate at least one method of data collection that describes and interprets the context in which the interaction occurs and one that is designed primarily to illuminate the process of interaction itself' (Fielding and Fielding, 1986: 30–5).

While we appreciate that in any study of 'process' there is a dialectical relationship between structure and action, we derived the bulk of our understanding of the structural features of RENEW from quantitative content analysis of official documents and literature—including the overview (NOR 1988) and the leadership book with detailed instructions (Martin, 1982)—and from the questionnaires completed by parishioners and members of small groups, especially in our parish case study, but with a considerable amount of comparative data collected from six other parishes. In our main research parish, St Matthew's, a total of 1177 questionnaires were completed by adult Sunday Mass attenders and by 689 small group members over the five seasons, and similar questionnaires were completed by 1,204 parishioners from three other parishes at the end of Seasons 3, 4, and 5. As a result of generous collaboration from the parish priests and evaluators, we were able to collect some data from seven parishes in the diocese. The distribution of these seven parishes in terms of their reported proportions of Mass attenders involved in small groups in Season 1 is indicated in Table 1.2. This shows that these parishes were, if anything, more committed than most parishes in the diocese to the small group process, one of the key elements of RENEW.

In addition to the theoretical ideas discussed above, which informed our study at various stages, there was also a sense in which the theory we developed was 'grounded' (Glaser and Strauss, 1973) in the ethnographic and other data that we collected. Most of our interpretative understanding of the RENEW process came from these

TABLE 1.2 *Distribution of Research Parishes (Reported Small Group Participants as Percentage of Mass Attenders)*

Parishes	<10	10<15	15<20	20<25	25<30	30<35	35<40	40+	Total
Research	–	1	–	1	2	1	1*	1	7
All	6	9	26	20	17	15	12	8	113

Source: Diocesan RENEW Evaluation Returns for Season 1.
* Our main research parish, St Matthew's, was thirteenth in the reported listing of small group participation in the diocese in Season 1.

more ethnographic styles of research. In particular, all three of us undertook a considerable amount of both observation and participant observation over the whole period of the study, especially at the parish level, but also at deanery and diocesan meetings connected with the RENEW programme and during the subsequent post-RENEW period. Regular field notes were kept throughout and apart from more formal data collection procedures, we systematically noted chance remarks and conversations about RENEW at both formal and informal social occasions. In this way we hoped to reflect more closely what ordinary Catholics actually thought rather than what they thought they ought to say to an inquiring outsider.

In response to requests for information about the decision whether or not to take up RENEW in a number of other dioceses in England and Wales, we received helpful written comments from two bishops, one senior priest, and four lay people who had attended briefing sessions at Newark in the mid-1980s. We were also sent written comments on their experiences of RENEW by one South African and three Scottish bishops and by two other informants who were involved with diocesan RENEW teams in Scotland.

Our final method of data collection was the focused interview. We interviewed Mgr. John Carroll and two other members of the international RENEW team; Bishop Patrick, Bishop of Downlands; Mgr. Francis Johnson, who had visited Newark in the mid-1980s; Mgr. Liam O'Brien, Director, and the three other members of the diocesan RENEW team; all three members of the core group and six parishioners and small group members in St Matthew's parish; a person employed by a diocesan agency and the parish co-ordinator from St Joan's parish; and one group interview with members of a RENEW small group in St Luke's parish from which emerged a project to help the homeless. All these interviews, which typically lasted 1½ hours or more, were tape-recorded for subsequent transcription and analysis. Informal interviews were also obtained from four members of the RENEW team and three small group leaders in St Cyril's parish.

The similarities between community development projects and the RENEW programme, which we noted above, suggested that a method of 'soft data' analysis developed by Norris (1981) to research a community development project, might be a fruitful way of examining RENEW. The method sorts statements and actions of participants into constantly recurring concepts, indicating a framework of 'second order constructs' in the kind of orderly scheme which Schutz (1962) suggests that research workers impose upon their raw materials, or which Glaser and Strauss (1973) anticipate emerging as 'grounded theory'. Such a scheme will be discussed in Chapter 5. The method was expected to elicit a sociological interpretation of possible confusions resulting from conflicting perceptions of statements and activities which might affect the implementation of the programme. It was hoped that it would facilitate the development of a coherent and illuminating theoretical interpretation of the RENEW process.

In sum, we collected a formidable amount of data over the five years of our study. With three different investigators and the triangulation of methods, types of data, and theoretical perspectives, we believe we can legitimately present a sociological interpretation of the RENEW process in our case study of the Diocese of Downlands, one which takes account of RENEW's structural features and also the interpretation of the process given by the various participants. In the course of our analysis we will propose for consideration a model of types of spirituality, historically and comparatively. Although examples are drawn from Roman Catholicism in the first instance, in principle the question of the sponsorship and control of types of spirituality is one with much wider relevance.

1.5 Outline of Book

In the early stages of our work, as we grappled with some of the first data from our main research parish, St Matthew's, we began to conceptualize types of religious renewal in terms of two dimensions: directive and non-directive organizational characteristics, and traditional and progressive religious concerns (Hornsby-Smith, Fulton, and Norris, 1991: 113). In Chapter 2 we develop our analysis further. Four types of spirituality are postulated in terms of a structural or organizational control dimension, and a cultural dimension in terms of modernity. This typology is validated in a critical comparative analysis of renewal movements in the Church both historically and in recent times. It provides the basic conceptual framework for the analysis of our own research data.

The following chapter draws on our interviews with key informants and ethnographic accounts to outline the process by which RENEW came to be adopted by the diocesan leadership, in the first instance, and subsequently how the individual parishes were incorporated into the diocesan effort. The focus is on the process by which the bishop, over a period of several years, came to recommend the adoption of RENEW as a response to the expressed needs of the diocese, and to persuade the clergy, in the first instance, and secondly lay activists and representatives, to agree to participate in and promote the programme. The chapter will offer an interpretation of the bishop's reasons for selecting RENEW in the context of institutional decline and evidence from earlier diocesan consultations of a strong desire for adult religious education on the part of the laity.

In Chapter 4 we continue to show how this decision by the diocesan leadership was transmitted to the parishes and how activists mobilized their parishes to participate with commitment in the diocesan effort. There were a number of key stages in this process including a series of deanery meetings, attended by the bishop, at which presentations were made by the appointed diocesan RENEW team, a series of 'overnight' seminars at which parish 'core' teams were socialized into the advantages of the proposed programme, the selection of parish committees and team leaders who, finally, were charged with the task of mobilizing ordinary parishioners to participate in a wide variety of ways for the five RENEW seasons. In this chapter we will draw, in particular, on our ethnographic field notes and interviews in two parishes.

The core of our empirical findings are reported in Chapters 5, 6, and 7. In Chapter 5 we examine further, in terms of our typology, the nature of the spirituality promoted by the RENEW leadership. We examine the wealth of qualitative (or 'soft') data which we collected from a variety of sources, including log notes of field work at deanery or diocesan meetings; transcripts of interviews with members of the Newark international team and members of the diocesan RENEW team; and a wide range of documents including official Newark publications or diocesan adaptations of them. The experience of RENEW in the parishes is the focus in Chapter 6. We report the results of questionnaire surveys of both parishioners and members of the RENEW small groups in several parishes in the diocese after each of the five seasons. In Chapter 7 we examine the conflicts within the diocese, and especially the justice and peace movement, over differing conceptions of and differing pastoral responses to a wide range of social concerns.

Chapter 8 will trace developments in the diocese in the three years following the end of Season 5 of RENEW. At the diocesan level it will report on the *Planning for the 90s* consultation in the context of the decade of evangelization. From this emerged the identification of seven priority areas and, after a process of negotiation with the priests in the diocese, a 'vision statement' and the request from the bishop that all parishes prepare a strategic plan by March 1993. In the main research parish, St Matthew's, this process had been anticipated and an ethnographic account of the emergence of its Parish Plan for Mission will be offered. This chapter also includes our own assessment of RENEW in the light of the research findings we have reported.

In the final chapter an attempt is made to draw together the different strands of this study and interpret them in the light of the typology of spiritualities. Our data point to the close relationships between power, social control, and organizational innovation, on the one hand, and dominant Church culture and innovation and change of religious culture, on the other. We conclude with some observations on strategies for renewal and revitalization within the Church that point to the wider applicability of our typology both comparatively and historically.

2

A Theoretical Frame

2.1 Dimensions of Spiritualities

In this chapter we establish a theoretical frame by which to identify types of spirituality, and to understand what particular type RE-NEW represents. It is useful to begin this chapter by looking at what the term spirituality means. Popularly, it is seen in individualistic terms, even when entire social groups are being characterized. In addition, the term tends to have other-worldly connotations, at least in traditional Roman Catholicism. Almost by definition, spirituality is removed from matters of politics, argument, and struggle between people. Consequently, it takes on the significance of 'piety', something entirely separate from the realm of the social, and eminently individual and removed from this world. As such, it does not question the organizational and political direction taken by the religious community of which one is a part and implies either indifference to political issues or a delegation of the political aspects of religion to the religious leadership. Even when religious leaders themselves are seen as pious, their piety is viewed as something separate from the application of their managerial skills and leadership qualities. To look at their piety, one brackets their religious politics, both internal and external to the group, or even the way they might generally treat people. As a total form of spirituality among the followers, piety is essentially passive and involves the surrender of organizational and this-worldly dialogue. It will be upheld by a religious leadership which desires total control of religious politics. The only type of religious politics which is likely to be assumed by the pious is support for the status quo.

Clearly, we are dealing here with a traditional representation of what a religious or 'spiritual' person is. It is a view which conflicts with the perspective which is being adopted in this book. *We hold that it is better to understand 'spirituality' as having both cultural and organizational dimensions. It also involves facing up to the kind of social world we inhabit and taking decisions and action in its regard.* The latter is true particularly of Roman Catholicism which has always had, and explicitly so since the fourth century, *a social project*. We will try, first of all, to clarify these statements.

Spiritualities are borne of religious movements as much by the example of charismatic individuals. They are ways of understanding, thinking, feeling, and acting out the religious quest. In addition, they are the property of groups. They are group forms which not only witness to a definite commitment on the part of an individual but characterize the lifestyle of groups. In other words, such groups live out their lives in a particular, organized way, as well as being affected to varying extents by the overall form of religious organization characteristic of their mainstream religion. In addition spiritualities have a social context to which they are a response and by which they are conditioned. They have a relationship with the historical, social, and political settings within which they have occurred. In sociology, these settings are often referred to as the structural factors influencing or entering into the spiritualities. In this chapter, therefore, we will be concerned with two particular aspects of spiritualities and religious movements, one a *structural* feature and the other a *cultural* one, which both together form the essential aspects of spiritualities generally. After specifying these conceptually and historically, we will proceed to look at the key transformation in contemporary society which affects both the culture and structure of all religious forms in today's world, namely the process of modernization, to which process, we maintain, religions have to respond if they are to survive in any substantial way. To clarify it, we shall also need to look at some other religious movements and spiritualities before returning to our analysis of RENEW.

2.2 Forms of Organization

The structural feature of spiritualities and movements we consider of key importance is that of *organization*. 'Spirituality', then, is not simply an inward process of the soul, or of souls in communion, without any link to the practicalities of human relationships. It is as much shaped by the form of organization—by the relationships of power which are taken up—as by its own specific charisma and inspiration. As we will see, organization significantly determines the very possibilities and forms of renewal.

Forms of organization are often delineated in sociology by their organizational type. The word 'organization' denotes co-ordinated activity, decision-making and implementation, with each member of a group assigned to a particular role with particular duties.

Organizations can be of varying kinds. Those which relate to matters of belief and commitment—particularly religion and politics—are ways of preserving, unfolding, or making present the original charisma of the founder or founders, a process known as routinization (Weber, 1968: 246–54). A further characteristic determining their type is the way in which decisions are made and implemented within or by the group or movement. The form which power takes on in this process is closely related to questions of democracy and hierarchy. It is true to an extent that personal preference will influence the form of organization one chooses. However, it is also true that organizations simply evolve, sometimes in response to the culture held by the members, whether the source of that culture be religious or not. In the case of Christianity, the central most powerful force was, in all likelihood, the ideal of community so clearly portrayed in the apostolic writings of the first century, from the Acts of the Apostles through the letters attributed to Paul and to the Johannine tradition. Up until the early fourth century and the coming of the Christian Empire under Constantine, the local Church or group of Churches was the principal organizational basis for this sense of community, led by presbyters and probably bishops, if one follows the writings of Ignatius of Antioch. From the fourth century, power in the Western empire developed around the Bishop of Rome and in the Eastern empire around the patriarchs of the main Christian centres. The consequence of the domination of Christianity was that, by the early Middle Ages, the local community was replaced to a considerable extent by Christendom, or by a society which as a whole claimed to embody Christian social order. This 'societalization' of the community ideal as represented by Christendom was to remain dominant until the Reformation, but had certainly lost its pre-eminence, even in Catholic lands, by the time of the Enlightenment, a process which will be considered later in this chapter. However, a diminished version can still be said to persist where monopoly Catholicism (Martin, 1978) still prevails.

Whatever the form of the ideal pursued, researchers in the field of organizational analysis have tended to accept that some forms are more appropriate to certain ends than others. One particularly insightful model of organizational forms was developed by Burns and Stalker (1966). Though their work was originally done with the modern business enterprise in mind, it can be applied to other organizational forms. They found that firms which produced routine products and required little novelty operated best with a top-down, hierarchical management structure, one which required little original thought and action once the product was on line. They termed this form of organization *mechanistic*. However, firms which required new products or frequent modification needed a high level of flexibility in their organization to enable them to adapt to an ever-changing scene. Such flexibility was provided by the introduction of group management teams, which often experienced a great deal of inner conflict, but whose working together and decision-making were much more effective than the hierarchical, top-down form. Burns and Stalker called this co-operative type *organic*.

We are not suggesting here that religion is simply a matter of products and consumers. A key difference between economic, market-oriented organizational activity and that of a religious institution, is that the best line of response in religion—for followers as well as leaders—is not market-led but value dominated. As such it is not invented or necessarily the most enjoyable and comfortable. What we are suggesting is that all modes of decision-making and group action within any form of organization tend to be strung out somewhere on a line between the organic and mechanistic types, and that this is as true for religious organizations as it is for economic or political ones. We are also saying that the form of the organization has certain effects on what the organization succeeds in doing; in the case of religious organizations, the form has an effect on the members and their outlook on their faith, life, and social milieu. This effect is not to be understood in a deterministic way; there are also other factors which affect the success of Churches, some of which may not be easy to formulate or to grasp in their entirety.

Within the ambit of Roman Catholicism, there has long predominated a mechanistic model of Church order which has sought, not always successfully, to control and guide (usually assist rather than initiate) its religious movements and its interaction with secular society. This model has been buttressed by the Church's theology of authority and ministry. However, the Church's hierarchical structure is additionally based on the priesthood and is of the clerical type, that is, based on a radical distinction between clergy and laity, with the cleric being the religious specialist and professional. In addition, the priest has always been male since the emergence of the clerical state in about the fourth century CE. Usually clergy have been recruited from various class or status groups within society, though the lower middle classes have tended to predominate. Consequently, we would argue that, given its strongly hierarchical nature, the Roman Catholic Church is likely to have great difficulty in responding appropriately to social change. It can make changes from the top downwards, but whether these are the appropriate responses to the circumstances is another matter. We would further suggest that appropriate responses might be impeded by current doctrinal positions. For example, the present dominant interpretation of the teaching on papal infallibility (divine assistance against error on matters of faith and morality) and on papal primacy (the direct subjection of all believers to papal authority), despite the fact that both are severely limited in theory by specific conditions, tends to 'creep' along in the minds and actions of both clergy and laity to include the belief that infallibility implies divine guidance in understanding what is right and wrong with the world, and that the leadership also knows better than the laity what kinds of changes are required in the organization and activity of its members. Such interpretations have a strong hold despite historical examples of error in the case of disputes over matters of fact: for example in 1307, the papal Bull *Unam Sanctam*, when the pope declared worldwide secular powers subordinate to the spiritual power of the papacy, and in the 1630s in the treatment meted out by the Holy Office to Galileo for daring to maintain that the earth went around the sun. All hierarchical organizations handle mental and social changes with great difficulty. So it is only to be expected that any renewal movement in the Church which implies or demands change in the hierarchical structure and practice will not make much headway.

It is also important to remember that the papacy still retains aspects of the kingly functions it has exercised in varying degrees for 1,400 years and one of these is the tendency to monopolize political relationships between the Church community and state institutions. That is, even after the collapse of Christendom, it seeks to develop through diplomacy not simply relationships between the Vatican and the various states, but relationships between the local Church as a community and its local state form. This may seem far-fetched. But one should notice that the fear of liberation Catholicism in third-world countries comes precisely from the politicization of the local Church community, one which inevitably involves their clergy and the interpretation of their religious faith. We are suggesting that the faith problem which arises for the Vatican—that local religion is becoming politicized and that this seems to tarnish the faith with politics—is in part a *result* of the traditional monopolization of religious politics by the Vatican, one which has tended to reinforce the interpretation that the political is separate from the religious and that the integrity of the latter—particularly the *magisterium* of the Church or its leadership as doctrinal teacher— is threatened as well as the purity of the faith.

Social control is a feature in any organization, but this is particularly true of the hierarchical organization. It is specifically designed not to allow deviation from established rules and to impose top-down decision-making. According to the dominant ideology of the time and of its current style of leadership, it will be able to absorb, or cope with developments coming from its grass roots or popular base, but it is unlikely that its policies will ever be significantly changed in the direction desired by movement from below. A particular consequence for religious organizations of this type is therefore an inherent tension between hierarchy and base. Such a situation, it would seem, can only be resolved structurally by one of five outcomes: (1) the total destruction of the hierarchical form itself; (2) schism, or the splitting of the Church itself into two or more Churches not in communion with each other; (3) the total suppression of certain, sometimes all, inputs from the base or from certain movements within the base, and their organizations; (4) some degree of absorption of change from the base without basic modification in the organizational type; and (5) a positive interactive relationship between leadership and people, with changes occurring consequently in both hierarchy and base. Continuity of the hierarchical type itself within Roman Catholicism shows that the first possibility has so far been avoided. The second, schism, has occurred, with the two greatest being that between the oriental Catholic (Orthodox) Churches and the Roman, and that between the 'protesting' Churches and the Roman Catholic. If our perception of modes of organization is correct, we will expect to find in history the third and fourth cases (total suppression of movements from below and some degree of absorption and rejection without modification of power structure) in greater or less frequency. But the last—interactive substantive change—we would expect to find more or less commonly according to the extent of inhibiting hierarchical control both centrally and locally in any given historical period. In order for interactive change to exist in the longer term, the organization itself would have to accept openly organic structural changes and certain of its dominant beliefs (those on infallibility and primacy) would have to be refined.

This leads us to suggest the likelihood that one of the basic problems within contemporary Roman Catholicism, one which has existed for a millenium but is now reaching crisis proportions, is a product of its mechanistic religious organization. Only where the Church exists as a religious organization within a pluralistic society is part of that basic tension alleviated. But even there it will tend to continue in the top-down mode of reform and decision-making, and run the risk of never reaching the people who really make it up, with consequent loss or lapsation where no religious policing system is available. Where it remains the religion of the majority in a society or nation-state, it will continue to seek dominance in the overall culture and to have its moral and social teaching reflected in the ordinances of the state itself (see Martin, 1978).

A useful distinction to bear in mind, especially when dealing with hierarchical (mechanistic) structures, is that the growth of spiritualities and renewal can be initiated in two ways. Where spiritualities emerge from the grass roots upwards, the leadership will seek to incorporate what it sees to be good and beneficial and 'cool out' or drain off what it perceives to be bad. Alternatively, spiritualities may be initiated from the top downwards, led by pope, Vatican or bishop, or by a local priest. In this case the leadership is already in control. Furthermore, priest-sponsored movements can ultimately be stopped, if they are perceived as threatening, by removing the priest, though there have been successful separatist movements initiated in this way. Examples of the latter are the reform of the clergy by Gregory VII in the eleventh century, the setting up of the seminaries for the formation of priests after the Reformation, and the development of Catholic Action in the late nineteenth century. RENEW has the appearance of a movement in this tradition, though there are ambiguities which suggest a greater degree of process than programme and the possibility of bottom-up renewal in the activity of its small groups and local organization. Our task in this study of RENEW is to see how successful at generating change the programme, process, or movement is. It is also to see whether top-down initiated movements are likely to be highly limited in their capacity to renew Church members, or if instead they show promise of developing burgeoning spiritualities.

In conclusion to this discussion of organizational structure, and by definition, to introduce more organic elements into the organization would signify a major transformation of the Roman Catholic Church which might have knock-on effects on its relationships with other Christian Churches. Of course, increase in organic decision-making would weaken aspects of hierarchical control and hence also the authority and self-interests of those in power. For fear of the loss of both what is seen as truth and as power, organic management structures are likely to be resisted by incumbents.

2.3 *Religious Cultures and Modernity*

The second essential aspect of spirituality is its cultural content and includes both the particular conceptualization of the divine and that of the social world. Together these constitute religious culture. On the one hand, in Christianity the content of the revealed message can present varying images and experiences of the divine. On the other, various images both of the surrounding and of the ecclesial society are purveyed and lived out. All religious people must take on an attitude which relates belief to their social environment. They are unable to avoid this, as religion has at its heart both a dimension of transcendence/immanence, relating the individual to the experience of the holy, and a social one, by which consciousness makes sense of and appropriates into life activity that transcendent/immanent experience. Religious experience is only possible to the already socialized human being, whose identity is normally maintained by ongoing social relationships, and the social predisposes, envelopes, and follows from it. We suggest that of crucial importance to the survival of Roman Catholicism is the extent to which its membership has a traditional or a modern religious culture.

At this point, and in order to explore religious culture further, we have to begin to examine what is meant by modernity. We are passing through a period of history known as modernization, some would say even post-modernization. It involves huge transformations in the world economic order, and, while it promises a great deal of good for humanity, it also appears to be partly responsible for the growing distance between the haves and have-nots within the world as a whole. The Second Vatican Council was an event which sought to galvanize the Roman Catholic Church to respond to the new situation and to renew itself in so doing. RENEW itself is a direct response to a growing awareness that talk in the Church cannot by itself solve the issues and that some form of transformative process in action is required.

'Traditional society' or 'pre-modernity' are catch-all concepts, and as such tell us very little. Historically, the periods where traditional religious forms tended to dominate are so vastly different from each other that they fail to address specific cultural content except as negative statements. In the present context, we use the term 'traditional culture' to refer to the kind which dominated the Christian era roughly from the early fourth century to the early sixteenth, including the late Renaissance period and the beginnings of the Reformation. During that time, and despite elements of what we might now see as typical of the modern, traditional forms dominated the Christian empire, the period of the political papacy in the residual empire, the Middle Ages, and the period of their decline. From the sixteenth to the nineteenth centuries, there was a period of transition, before the full emergence of modernity in the twentieth century.

Traditional culture, in the sense we are using the term, indicates a form of life which is relatively stable, with a relatively unchanging social structure, based on a mode of production fairly close to subsistence level, with the majority of people working the land. In such a society, time has a regular rhythm and distances are fixed and measured in days on horseback or by foot. Experience is localized, the interpretation of the universe fixed, and the world usually enchanted—at least in Western traditional cultures—with both folk religion and official Christianity encouraging supernatural and preternatural perceptions. In medieval Europe, huge areas were dominated by the link between feudal and semi-feudal lords and the clerical Church. The moral order was permeated by the certainty of death, hope in the afterlife, and a sense of the futility of earthly existence, a sense which was mainly counterbalanced by a trust in God's providence and a belief in the established order of Christendom.

Modernity is a world of rapid change in the experience of time, which becomes 'disembedded' from experience and measurable; it is a world where the experience of space also changes and becomes different from place and is, therefore, no longer measured in terms of one's locality (Giddens, 1990: 17–29). The modern world can be identified historically as that world which is inhabited by nation-states, industrialization, mass production and consumption, the commodification of labour, and the existence of a plurality of cultures following on from the decline of the cultural dominance of traditional religion. One can isolate at least four major elements within the cultures of modernity which have fundamentally changed the framework for the operation of religions situated within their social boundaries. These elements include what we can call 'the moral gains of modernity', though they have their down-side counterparts which will also be examined. They are: (1) the recognition of the *autonomy of conscience*; (2) a considerable *autonomy of consciousness*, especially in the development of scientific knowledge and human dominance of nature; (3) the growth of *human and political rights*; and (4) the *globalization of socio-ethical responsibility*. These differ somewhat from the formulation offered by Giddens (1990) but they are more historically focused and relate more directly to the religious experience of the West. Among the negations of such values which Christians and all humanistically oriented people are aware of are totalitarianism, ethnocentrism, the emergence of total war and the nuclear bomb, widespread famine, and the destruction of the environment. These positive and negative aspects of modernity which we will briefly explore are summarized in Figure 2.1.

The coming to dominance of these cultural parameters, which

Moral and Material Gains of Modernity	Failures and Negativity of Modernity
Growth of semi-autonomy	Totalitarianism
Growth of personal ethics	Political oppression
Growth of religious consciousness and of reason	Mind control
Growth of democracy	Violence and torture
Growth of living standards to permit a life span of a meaningful bodily cycle	Global wars Ethnic conflicts and wars Terrorism
Growth of science, industry, and technology to the benefit of humanity	Industrialization of warfare Massive deterioration of world ecosystem
Improvements to diet Availability of food Improved housing, warmth, comfort	Famine Mass poverty

FIG. 2.1   Positivity and Negativity of Modernity

shift the framework for the experience of religion in the subject's consciousness, is associated with four sets of historical events or processes: (1) the Renaissance and Reformation; (2) the scientific and technical revolution begun in the seventeenth century and the Enlightenment and Industrial Revolution of the subsequent two centuries; (3) the North American and French political revolutions and development of the modern democratic state form; and (4) the contemporary processes of globalization. We will consider these various aspects of modernity briefly and in turn.

While the *Renaissance* brought to prominence again the Greco–Roman artistic exploration of human life and its forms, the *Reformation*, itself a religious movement, stressed among other elements the relative freedom from human authorities of individual religious experience and conscience. The Reformation also led to an improved autonomy for the secular world and for the natural environment. The latter was purified from the magical influences of the sacred power attributed to relics, holy wells, and springs, as God was more and more encountered personally through faith in Jesus Christ. Along with the destruction or decline of belief in the accumulation of merit and in the monastic and religious life as the better and safer way to heaven, the Reformation helped to open up this-worldly asceticism and secular activity in general as a genuine way of life for the religiously committed. It also aided the project and validity of science but with a prime emphasis on the concept of human dominance over nature. These dimensions were inherited by the *Enlightenment*, which stretched the understanding of human autonomy. It also involved a critique of religion, often in contradiction to official Church teaching, and exposed its traditionalist mentality and the continuing attempt in the Catholic world to dominate and restrict the culture of society. The *scientific revolution* which brought with it the knowledge of the constitution of material reality, thus aiding the technical developments of the *Industrial Revolution*, led to advances in production and travel which were more numerous in 200 years than those of all previous human history. The dominance and manipulation of nature which these developments have brought, open up the possibility of longevity for most human beings, as well as the ability to support vast populations at a level of prosperity, in terms of food, shelter, and clothing, hitherto enjoyed only by kings, and surpassing those personages' abilities to travel and to enjoy themselves. Thus the development of human cultures and products well beyond subsistence level, and the possible enrichment of cultural (and religious) life were facilitated.

Part of the Enlightenment, and the *political revolutions* in North America (1776) and France (1789), was the assertion of the rights of the human individual and the empowerment of humanity to shape the economic and political sphere, a power which, while only partially realized by each, was previously not believed to exist. In traditional consciousness, people were basically unequal. Though ancient Greece possessed for a time a form of democracy and bequeathed it to its western posterity, it had been constructed on the bedrock of slavery. Likewise the world of production and politics were given and largely immutable. Kings and barons ruled by right and, in the West, could only be overthrown if they were tyrants. Their positions in the medieval and ancient world were otherwise assumed to be justified and often reinforced by divine legitimation. Most people were seen by the intelligentsia of the ancient world and by clerical élite of the Middle Ages as incapable of perceiving the truth, whether factual or moral, and in need of guidance by the clerical Church, which by the thirteenth century had become so powerful as to be seen as the only safe arbiter of secular arguments otherwise only resolvable by force of arms. Similarly, poverty was a misfortune. The control of wealth by the aristocracy and small merchant class was seen largely as a fact of life and an inviolable right, despite Aquinas's teaching on property as a contingent and not a natural right. In the early medieval world, the entire social order was governed by a religio-political alliance of secular and religious leaders. Indeed, because activity in the world was defined specifically as secular, the secular world became of lower status than activities which were defined as religious, such as those of the monastery. It is because of this global definition of the religious and the secular by the clerical leadership itself and agreed to by its feudal élite, that the medieval order existed as it did, confirmed by the religious élite and justified by its own religious ideology.

The transformation in consciousness, wrought by eighteenth- and nineteenth-century political and economic practice and by the thinkers who in part envisaged and in part articulated the changes, thus promoting them further, broke with these forms of interpretation of the person and of the political-economic mode. These developments were a consequence of the Reformation and of the new attitudes towards this-worldly activity which that religious movement inaugurated. It is true that those very same religious institutions challenged the political order in some countries and enhanced the community's contribution to political decision-making through parliaments and assemblies, enhancing also human effort in the transformation of the economic order through a this-worldly religious calling (Weber, 1930). However, it is also true that there was resistance to economic and political power passing beyond the confines of the middle and upper classes of society. The Reformation was a middle-class as well as a religious revolution. It was left to the economic revolution of industrialization, and the political revolutions in France and North America to take the further steps of opening up the human capacity to transform the political and economic orders in more total ways against the background of an ethic based on the human person, one which has come to be recognized—at least officially—as a guide to international law and to the formulation of the majority of state constitutions.

Partly as an effect of these developments, a certain globalization has taken place. By this term we mean in general the dramatic increase in communication, travel, and transport over the globe and an accompanying development of exploitation of the world's resources. The developments are uneven in the classic sociological sense. Some areas and social groups develop earlier than others, and the slow developers end up easily subsumed under the power of the early developers. Thus some peoples and social groups are dominated rather than liberated by the ensuing social relationships, be they economic, political, or cultural. The entire human world is locked into a set of power relationships which not only have mutual effects but also affect the whole planet, threatening both its and the entire human race's survival. This is most clear not only in the threat of nuclear and global warfare, but also in the ecological crisis, which cannot be solved without global co-operation.

All these positive and negative realities of modernity also bring with them corresponding dangers. The most important of these, or the ones we have become most aware of, are totalitarianism, mass destruction through nuclear and conventional warfare, the destruction of the environment precisely through its dominance and exploitation, and the concomitant destruction of huge swathes of humanity additionally exploited by dependency relationships. Because of these dangers, and their concomitance with globalization, there emerges also *the globalization of socio-ethical responsibility*.

Clearly, there is more than one 'project' to modernity. It is not an abstract reality but real. People may have different motivations in living out modernity, ranging from the pursuit of wealth for personal gain—even to the detriment of others—to human liberation, by which we mean freedom from hunger, want and warfare, growth to intellectual, emotional, and physical fulfilment over the life-cycle, in addition to commitments to a variety of ways of life, such as those provided by religion. Such aspects exist also in concrete ideological forms such as Liberalism, the Enlightenment, and Marxism, in addition to other humanistic and religious forms. We wish to emphasize the positive gains. They have a cumulative effect on human consciousness, particularly on critical and ethical perception. But we are also faced with the failures of modernity, some of which can totally destroy all possible gains, others which can destroy all the gains for massive sections of the population. What we want to stress here is the way in which modernity forms the situation within which and to which religion has to respond if it is to become a part of the modern world. There is a contradiction at the very heart of modernity which now has to be openly recognized.

The modern consciousness carries with it not only new possibilities of empowerment (which includes the enfranchisement of each mature individual), the emergence of a political consciousness, the growing understanding of the processes of wealth production and consumption, and the exploitation of material resources. Against this there are new possibilities of domination, slavery, and destruction resulting from the development of science and technology. We are suggesting also that this modern consciousness also poses radical choices to the religious consciousness. The crisis of modernity puts religion on the spot, with believers having to make a complete reappraisal of their situation. To this radical crisis of modernity, religion, if it is to remain genuinely human, has to respond. This response, we suggest, can lead either to a reassertion of the traditional ways of living out the religious life, or to their transformation, by facing up to modernity, welcoming and supporting its moral gains as expressions and realizations of the religious quest, and fighting constructively against its concomitant failures, which the Christian consciousness must see as evils against which there must be a total commitment to combat.

2.4   *The Crisis of Modernity*

The crisis of modernity is the furnace in which all religious forms now have to be forged. To see religion in the modern world only in terms of decline might be to pre-empt religion's capacity to survive or to transform in the context of rapid social change, and leave it no space for existence in the modern world except in its interstices. Our view might here be dominated by the vision of the collapse of medieval religious hegemony and institutional dominance. Probably, religion has only a limited number of ways of survival in the modern world:

(1) It can withdraw from the world and live in isolation as much as possible from the processes of modernity. This is the response of certain sects, such as the Amish in the USA, and can involve the almost complete denial of modernity.

(2) It can enjoy the benefits of modern technology, democratic politics, and aspects of the broadly modern culture while prefacing to it all a fundamentalist religious belief structure, such as creationism. This type is currently perhaps the most visible form of Christian and Islamic response to modernity. In the USA, fundamentalist Christians now outnumber those in the broadly liberal Churches.

(3) Another type of response is to come to grips with the problems modernity poses to the religious conscience and consciousness itself. This, we are suggesting, requires a transformation of the religio-moral consciousness. Gramsci called such transformations 'intellectual and moral reformations' (Fulton, 1987). Religious institutions have to internalize the moral gains of modernity in such a way that these gains become a part of the religious perception of social reality. We argue that this is what happens when religious groups accept key elements of the morality of modernity which have not of themselves sprung from religious revolutions. For example, the concept of religious autonomy propounded by Luther was limited to individual consciousness and was subsequently developed under

the pressure first of the Enlightenment and later with the steady enlargement of suffrage and other human rights for both women and minorities.

In the context of a modern society where a high degree of institutional specialization exists, the traditional religion of either (1) or (2) above, aids introversion and preoccupation with the self, particularly where central communal rituals become the sphere of the cleric and are marginalized in the experience of the individual. In other words, there is a certain affinity between the traditional religion of the later Middle Ages and the privatization of modern religious experience. Such a link was mediated in the Middle Ages by the decline of participation in the central community rituals of Christian worship and their substitution by the more individualistic rituals of relic worship and devotionalism, while in the modern era, a link is also provided by the processes of privatization of the religious institution and its replacement by the state and the institutions of modern production. Aspects of privatization are also a feature of post-Tridentine ritual and the devotional movement within Roman Catholicism.

This process of privatization also illuminates an important link between modernity and the problem of the renewal of religion. The process of modernization forges the steady differentiation of the political sphere from the religious in a particular way. Religion is no longer a sphere which operates out of both the economic (barons and lords) and the religious (princely bishops) in alliance. As we noted earlier, the 'societalization' of the community ideal was to remain dominant until the arrival of modernity, and to an extent still persists where monopoly Catholicism still prevails.

Linked to this process is the increasing abandonment of societal relations based on the local community, as towns and the associational lifestyle characteristic of the central institutions of modern society emerged to replace communal-type relationships. Traditional society was based largely on face to face and emotionally relevant relationships, even though many of these relationships might have been emotionally negative rather than positive. However, because such relationships were face to face, they allowed a direct reference to the way Christian community itself was understood, that is, in its face to face interactive mode, experientially. The development of modern relationships, which are formal and impersonal (filling out a tax form), usually requiring indirect contact (letters, telephone calls), left a gaping hole in the experience of community not just in secular terms, but also religious, as overall relationships no longer had a religious societal reference. The implication of this development was that if religious organizations did not work at the creation of the religious community in a very strong relational way, the very nexus of Christian religious survival—face to face positive relationships—would break down. This means that Christian Churches cannot possibly survive without the successful and positive construction of face to face community experiences. Christian survival is now based on the positive construction of community-style relationships. In this way, creative liturgy and Christian face to face bonding become positive imperatives. Such a positive construction has probably not taken place within the tradition of Roman Catholicism since the pre-Constantinian era. The failure to undertake it leads, first, to the privatization of religion, then secondly, following the death of the individual, the death of the Church as its individual members disappear.

In this modern world, with its representative democracies and massive improvements in human potential and yet with all its dangers of Armageddon, what has been the effect on religion? While within Protestantism, those rights and abilities have more readily been recognized (though group rights in the form of minority rights have found difficulty in coming to fruition), within the Catholic frame of reference, human rights and empowerment in the economic and political sphere have come much later, and have been shaped in their own particular way. Aspects of the Protestant recognition of the autonomy of conscience have only recently come to be respected by the leadership in the Roman Catholic Church, in allowing space— at least in practice—for individuals to follow their own conscience even in the face of Church discipline. But other aspects of the recognition of persons, such as gender equalities, are still far from the general consciousness of the male clerical centre.

In addition, the political role of the Roman Catholic Church has been split between a centralized papacy and laity at the local level. The papacy has focused on the preservation of the religious rights of Roman Catholics to practise their faith through the techniques of international diplomacy. The political consciousness of laity, however, has been largely left to be worked out at the local level. However, it has been 'guided' from the centre by particular political ideals, though the imposition of Vatican thought has had only limited success. One such ideal has been a certain *integriste* view of the social order and the use of the functional model of society to elaborate Catholic beliefs. This views each individual and group in society, whatever their state of equality or inequality, to be working for the good of the whole, similar to the parts of a living organism. Such a view has had a significant effect on the development of monopoly Catholic states. The Church in some of these is now in a phase of decline (Italy, France) while in others it is either still succeeding in imposing a partial religious domination on the state (Spain, Ireland), or maintaining its power (Poland).

However, at the level of intellectual reflection, a corrective to such thinking has been the relatively recent recognition of the inequities of the economic order, so that unbridled capitalism was criticized by Leo XIII in the 1890s and finally condemned by John-Paul II in the 1980s almost as severely as totalitarian communism. Yet, up until the 1960s, the approach by the hierarchical centre to 'social problems', by thinking about them in the abstract and without any engagement at the local level, was a measure of the distance which existed between the Vatican and the real world. Where the popular consciousness had found its own economic, political, and religious answers, this frequently incurred real opposition from Vatican diplomats rather than papal support.

The diplomatic approach had in the past resulted in a social ethic promoting a false sense of community, one which relied on fundamental inequalities between the powerful and the dispossessed. But the vision of charity as an interpersonal relationship bereft of any genuine consciousness of the radical inequality embedded in economic relations, still tends to dominate clerical and popular consciousness today. We are suggesting that the 'charity' approach is typical of a society where poverty and starvation are seen as beyond the human capacity to comprehend or resolve. Such a mentality is not the outcome of a post-modern awareness but a characteristic of a traditional culture still mainly unaware of the human ability to affect economic structures.

In order to spell out what is meant here, a practical example may be helpful. Consider the dramatic increase in conscientization over the issue of famine in the world. Parts of the so-called developed world have begun to respond to it on a considerable scale, though rarely at the level of nation-state institutions. One could say that the response to media coverage and to appeals by charities has been almost intuitive among the masses of people. They are conscious that they must intervene, and to put such responses down to knee-jerk reactions is in all probability to underestimate the strength of people's moral convictions.

Behind this sense of moral obligation is the fact that famine is both in part caused by, and can be in part solved precisely because of, certain aspects of globalization and the global economic system. But a further step must be taken, though it appears as yet only in the rhetoric of aid agencies, namely that we have a responsibility to solve the problem in the long term as well as in the short. Because famine is in part a result of the interdependence of the world system, and follows on from the system of cash crops and its failure, and from the use of weapons of mass destruction produced and sold by the developed world, and because it can in part be solved by the application of modern technology, planning, and transport on a global scale, the issue has become one of social justice and no longer one of 'charity'. The continuous relationships of power between rich and poor countries, or between rich and poor within a country, are no longer ones of charity but of social justice. The ability even to think in these terms about such issues was not a feature of traditional societies, though aspects of it did occasionally seek to emerge, as in the Peasants' War in Germany in the sixteenth century and the Diggers' movement in England in the seventeenth. When it did occur, interestingly, it was within the boundaries of a religious consciousness.

Because modifications to the political and economic structures of society are recognized as possible, and because the entire world can be clothed, fed, and adequately sheltered by means of present human resources, it is no longer possible to consider 'charity' in the popular sense as complying with 'charity' in the Christian sense. The new way to realize Christian charity is to implement the necessary political and economic changes. This is precisely where the obligation to act justly to all tallies with the biblical injunction to love one's fellow humankind.

'Charity' became the word which designated the corporal works of mercy in traditional Christian societies, mainly because such works were then the mark of the true Christian going beyond what was believed to be the minimum action of basic human compassion on behalf of others and which even the heathen might be expected to perform. But now the minimum action, justice, and the upholding of 'human dignity', has passed another threshold. Not only have we come through modernity to recognize the systemic nature of the production, distribution, and exchange of goods and services, with all elements in it dependent upon and responsible to each other, but also through modernity the entire globe has become one interdependent economic system. Poverty and hunger were once totally beyond the geographical reach of a better-off humankind, but this is no longer the case. Consequently, the solution to poverty is not in handouts, but handouts followed by empowerment, to enable people to take charge of their own role in the international system of relationships, and develop their means of production to the level where they can become self-sustaining communities. It is the entry of world-wide poverty into human consciousness which creates the justice obligation for the humanity of the First World towards those of the developing world, and it is no longer a question of mere charitable activity.

This recognition of the West's and the individual's responsibility for events in the Third World has, however, not reached the consciousness of the majority of the world's governments which claim that they cannot afford the 1 per cent of their national product which the United Nations has invited them to donate for the development of Third World countries. This is a point where a Christian conscience could enter. At the moment, the Churches already assist in the spreading of conscientization about the world's needs through their aid agencies. However, despite the fact that they make a small though significant impact, it is perhaps nothing compared to the impact they could develop if they were to see world-wide poverty as the great social sin of the world. While some people salve their consciences with an annual cheque, there is little evidence of a concerted political campaign. While such an orientation has been formulated within liberation Christianity, in general such movements remain marginal to both the Reformation Churches and the Roman Catholic Church.

Elements of such perspectives are to be found in recent papal encyclicals, particularly those from the 1960s dealing with the Third World, even if social class relationships in general have yet to be fully explored. In this way, papal teaching has fallen into line with much humanistic reflection on the globalization of human relationships. Although the ability to control economic forces remains far from total, the 'system' is better understood and our ability to affect the lives of peoples all over the globe is recognized. The globalization of religious and ethical outreach reflects much common cause for religious and secular faith alike, and yields, at the same time, a key point of contrast between traditional and modern spiritualities. At the moment there is a tension between papal teaching on the subject and papal practice which is wary of allowing such a belief to become politically operative in the minds and hearts of Catholic populations. So the papacy continues to have problems with the political practice of liberation theology while at the same time it preaches the same theory.

Modernity is thus a set of processes which either remove, fossilize, or dramatically change religious consciousness. The consequence is that the institutional Church is faced with either accepting the new understanding and acting on it, with consequences for its internal hierarchical ordering, or retreating to a sense of community characteristic of and only possible within the regime of traditional society. For that mentality to survive, religion and politics have to be kept apart and religious responsibility denied. The present papacy has a considerable consciousness of the West's responsibility for the Third World. The sad thing is that it does not appear to appreciate that responding to this has both a religious and a political dimension. Empowerment in the one requires some form of empowerment in the other.

2.5 Responses to Modernity

The state of Roman Catholicism today is pluriform with continuous and forceful attempts by the centre to reduce this pluriformity to hierarchical unity. We suggest that in fact different movements, some already institutionalized, represent different responses to modernity and to its crises. Three movements in particular illustrate the alternatives which we have outlined. They are Opus Dei, charismatic renewal, and liberation Christianity. They encapsulate what appear to be distinctive ways of confronting the dilemmas.

It is not possible here to go into any detail on these movements (for Opus Dei, see Walsh, 1989; for charismatic renewal, see McGuire, 1982 and Neitz, 1987; for liberation Christianity, see Smith, 1991). A schematic interpretation, along the specific lines with which we are concerned, has been given in Figure 2.2.

The main point we wish to note here is that organization and culture are the two main interpretative dimensions we have suggested and applied. Their use appears to contribute to the understanding of the place which each movement or organization has in contemporary Roman Catholic spirituality. The major difference between the three movements and RENEW is that all three began independently from hierarchical control. The founder of Opus Dei, Escrivá, sought early on to get papal approval; in fact the search for patronage was typical of his approach. However the Vatican showed clear divisions in dealing with it. It gradually made headway through internal patronage, but only emerged victorious with the arrival of John Paul II, who has seen it as an ideal vehicle for his vision of the re-evangelization of the Christian world.

Charismatic renewal also began outside of hierarchical control. Indeed, such was the early fear of loss of control of significant sections of the Catholic community by the Vatican that internal wranglings among bishops could only be avoided by clerics asserting

	OPUS DEI	CHARISMATIC RENEWAL	LIBERATION CHRISTIANITY
ORGANIZATION:	hierarchical (mechanistic)	hierarchical and organic controlled 'inspiration'	organic
agenda setting:	hierarchically set		set by social circumstances
clerical/lay:	clear clerical control	clerical or lay facilitator	clerical or lay facilitator
gender:	male dominated, women subordinate	women equal or subordinate	women equal? (not enough data)
goal:	monopoly Catholic society, personal salvation	recover interior freedom, emotions, community, personal salvation	emancipation of self + group here and hereafter
CULTURE:	'bubble' of traditional religion	flexible but leaves society unchanged	modern/transformative
response to modernity:	accepts technology, rejects values	recover community + emotional life	response to oppression (individual + social)
response to history:	to decline of church power over dominant culture	to collapse of devotionalism	to political/economic oppression
empowerment:	obedience	empowerment of soul + emotions	empowerment of self + group
group style:	inner hierarchy (three levels)	face to face/elite/cult within a church	basic Christian community
central ritual:	Tridentine mass	charismatic meeting	conscientization (problem, scripture, prayer, action)
strategy:	infiltration of key cultural bases: universities, media	no clear strategy, tendency to social introversion	conscientization? (leading to political-economic action)
STATUS:	approved (recommended)	approved (after early hesitation)	seen as threat
CONFINES:	confined to RC, mainly latin	inter-Christian, most places	inter-Christian, developing world

FIG. 2.2 Roman Catholic Contemporary Institutions/Movements Compared

leadership and 'cooling out' its original strong ecumenical orientations. It is now thoroughly domesticated and well organized under clerical supervision and with the appropriate training of lay supervisors.

Finally, liberation Christianity emerged from earlier Catholic Action-type ministries, sponsored by the Brazilian hierarchy. Sheer shortage of clergy enabled a lay leadership to apply the techniques of conscientization to the religious and human development of poverty-stricken communities, with extraordinary success. But the creativity of the response was such as to shatter the traditional framework of religious action for participants, and was one with which the Vatican was simply unable to cope. The most dramatic expression of this negative encounter was the shouting down of John Paul II by the Managuan crowds on his visit to Nicaragua in 1983. Indeed, one of our main arguments will be that the present structure of the papacy is ill-equipped to handle modernity, as it requires considerable empowerment and space to create an appropriate religious response both to the evils and the moral gains of the modern world.

We have pointed out that RENEW is unlike all three movements in that it did not emerge at the periphery of Church authority, but rather from a hierarchical apex at the instigation of individual bishops. RENEW is structured, according to its founders, as an empowering movement specifically for the laity. Does it in fact do that? And what does it empower them to do? Are its promises fulfilled and if not, why not? We suggest that our examination of the twofold dimensions of culture and organization will help us answer these types of question.

2.6   *A Classification of Spiritualities*

In this chapter we have argued that a social and comparative study of spirituality requires the recognition and examination of the two key aspects, organization and culture. We have also added that a significant element in the response to modernity has to be a recognition of both its values and its moral imperatives, including the transformation of the previously supererogatory to the realms of social justice. As social phenomena, spiritualities are both cultures and sets of corporate actions. Their values and perceptions affect and are affected by the forms of organization which form an integral part of their unfolding and development. The culture of a group's spirituality involves the interpretation of the experience of

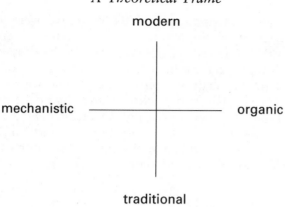

FIG. 2.3   Principles for the Classification of Spiritualities

the social milieu in which the group's spirituality is set, and the actual value response which the group formulates: its goals, its perception of the divine, the human and the world at large, its choice of virtues and its attitude to action in the world, its group style, and its dominant rituals. The organization of a group's spirituality is the form of agenda construction, decision-making, and chain of command and execution which the group adopts, and involves such issues as hierarchical and organic decision-making, clerical–lay and male–female relationships, and the strategy or strategies the group employs.

From these two dimensions of traditional/modern cultures and hierarchical/organic forms of organization, we can obtain four combinations of culture and organization which provide us with a set of possible spiritualities in the contemporary world of Roman Catholicism. The axes are illustrated in Figure 2.3. The four types the axes yield will be developed further in Chapter 5.

In terms of fitting all contemporary realities into this type of frame, however, it is worth forecasting that it will be well-nigh impossible to do so neatly. Social reality, especially the religious, rarely fits neatly within any one cell of a classification. Certainly any attempt to classify past spiritualities would clearly require further elaboration to situate them more firmly in their historical period and locality. But we do maintain that a spirituality or movement is likely to fit predominantly into one or other cell for at least one period or phase of its existence and that understanding it in this way is likely to provide sufficient significance to mark it off from other phases, spiritualities, or movements.

At the beginning of our study of RENEW, we were struck by what seemed to be a top-down organizational programme and ambiguities in the preferred religious culture. In the chapters which follow, we will report our findings from our case study of RENEW in the light of the typology of spiritualities which we have drawn up. We commence in Chapter 3 with an analysis of the process by which the Bishop of Downlands came to recommend RENEW to his priests and later the laity in his diocese. Of particular concern here will be the extent to which the offer of participation in RENEW followed mechanistic or organic paths.

3

The Adoption of RENEW

3.1 The Search for Renewal

In the previous chapter we proposed a model of spiritualities in terms of two dimensions: organizational structure and cultural type. In this and the following chapter we will be concerned chiefly with the first of these dimensions: the nature of the organizational framework in the research diocese within which the decision to adopt the RENEW programme was taken and implemented. Our concern is a sociological one. We aim to describe the process by which the decision was taken to adopt RENEW and the mechanisms and strategies employed by the religious leaders and initiators in the diocese to persuade the mass of priests and lay people in all the parishes in the diocese to accept their recommendation and to mobilize them, with more or less enthusiasm or reluctance, to participate in the three-year undertaking; to identify the dominant ideologies implicit in the RENEW programme and expressed by its advocates and the diocesan leadership in order to legitimate its promotion; and to offer a sociological interpretation of the processes involved.

We have used pseudonyms throughout for the diocese, parishes, individual informants, and various diocesan and parochial publications. Dates of interviews and quotations from publications have been given to enable social researchers to verify our sources and to demonstrate that our data are reliable enough to sustain our analysis. But our primary concern is *not* with the particularities of the Diocese of Downlands but with a generalizable analysis which might be applied to a much wider corpus of spiritualities. It is our hope that the use of pseudonyms will encourage readers to focus on the *processes* and their interpretation rather than on particular circumstances and personalities.

The adoption of RENEW in the Diocese of Downlands can be seen as part of the general process of renewal called for by the Second Vatican Council but in the specific context of a prosperous area in south-east England in the late 1980s. We have previously noted the context of decline in the diocese, both in terms of weekly

Mass attenders and numbers of active priests, which were matters of some concern. In the period after the Vatican Council many Catholics also felt a sense of uncertainty and some unease at the loss of previous 'certainties'. In a series of consultations over a decade or more, lay people in the diocese had expressed a need, however inarticulately, for some form of adult religious education. It was in the context of these trends and felt needs that the bishop led the search for an appropriate response.

We will demonstrate that the bishop, in consultation with a few close advisers, took the decision to adopt RENEW in July 1986 and thereafter co-opted the priests, and later parish activists, in the promotion of the programme. We will argue that the sequence of events in the process of adopting RENEW demonstrated clearly a top-down or mechanistic organizational mode in the diocesan Church. Our data are derived in the main from tape-recorded, focused interviews (Merton and Kendall, 1956) with Bishop Patrick and a number of his close advisers, and with Mgr. John Carroll, the originator of RENEW in the Newark Archdiocese and the Program Director of the National Office of RENEW in Newark. Apart from this we have drawn on the reports published in the various editions of the *Downlands Times* (*DT*), the regular diocesan newspaper.

In an interview Bishop Patrick traced his path to RENEW from his experiences with small groups and communities in a parish in the early 1960s. These had a profound effect on him:

So I always realized that the revitalization of the parish was connected in some way with not only the Mass and the sacraments and the ordinary life of the parish, but also with the way that people got together, particularly with regard to meeting and studying the Word of God and relating it to daily life, and . . . sharing their faith.

Later experiences and reading Yves Congar's *Lay People in the Church* (1965), reinforced his view that

the development of small communities within the parish would help the overall mission of the Church in the parish . . . And if you look at the history of the Church, you will see that all religious revivals or renewals come from people being gathered together, listening to the Word of God and relating it to the needs of their life and their times. (Interview, 7 Oct. 1992)

This conviction was expressed further in his first pastoral letter as Bishop of Downlands in 1978. He indicated that there were 'three ways in which we can all build up the Church so that it really is a sign of God's presence in the world': liturgy, prayer, and community. He suggested that:

The third way of building up the Church is by realizing we are a *family*. By this I mean we must strive to form local Christian communities of all kinds. Whether we are talking about parishes, schools or societies we must start by looking at ourselves primarily as people, as a community, as a family. We need to experience a deep sense of belonging to the Church. The local community needs to be somewhere where everyone feels at home. We need to welcome everyone more, to make people feel that the parish and liturgy are theirs for the sharing. (Stapleton, 1990: 56)

The bishop has consistently promoted small groups and their role in adult religious education and formation. A year after the National Pastoral Congress in Liverpool in 1980 he encouraged 'small groups of parishioners to meet regularly to pray, listen to the Word of God in Scripture, and talk about their own particular situations in life', and a number of training courses for group leaders were arranged (*DT* June 1981). Two years later (in *The Sower*, Jan. 1983; *DT* Feb. 1983) he wrote enthusiastically of the week-long training sessions for formation groups held at St Winifred's, a diocesan pastoral centre. These were an attempt to counter three problems still apparent in Catholic parishes nearly two decades after Vatican II: the continued running of all aspects of parish life by priests, the lack of effective spiritual formation among lay people, and the reluctance of lay people to undertake active work. In retrospect, Bishop Patrick regarded this experiment as only

partially successful. I think the early effort ran out of steam, so to speak, partly because the organization was not thorough enough, and partly because I don't think that the real importance of the groups had come home to people. (Stapleton, 1990: 63)

In 1985 a large number of parish groups in the diocese participated in the national *Called to Serve* consultation in preparation for the 1987 Synod in Rome on the *Vocation and Mission of the Laity in the Church and in the World, Twenty years after the Second Vatican Council*. Bishop Patrick noted that there were about 500 groups in the diocese involved in that consultation:

And there were loud cries in that consultation for things that needed to be developed within the diocese. And I suppose the three most important things were: . . . liturgy, prayer; formation, in terms of forming Catholics in their Faith; and mission to the world, and . . . social concerns or issues of justice and peace. (Interview, 7 Oct. 1992)

It was about this time, in March 1985, that several bishops from England, Wales, and Scotland and their close advisers visited the Archdiocese of Newark for a week's seminar on RENEW in response to an invitation from an American foundation which was impressed by the achievements of Mgr. Carroll. Bishop Patrick was accompanied by Mgr. Francis Johnson, the Episcopal Vicar for Education. Bishop Patrick returned from Newark with two reservations about RENEW:

One was the American flavour which I didn't think would go down well in England. The second was the word RENEW [which] gave me the impression of . . . a sort of rather gimmicky thing to revitalize the Church . . . But . . . RENEW itself, what it was trying to do, I was totally in accord with, namely to develop prayer, liturgy, more . . . faith-sharing communities; the very simple orientation and development of issues of justice and peace, of social concern. And I always felt . . . that what people were looking for was a deeper faith. And I thought that what RENEW would be able to provide was the circumstances or the process within which many people would find a deeper faith, a deeper love of scripture and a deeper openness to society.   (Interview, 7 Oct. 1992)

Mgr. Johnson was very enthused by the spirit of the RENEW programme which he felt

had a very great deal to offer in getting people together around scripture . . . and getting laity involved in the leadership of the parish . . . But what it didn't seem to offer that our diocese had been asking for was the *content* of Christian formation, or the doctrine . . . Because there had been quite an on-going priority given to that . . . in our diocesan consultation.   (Interview, 12 Oct. 1992)

It is clear that one of the reservations about RENEW was 'a strong resistance among the priests to any idea of "another American programme"!' It does seem that the phrase indicates a reflex reaction to anything foreign. Mgr. Johnson, for example, noted that it was

because so much reached us from the States, like the Brusselmans First Communion programme . . . I think it was a kind of catch phrase . . . People were beginning to say 'in this country we've got a different culture from over the Atlantic; we shouldn't get everything from over there!'   (Interview, 12 Oct. 1992)

Another senior priest was more critical and 'felt some of the anti-Americanism was that knee-jerk stuff, wrapped up in having lost an empire and being really third rate' (Interview, 17 Nov. 1992).

Apart from this, the financial outlay of around $100 (at that time about £100) for the basic materials for each parish 'seemed rather hefty' though he did not think it was a major consideration at that time. Nor were the criticisms from right-wing Catholics in the United States, and the examination of its content by the US

Bishops' Conference, about which the RENEW team had been 'very open', major considerations at this stage.

In sum, around the mid-1980s Bishop Patrick, who had had a long-standing commitment to small groups and was seeking some sort of response to lay people's expressed needs for basic Catholic doctrine and adult religious education, and who had taken up the invitation to consider RENEW, did not, at that stage feel that it was appropriate for the diocese. As Mgr. Johnson observed:

it wasn't dead right for us at that time. Let's keep it on the back burner and let's see what our diocese wants to do . . . And we were talking about making up our own program of renewal and formation. But then [a] shift of emphasis came, much more towards scripture and Sunday liturgy and spiritual renewal. I'm not saying the content wasn't important; but not hitting quite so hard . . . (Interview, 12 Oct. 1992)

3.2 From Invitation to Decision

In a memorandum, 'How RENEW came to Downlands', which he had prepared for the *Downlands Times*, Mgr. Johnson outlined the various stages in reaching the decision in 1986 to offer RENEW to the diocese. Additional information was given in the *Report for Ad Limina [Visit] From [the] Office of Small Communities* (Feb. 1992). A report on the diocesan *Called to Serve* consultation formed the agenda of the Diocesan Pastoral Council (DPC) held at St Richard's Seminary in February 1986. In his pastoral letter of April 1986 Bishop Patrick summarized the results of the consultation and discussion at the DPC which 'indicated [a] widespread desire for [a] deeper understanding of the Church's teaching, formation as disciples of Jesus Christ, a real sense of community, greater sharing of responsibility in parish life, better communication and cooperation between bishop, priests and people, and above all, spiritual renewal'. At the DPC he had also expressed the hope 'that in the next few years, a pastoral plan would emerge enabling us to realize the dream expressed during the day' (*DT* Apr. 1986).

At a meeting of the heads of diocesan departments in May 1986 it was considered that 'RENEW had much to offer', though it perhaps needed adapting to the particular needs of the diocese, 'especially with more "Catholic teaching"'. Around this time, a meeting of the Council of Priests 'discussed pastoral strategy for the diocese, and centred on spiritual and catechetical renewal, linked with scripture and Sunday liturgy'. Mgr. Johnson observed:

That was the meeting when Bishop Patrick and I met eyes and thought 'they're talking about RENEW'! That was actually a turning point . . . What was coming up was this scripture and spiritual renewal, which was a slightly different slant, whereas before it had been much more on content and doctrine. And this was a newer development, a shift of emphasis, I should say. And that was where I think we thought that RENEW is something that would meet that need.   (Interview, 12 Oct. 1992)

An informant from the Sacred Heart parish told us that as late as Season 2 in the spring of 1989, a member of the diocesan RE-NEW team 'let it out' at a meeting of leaders that the main reason why RENEW was adopted was because Mass attendances were dropping. So this parish regarded RENEW as the diocese's answer to fears of evangelism by the local Baptists and a fundamentalist group such as the Riverton Community Church. In spite of the worrying aspects of declining Mass attendances and shrinking numbers of active priests, the bishop insisted that his main concern was:

How does the Church face in the culture of our day? How do you develop both a personal and communal faith of our people? . . . How do we actually, in this process, be proactive instead of reactive? How are we not just keeping the Church going, in terms of guarding and living the tradition of the Church? How do we make it new . . . fresh? . . . And so the purpose of RENEW was not just a reaction to those elements which threaten the Church today; it was much more an initiative, a process to enable people at grassroots level to actually deepen their faith. I don't believe that that can be done just by instructing people better . . . by exhortation, or good pastoral letter . . . I think that the answers . . . don't necessarily come from above, from bishops or priests. They come from the people reacting within the context of their own lives to the needs of their world, their society, and their parish and their community . . .   (Interview, 7 Oct. 1992)

The process was taken further at the June meeting of the DPC Committee which 'favoured using RENEW rather than trying to prepare our own programme from scratch'. Later, when encouraging the take-up of RENEW in the diocese, the need 'not to reinvent the wheel' (Stapleton, 1990: 81) became a strong argument in favour of the American programme rather than attempting from scratch and with limited resources, to construct its own alternative programme of renewal.

The next step was taken during the diocesan pilgrimage to Lourdes in July 1986. Mgr. Johnson has described how he, Bishop Patrick, Mgr. Tom Cook (the Vicar General), and Mgr. Jim Smith (the Chancellor), 'discussed RENEW and Downlands over dinner at the Hotel St Sauveur. The momentous decision was taken to invite

Mgr. John Carroll, the founder of RENEW, to present it to the priests and to the Diocesan Pastoral Council'. There then followed a series of telephone conversations with the RENEW office in New Jersey to arrange for Mgr. Carroll to give presentations to both the diocesan priests and the DPC in November 1986. However, there is little doubt that the decision to adopt RENEW was taken at this point, in Lourdes, because it appears that the bishop was actively seeking funding to undertake the RENEW programme some time before Mgr. Carroll made his presentations in the diocese.

Mgr. Bob Reilly has described his original hostility to RENEW and his subsequent Saul-like conversion from being 'set on persecuting it' to his current encouragement of it in his role as Director of RENEW in Europe. In an interview he recalled that when Bishop Patrick returned from Newark

he called together five or six of us to talk about it. I well remember I was sitting . . . at the bottom of the table, and I was very quiet because I was really angry as a pastor at this point. I was up to my eyes . . . I wasn't too long in (his new parish of) Beachcliff at that point, with trying to launch various sacramental programmes, renewal programmes, such as the First Communion programme, Confirmation programme, reconciliation programme, and so on. At the same time one was trying to launch [a] parish pastoral council . . . I was up to here with school governorships . . . Anyway, Bishop Patrick caught my eye at one point and he said: 'Bob, you've been uncharacteristically silent all during this meeting', and he wanted to know why. I said: 'I'm fuming . . . We haven't even got RCIA [Rite of Christian Initiation of Adults] moving yet!' . . . And the end result of all that was . . . Bishop Patrick turned to Francis Johnson and said: 'Francis, keep that return ticket in your pocket; we'll go over and have a look at RENEW another time. So we put it on the back burner at that stage, for I suppose at least a year . . . Behind the scenes I was Saul . . . set on persecuting it. I suppose I fell off my horse! When the RENEW team came over, Bishop Patrick then invited the heads of the various departments in the diocese, the agencies and so on, to come to St Winifred's . . . to hear a presentation by a number of people from RENEW. I still was quite negative, putting it gently . . . And the moment of conversion, for me, to RENEW came when . . . they had been placing great emphasis on the fact that RENEW was based on an axis of prayer and organization . . . They attributed whatever success it was having, in no small measure, to the harnessing, as it were, of the prayer-life of the people of the diocese, invoking the spirit . . . of a 'new pentecost' . . . that we would be open . . . to the guidance of the Holy Spirit, for His Church . . . And I found myself saying: 'well, Bob, if it is true that the Holy Spirit in fact can and does renew His Church . . . who are you to get in the way?' And my opposition, as it were, melted at that moment. (Interview, 21 July 1992)

Mgr. Reilly recalls showing the RENEW materials to a friend, a senior businessman, whose judgement at the time was that in his business RENEW 'would be marked down as "high risk". If it comes off . . . the dividends will be high . . . If it doesn't . . . there will be a lot of egg on a number of people's faces!'

It was at a meeting of clergy advisers that it was agreed that 'something had to be done' and Bishop Patrick thought that

maybe we ought to have a look at RENEW again . . . Some of the initial work that would take us a very long time to do has been done by them . . . So I asked two other people to go over [to Newark], the Vicar General, [Mgr.] Tom Cook, and Jane Morris [the Diocesan Youth Officer] . . . I think that what made me go back to RENEW was that I couldn't find, frankly, anything which combined so many of the things that I wanted in any other process . . . Everybody was saying to me who I listened to in the diocese 'there needs to be some kind of process which would activate . . . the diocesan process at this time to respond to *Call to Serve*. And to wait for another two, three, four years would not be right. So in a sense I said 'well, we'll have to . . . '.   (Interview, 7 Oct 1992)

It is perhaps helpful at this stage to pause in the review of the process of adopting RENEW in Downlands and note that in spite of some talk about lay empowerment, the decision to adopt RE-NEW was clearly top-down and taken by the bishop in consultation with his closest advisers. There is no evidence of an in-depth consideration of alternatives, or that the mass of priests or lay people in the diocese were seriously involved in the decision.

It might also be appropriate here to ask why it was that the decision-makers in other dioceses came to other decisions about RENEW. In response to our enquiries, we received written contributions from two bishops, a senior priest, and four lay people, from four dioceses which had sent them to Newark for briefing purposes in the mid-1980s, but which had decided not to take up the RE-NEW option. Some felt that indigenous programmes of renewal were more appropriate. Thus one of the bishops

came to the conclusion that we were not ready for such a programme . . . there must be a balance between where people actually are and the direction in which they should be moving. It was felt that the priority was to lead people to appreciate, at least in part, the genuine level in ecclesiology which has been achieved during the second half of this century. To do this a transparochial service had to be provided which eventually would nourish the parish as a Church Communion.   (Letter, 22 Feb. 1994)

A senior priest in his diocese was so disappointed with the decision that he attempted to run a RENEW programme in his own parish.

Another bishop 'decided not to pursue the option of RENEW mainly because of one factor—that many of the aims and objectives of RENEW were already in operation in the diocese' which had generated its own pastoral plan. An additional 'major factor was that any material for RENEW had to be purchased . . . at a cost that was felt to be inflated' (Letter, 2 Mar. 1994). A senior priest from this diocese elaborated:

RENEW was not in principle any different from the sort of MISSION that enlightened parishes were organising in the 70's . . . [the] 'base Communities' were not really more than street groups [or] 'Eucharistic' . . . and . . . for long-term groups they were too overloaded by 'content from on high' . . . [and] would tend to be 'middle class' . . . the philosophy/theology of RE-NEW missed the real point of the Justice issue and the Option for the Poor, and that it was intentionally designed to meet the inhibitions of the affluent in relation to these issues, avoiding any analysis and any real solidarity. What was called Justice, seemed to me no more than the old approach of Charity for the Needy by the well-off . . . I think though that the real reason for our diocese not taking it on was firstly that we felt that the [diocesan] clergy would not readily co-operate with something so pre-packaged . . . and so heavily structured at diocesan level and secondly that it seemed too expensive . . . (Letter, 10 Mar. 1994)

A senior lay person from a third diocese had judged that RENEW 'was not the right thing *at that time* to offer' to the diocese. Noting that her judgements of RENEW had been made seven years previously, she recalled that she saw RENEW as a package incorporating into one structure, methods and insights already familiar from RCIA and other forms of parish catechesis, and from movements such as the Young Christian Workers (YCW). Such developments were already taking place in the diocese. She also recalled feeling doubtful about the culture of the programme (Personal communication, 11 May 1993).

Finally, three lay people from a large metropolitan diocese organized in areas testified to the critical nature of such contingencies as the sudden transfer of a bishop to another diocese and a reticence to pre-empt decisions involving a new appointment, conflicting priorities among area bishops inhibiting initiatives which embraced the whole diocese, and recent diocesan administrative reorganization, which would have made it difficult to initiate RENEW at that stage. Our informants differed over the importance of the cost of the programme at a time when the diocese was attempting to reduce its debt by increasing demands on the parishes. One bishop who was an admirer of Helder Camara was said to oppose 'the RENEW process which had to be imposed from above'. This informant also suggested that catechetical co-ordinators were opposed to RENEW because it was felt to interfere with the RCIA process and there were also misgivings about the effect on traditional ecumenical activity during Lent. Finally, the point was made that the bishops had so many national and international responsibilities that they did not in practice do much long term planning (Letters of 23 and 24 Feb. 1994).

In the Diocese of Downlands such concerns were not so prominent and the strategic decision was taken by the bishop and his close advisers that RENEW was the best option available to meet the felt needs of the diocese, since the alternative of a home-grown programme would take too long to develop. There was no point in 're-inventing the wheel', and it would be a relatively easy task to adapt the American programme for local consumption. Having taken the decision, the next task was to obtain the compliance of the diocese. In both Downlands and those dioceses which had not taken up the RENEW option, however, a common theme is the top-down nature of the decision-making process. Advisers were consulted but the decisions were almost invariably top down rather than collaborative.

3.3   From Decision to Persuasion

We have seen that the *decision* to adopt RENEW had been taken in Lourdes in July 1986. What followed would be the important stages of first, persuading the diocese, primarily the priests and then the laity, to agree to participate in what would be a major diocesan undertaking, and secondly, to put in place the appropriate resources and organization to implement the programme. Mgr. Johnson's memorandum is succinct:

Mgr. John Carroll gave presentations to the priests and Diocesan Officers at St Richard's Seminary, . . . and to the Diocesan Pastoral Council at Middleton (on 18–19 November, 1986). The priests were not fully satisfied and wanted more information about RENEW, but both gatherings gave Bishop Patrick an overwhelming vote that he should seriously consider offering RENEW to the Diocese.

This brief statement fails to convey the sense of tension and conflict which was expressed at this stage in the process of adopting RENEW. Bishop Patrick described the presentation at St Richard's as 'the most dramatic meeting I've ever had in my life . . . I have to say it wasn't an easy meeting!' (Interview, 7 Oct. 1992). Jane Morris, who made a presentation at the meeting, recalled that people

were a little nervous of what was going to happen because there was . . .
a three-line whip to get everybody there . . . It was a very tense meeting . . .
This was the first time these [clergy] were hearing it, so of course it was
a threat . . . They needed time to absorb it and make it their own . . . And
I think people were very nervous of buying into something which seemed
to be imposed from another culture on them . . . But I thought there was
a huge amount of potential for making it our own and using it for the
pastoral development of the diocese. . . . OK, there were a few little cultural
quirks here and there but we didn't have to buy them. But the basis was
actually good sense; I thought it was scriptural, . . . gospel-based. (Interview, 25 Nov. 1992)

Mgr. Johnson observed that the meeting with the priests of the
diocese at St Richard's

was a slightly hairy one! . . . There was a bit of personal feeling . . . I don't
think I've ever experienced anything quite (like it) . . . When I went in
people were sitting in the back of the room, with several front rows empty.
And I spent several minutes trying to get people to move to the front . . . John
[Carroll] must have read the vibes of the meeting as well. There was a lot
of antagonism about . . . I suppose it was part of this thing, another
American programme; the bishop had gone to the States and been enthused and come back [and] wanted to sell it to the diocese, you know.
So there was certainly some negative feedback in that meeting. But in the
questions and answers [at that meeting] there was some quite strongly
critical questions . . . Although it wasn't an easy meeting, he wasn't given
the cold shoulder in words. But I think he was in vibes! (Interview, 12
Oct. 1992)

One parish priest expressed his reservations, and he suspected
those of other priests too, about the style of 'consultation' employed
by the bishop:

The trouble with doing things this way is that you are always being presented with something, you know; 'there's the question, here's the answer;
do you accept the answer?' Rather than saying: 'here's the question; what
answers are there that we can have to this question?' So my criticism of
that consultation . . . is that you are always being consulted on . . . an answer
rather than being consulted on the question. (Interview, 22 Feb. 1989)

He proceeded to illustrate this by reference to an earlier consultation about the appropriate arrangements for the administration of
Confirmation in the diocese. This priest was initially not at all
enthusiastic about RENEW and felt that the diocese ought to have
been able to produce its own materials 'more in tune with our own
needs'. He argued that there were developments and processes and
activities on-going in the parishes which were interrupted by programmes such as RENEW. In his parish a particularly sad effect

which had upset many people was that the well-established ecumenical Lenten groups were suspended for two years. Energies needed to be concentrated on the needs of the local community rather than dissipated in the large number of meetings which the RENEW programme entailed.

It seems that the meeting with the parish representatives at the DPC the following day went much more smoothly and Mgr. Carroll's presentation 'was very well received' and there was 'an overwhelming feeling of "gosh! Let's get on with it"'. While the lay people 'were very keen ... the priests were much more guarded'. Mgr. Johnson recalled that the bishop asked for a 'straw vote' at both meetings and received overwhelming support at both meetings to the question: 'would you vote that I should seriously consider offering RENEW to the diocese?' Given their evident hostility, the vote of the priests was perhaps surprising. A priest informant told us that at the priests' meeting four priests did not put up their hands. He observed: 'They were brave men!', an indication of the pressure felt by the participants. But 'they were not saying "yes, we want it" but "yes, give it serious consideration"'.

INTERVIEWER. Was the bishop trying to persuade them at this stage or was he [still] sounding them out?
RESPONDENT. He was trying to persuade them ...

Mgr. Johnson observed that:

[After the November meeting] the bishop obviously realized the priests weren't ready for it yet. And so he went through that process of writing and asking for their views. And I think ... probably the response he got was, while there were questions and doubts and so on, there was pretty positive feeling about doing something of this sort. (Interview, 12 Oct. 1992)

The *Report for Ad Limina* in February 1992 noted that after the two meetings in November 1986:

Bishop Patrick visited every deanery, inviting parish clergy to put in writing by Easter 1987 their own personal position on whether or not the diocese should go ahead with RENEW, each parish being free to participate or not. (Para 2.3.2)

At the seminary meeting Bishop Patrick had said:

I wouldn't do it unless over 70 per cent were in favour. Nor would I do it until I'd explained what I had in mind more fully and they'd had a chance to absorb [it], which meant my going round all the [priests in the] deaneries. And eventually they all had a kind of vote with their comments on whether we should adopt it or not. (Interview, 7 Oct. 1992)

Mgr. Bob Reilly recalls that the bishop said to the priests:

This is RENEW; I'm offering you this. Now if you're not going to do it, I would expect you to come up with a comparative programme of renewal for your parish, because you're not going to stay where you are. Your people have said, people in this diocese have spoken, the priests in this diocese have spoken. We're not going to stay where we are. There's no such thing as just sitting here.

Mgr. Reilly noted that a similar position had been taken by an American archbishop in 1992 who had told a diocesan meeting: 'Well, you're free. But you're not free to do nothing! I'm offering you RENEW' (Interview, 21 Sept. 1992). The Council of Priests aired the matter again at their meeting in January 1987 and over the next two months the bishop visited each deanery conference (of priests) 'to say more about RENEW and his hopes for the diocese'. The Council of Priests met again in April 1987 and around this time the priests voted for RENEW to go ahead.

It seems that the original intention was that Mgr. Cook would be the Director of RENEW in the diocese following his visit to Newark with Jane Morris in the summer of 1986, but unfortunately he became seriously ill and died in May 1988. In the event the bishop appointed Fr. Liam O'Brien to direct RENEW in the diocese in the summer of 1987 and the August/September issue of *Downlands Times* announced that

The two-and-a-half year programme of spiritual renewal will begin in autumn 1988, after several months of preparing materials and training parish teams . . . Fr. O'Brien is at present taking part in a detailed briefing on "Renew" in New Jersey, its international headquarters. Bishop Patrick will appoint further members of the "Renew" team in due course. (1987)

In his article on RENEW in the diocesan silver jubilee book, Canon O'Brien reported that 'The RENEW office was set up at St Winifred's, and opened in August 1987. Sister Mary Richards . . . joined Fr. O'Brien. She brought with her experience of RENEW in New Zealand . . . Jane Morris was coopted to work part-time while remaining full-time Youth Officer [sic!]' (Stapleton, 1990: 81).

It is interesting to note the backgrounds of the three members of the diocesan RENEW team: a priest who had had 14 years secondment in Lima, Peru, and practical experience of basic Christian communities and the themes of liberation theology; a religious sister who had had experience of RENEW in New Zealand and the involvement of the charismatic movement; and the diocesan Youth Officer who was well known in the diocese. Some observers have noted that it is not uncommon to appoint the diocesan core team from outside existing diocesan agencies. It has been suggested that this enables a fresh approach to renewal to be taken in a situation where bureaucratized diocesan agencies appear to have lost their effectiveness. In the present case, while relations between the RENEW team and the Downlands Christian Education Centre (DCEC) were not easy, the reasons appear to have been due to space limitations which necessitated location of the RENEW team separately, more than ideological differences. In the summer of 1987 all three members of the diocesan team attended training sessions at Newark prior to planning the implementation of RENEW in Downlands.

Half-way through the RENEW process, Jane Morris, who had worked for the diocese for nine years and who was tired from doing two jobs and felt she had been out of teaching for long enough at a time when there were major changes in the schools following the introduction of the National Curriculum, felt it was time to return to teaching. She was replaced by Ann Potter, another teacher who was well known in the diocese.

Once the decision had been taken to adopt RENEW, the question was raised about the appropriate starting date. Jane Morris advised the bishop to wait another year in order to 'spend longer orienting people, making sure the material was there ... up front' (Interview, 25 Nov. 1992). Bishop Patrick, however, decided to launch RENEW in September 1988 and explained his reasons:

A certain feeling of urgency ... I may have felt that the time was right now and that if we waited another year we'd never be more ready and that people were a bit 'on the boil' and to wait for another year, we may never have started ... But I think the point Jane made to me was a fair one. (Interview, 7 Oct. 1992)

3.4 From Persuasion to Implementation

It is clear from the above account that the *decision* to run RENEW had been taken. Yet the clerical leadership in the diocese continued to claim that each parish would be able to choose whether or not to participate. Thus in his article on RENEW, the Director of RENEW in the diocese wrote that:

There were open meetings in every deanery, followed by 'Overnights' at St Winifred's and St John's (two retreat centres) for parish clergy and two lay people from each parish. These had the task of reporting back to their parish, after which the parish was ready to decide whether to participate or not. By Easter 1987 the parishes had made up their minds. (Stapleton, 1990: 81)

This summary is inaccurate and gives a misleading account of the sequence of events. The 'information nights' at which the RENEW team and the bishop presented RENEW in each of the twelve deaneries in the diocese were held in October 1987. A meeting of priests was held in early November 1987 and seven 'overnights' for the briefing of the parish priests and two lay members of their parish were held in January–March 1988. The process of consulting the parishes could not, therefore, have been completed before Easter 1988, but the schedule of information nights, overnights, training sessions, and dates for each of the five RENEW seasons was circulating in the autumn of 1987.

This process of persuading the priests was by no means easy. One priest told us in conversation (4 Sept. 1989) that he was disgusted at the way the decision had been taken. He regarded RENEW as 'innocuous and insufficiently radical . . . introspective and cosy'. The Church should rather 'go out and get hurt . . . and take risks'. RENEW was 'like giving a starving man a spoon of semolina'! In his view 'it was a time to act . . . [not just] preach'. We have previously noted that Mgr. Bob Reilly was another priest who was initially extremely sceptical about RENEW.

Another of our priest informants suggested that the bishop was a little intimidated by his priests and was prevented from initiating 'anything which will upset the clergy'. We have seen, however, that the bishop 'took on' the priests who were extremely hostile as late as November 1986. By eliciting their agreement to his 'considering' RENEW, undertaking an active programme of persuasion in meetings with the priests at deanery level over several months, and challenging them either to participate in RENEW or to come up with a relevant and viable alternative, the bishop successfully co-opted the priests of his diocese by Easter 1987. Canon O'Brien noted: 'Of some 120 possible Church communities, only three opted out, two of which came in once RENEW was under way' (Stapleton, 1990: 81). The period of persuasion was over; now it was a matter of organizing a major diocesan programme in little over a year.

The clerical leadership in the diocese has suggested that parishes still had the option of not taking up RENEW. In our judgement this claim cannot be entertained seriously. We have already noted that a full timetable of events leading up to a September 1988 launch was in place long before the 'information nights' held in every deanery throughout October 1987. It is also interesting to note a strange usage of the term 'deanery' by the bishop and priests. In a number of our interviews, they referred to deanery meetings. This confused us until we began to appreciate that, almost invariably, the clergy were referring to meetings of the priests in each deanery. This neglect of the laity in such casual usage is perhaps a significant indicator of where real decision-making actually took place and by whom. We suggest that the evidence which we have presented indicates clearly that the key decision had already been made by the bishop in consultation with a small group of priest advisers and that they had then successfully co-opted the chief officers of the institutional Church, the parish priests. The next stage was to co-opt the lay people in whose interests the programme was being run. In reality, we would suggest, their power of choice in the parishes was minimal. There is also evidence in some of our interviews that some people in some of the diocesan agencies felt that they had been marginalized by the setting up of the RENEW team and that the ongoing work of these agencies had been disregarded (Interview, 1 Feb. 1989).

This interpretation is supported by the following ethnographic account of the setting up of the core group in St Cyril's parish and their 'overnight' experiences. Some time after a meeting of the priests of the diocese with Bishop Patrick in November 1987, parish priests were contacted by the three-person diocesan RENEW team to bring to a diocesan 'overnight', in one of the diocesan pastoral centres, two lay parishioners who might be seen as key parish members and likely to be open to the development of new schemes for parish-oriented renewal. It was then up to the priests to proceed to the next stage of setting up what was likely to become the local parish RENEW core team.

St Cyril's parish stretches over an area of about five square miles of Conservative-voting suburbia around the southern edge of London. With the arrival of a new priest in the mid-1980s the traditional pre-Vatican liturgy began to change and the parish was moving in the direction of greater openness to religious change and spiritual development when RENEW came on the scene. While the parish priest was progressive in liturgy and catechesis, he did not see issues of social justice as a political-religious matter.

In this parish, the first stage of forming the nucleus of the parish RENEW team was accomplished in the following way. Two weeks or so after the bishop's own overnight with the clergy in November 1987, the parish priest and his temporary assistant priest approached one married male and one single female parishioner to join them in participating in one of seven weekend 'overnights' (Friday evening to Saturday evening) in one of the diocesan pastoral centres. The priests' explanation was that the bishop was issuing an invitation to the parish to join in a programme of Christian renewal and that the group of four were to act as parish delegates in assessing and possibly adopting the programme. A letter of thanks for accepting came two weeks later from the bishop, and the parish group was invited to attend the last session in March 1988.

About two weeks before the overnight a letter was received by each member of the group from the diocesan RENEW team. This clarified the purpose of the overnight:

What we hope to do at this Overnight is to provide you with clear information about the purposes, goals, spirit and organization of RENEW for your own sake, and also to enable you to share this with your Parish at large, so that you can commit yourselves to personal spiritual renewal, and the renewal of your Parish.

Like an invitation to reject sin, who could resist such worthy purposes? Clearly, the invitation to listen and the process of commitment to RENEW in the parish were not seen as separate issues, at least by the author(s) of the letter, despite the insistence on 'choice' in the RENEW literature.

Part of the overnight was devoted to prayer and meetings of each parish group separately. The bulk of the time was otherwise devoted to general sessions of communication and prayer. The overnight itself concentrated on the presentation of the RENEW programme, always introduced by prayer and reflection, and followed by some discussion and additional clarification. The final act of the overnight was led by the bishop and was the final decision-making process or prayer commitment by the participants from the parishes. Stress was laid on the view that everything about RENEW had to be freely undertaken.

Nevertheless, one of the co-ordinators in St Matthew's parish admitted that while it was sold as a free choice: 'it was a *fait accompli*, and I think you almost had to be pretty strong to resist.' However, she felt that if the bishop thought it was going to do something positive for the diocese as a whole, then it was inevitable that he would want to sell it pretty hard. So she could 'see why there wasn't really so much of a free choice in the end' (Interview, 24 Oct. 1988).

This interpretation is supported by the documentation available to the members of the parish core groups at their 'overnight' training sessions in January–March 1988. They were, for example, invited to 'learn about RENEW and its process' and to 'consider how to communicate this to the rest of your parish in order to enable a decision to be made about RENEW'. After communicating information about RENEW to the parish, 'a decision needs to be made on RENEW and notified to the Parish'. The 'overnights' were seen as the first of nine stages on planning RENEW for their parish and the ninth stage was the start of Season 1 on a predetermined date, Sunday, 2 October 1988. At no stage was consideration given to any alternative means of pastoral renewal.

In the booklet *Seven Questions About RENEW* prepared by the diocesan team and presented to participants at the 'overnights', the answer to the question 'What is RENEW?' was:

RENEW is a spiritual renewal process to help parishioners develop a closer relationship with Christ, to make an adult commitment to Jesus as central in their lives and to open them to the power of the Holy Spirit so that they become more authentic witnesses.

Since RENEW invites the total parish, including inactive members, to participate together; since it is renewal encouraged by the parish priests and organized by parish leaders; since all phases of RENEW are experienced in the parish, it is more than renewal of individual persons. It is parish renewal and creates a spiritual climate throughout the parish community.

The Christocentric emphasis locates RENEW within one of the main spiritual traditions of Christianity. The conscious reference to the Spirit as the power behind the process emphasizes a change generally in Roman Catholic spirituality since the Second Vatican Council. The move from an individual spirituality to a group one is to be achieved through the parish and in smaller faith-sharing groups.

The answer to a second question 'What will RENEW do for the parish?' is more goal-oriented and practical. It claims to:

(1) Set a spiritual climate and provide a common experience which will be a unifying force in the parish.
(2) Call forth unparalleled prayer.
(3) Find and develop new parish leaders.
(4) Bring many inactive people to involvement in Church and community.
(5) Occasion the return of many parishioners to the sacraments.
(6) Offer in one process basic formation in prayer, scripture, community-building, justice, liturgy, evangelization, family-life and support for the Adult Catechumenate (RCIA).

The promise is to deliver a type of parish life and personal spirituality which parishes have rarely achieved in the past. There seem to be elements of the 'hard sell' or marketing of religious products typical of American evangelism and which Berger (1973) and

Luckmann (1970) forecast would be a characteristic of religion in the modern world. The offer is comprehensive and promises success to those who follow the programme with commitment. As such it is reminiscent of the community development programmes of the 1970s and 1980s.

The overall framework of the overnight: being sponsored to attend, the sense of responsibility to the parish, the amount of information to absorb and the decision-making process within twenty-four hours, all made it very difficult to decline. Few, if any, of those attending failed to participate in the concluding ceremony of commitment. The pattern of the overnight resembled the Ignatian spiritual exercises in so far as commitment to RENEW was assumed to follow from the presentation, meditation, and prayer. However, two features in addition to the spiritual exercises were the pattern of small groups, which were supposed to become the main agents of renewal in the RENEW programme, and the theme of a this-worldly 'calling' or vocation of lay people. The overnight began with prayer and reflection on God's call. The latter part was devoted to commitment by each parish core group to the task of selling RENEW in the parishes.

How might one interpret the overnight sociologically? It is difficult to avoid the conclusion that it was a sophisticated device for co-opting key lay members of each parish who had been sponsored by their parish priests. Having committed themselves to adopting RENEW, priests now had the task of selling RENEW to their parishes. While nominally parishes could choose not to undertake the RENEW programme, the social pressures of the intense overnight experiences and the invitation to participate in personal and communal spiritual renewal under the direct sponsorship of their bishop and parish priest was not one which could easily be resisted. The whole overnight experience was designed to incorporate the laity into the diocesan project, not to deliberate on its pros and cons in rational discussion of alternative options. Rather the whole exercise confirms our interpretation that RENEW was a top-down programme of diocesan-wide parish-based renewal.

3.5   Conclusion

A useful concept for understanding the processes which were going on during this period of adopting RENEW is that of *co-optation*. Selznick defines this as 'the process of absorbing new elements into the leadership or policy-determining structure of an organization as a means of averting threats to its stability or existence' (1966: 13). He further distinguished

Formal cooptation, when there is a need to establish the legitimacy of authority or the administrative accessibility of the relevant public; and informal cooptation, when there is a need of adjustment to the pressure of specific centres of power within the community.   (1966: 259)

Selznick hypothesized that 'cooptation oriented toward legitimization or accessibility will tend to be effected through formal devices', such as the formal co-option of opponents into the administration. This device 'is especially useful when its object is the creation of public solidarity' (1966: 260). One final element of Selznick's theory is helpful: that 'the grass-roots utilization of voluntary associations represents a sharing of the burdens of and responsibility for power, rather than of power itself' (1966: 264).

The suggestion being made here is that sociologically, a process of formal co-optation of the priests of the diocese was set under way at this time. In this way it was hoped to legitimate the decision to adopt the RENEW programme and to share the burdens of implementing it while still retaining overall control of its course at the diocesan centre.

We are here dealing with the concept of power which, as Lukes (1974) points out, is a complex phenomenon of three dimensions and involving not only observable decision-making in situations of conflict, and the ability to control the agenda and both decisions and non-decisions, but also the consideration of contradictions between the interests of those exercising power and the real interests of those they exclude. Particularly helpful for our analysis is Schattschneider's observation that:

All forms of political organization have a bias in favor of the exploitation of some kinds of conflict and the suppression of others because *organization is the mobilization of bias.* Some issues are organized into politics while others are organized out. (Quoted in Bachrach and Baratz, 1970: 8)

Bachrach and Baratz defined the mobilization of bias as 'a set of predominant values, beliefs, rituals, and institutional procedures ("rules of the game") that operate systematically and consistently to the benefit of certain persons and groups at the expense of others' and noted: 'the primary method for sustaining a given mobilization of bias is non-decision-making' which they define as 'a decision that results in suppression or thwarting of a latent or manifest challenge to the values or interests of the decision-maker' (1970: 43–4).

We suggest that in order to achieve his strategic goals, the bishop mobilized bias in favour of the adoption of RENEW. There is nothing improper or unusual about this; it is one function of leaders to initiate and promote action on decisions which they have taken after consultation and the sounding of opinions. In this case the bishop, as the religious leader of the diocese, had a long-standing belief in the effectiveness of small groups in generating commitment on the part of their members. He was aware of the repeated demands from active laity in the diocese for more adult religious education and spiritual formation and the real advantages of 'not reinventing the wheel' which the well-tried pastoral programme RENEW offered. Furthermore he was not convinced that the diocese, with its limited resources, could achieve a comparable programme on its own in a reasonably short time or that there were any viable alternative programmes. Consequently, having deliberated over the matter for a year or more, the bishop and his closest advisers had come to the decision at Lourdes that RENEW was an appropriate response to the needs of the diocese. Mgr. Tom Cook, the Vicar General, and Jane Morris, the Diocesan Youth Officer, had also been sent to Newark for a briefing.

The priests, however, were, for a variety of reasons, initially hostile or suspicious of the programme and were apprehensive about its likely implications for them in their own work. But instead of risking the rejection of the programme by the priests, the bishop set out on a process of persuading them, as key gatekeepers in their parishes, through a process of 'mobilizing bias' in favour of RENEW. Thus the key vote was not for or against RENEW but for or against its consideration. It seems that the priests were required to suggest a clear alternative if they were not happy with RENEW and by all accounts few did.

In this way the bishop's power was exercised 'by confining the scope of decision-making to relatively "safe" issues' (Bachrach and Baratz, 1970: 6), in this case the *consideration* of some sort of organized response to the perceived needs of the diocese. Bachrach and Baratz distinguish the 'two faces of power', decisions and non-decisions. In our case, it was decided to 'consider' RENEW but 'non-decisions' included not voting immediately on taking up RENEW and not offering for consideration alternative pastoral strategies, including the development of the diocese's own pastoral renewal programme from scratch. As one of our informant priests pointed out, consultation was focused on the acceptance or not of the proposed *answer* to the question, not on the evaluation of alternative answers to a *question* about appropriate pastoral strategies. This could be seen most clearly in the overnights which mobilized bias in favour of a commitment to the pursuit of personal and parish renewal by promoting the RENEW programme in the parishes. In the normatively charged atmosphere of the 'overnight', the participants had little choice but to commit themselves to mobilize support for the programme in their own parishes.

The evidence we have reviewed about the original decision to adopt RENEW as a major pastoral initiative in the Diocese of Downlands overwhelmingly supports the argument that there is an inherent conflict between the present mechanistic structure and organization of the Church and attempts to promote lay empowerment. Our case study shows that even full-time workers in the diocesan agencies were never directly involved in the decision-making stages of the adoption of RENEW. Furthermore, although the priests were involved at a much earlier stage than lay people, even here it was largely a question of the use of sophisticated processes of co-optation after the decision had been taken at the top of the hierarchically structured organization.

4

Parish Mobilization for RENEW

4.1 The Deanery Meetings

In this chapter we will continue our analysis of the organizational features of movements of religious renewal through our case study of RENEW in an English diocese. We have shown how the bishop, in consultation with his closest advisers, came to the decision to adopt the RENEW programme for the Diocese of Downlands in July 1986, and proceeded in a series of stages to co-opt in the first place the priests of the diocese by Easter 1987, then over 2,000 parish activists in a series of meetings in each deanery in October 1987, and finally sponsored activists from the parishes at the 'overnights' early in 1988. The diocesan RENEW team had been appointed by the summer of 1987 to implement the programme after appropriate training at Newark. In this chapter we will draw on our ethnographic accounts of the deanery meetings and of the process of setting up the parish core groups and teams to illustrate some of the ways in which the parishes were mobilized from the top down to participate in the diocesan programme.

On the night of 15/16 October 1987 the south of England experienced its worst hurricane for three centuries. Four days later the electricity had still not been restored to the bishop's palace so he was able to joke at the deanery meeting in Crossroads that he had come there to get a hot dinner. In fact his purpose in visiting Crossroads and the other eleven deaneries in the diocese throughout October 1987 was to present active laity with an outline of the RENEW programme and urge them to commit themselves to renewal by their whole-hearted participation in it. There never was the slightest possibility that lay people would have rejected such a serious undertaking sponsored by their bishop.

The bishop first introduced Fr. Liam O'Brien who had been appointed as Director of RENEW in the diocese. Fr. O'Brien noted that over 2,000 people had already attended the previous eight deanery meetings. The Crossroads meeting was attended by over 250 people. RENEW, it was stressed, was a *process* which aimed at spiritual growth in faith, 'not a programme with a beginning and an end'. The RENEW logo chosen for the diocese was an oak tree to symbolize the ever-living roots and fruits of the faith and an enduring ability to withstand the buffetings of life. The purpose of RENEW was the spiritual growth of the People of God in the diocese as a vibrant faith community. It was not a catechetical or adult education programme. He noted that in the hundred or more dioceses throughout the world which had adopted RENEW, the proportion of 'involved' parishioners had typically increased from around 13 per cent to 20–40 per cent. Such promises of effectiveness could not but impress committed laity concerned to involve more people in parish activities. Finally, he stated that there were three principal goals of RENEW: (1) teaching and witnessing to the Word of God and widening the audience; this was scripture-based and Christ-centred; (2) developing vibrant faith communities, a desire which he said had been repeatedly expressed to the bishop in the Synod on the Laity consultation *Called to Serve*; 'helping each other to become living Christians' in parishes which were 'open, caring and believing'; and (3) establishing justice formation and action, for example in one's own family, with neighbours, in the parish, country, and world, 'where what is unjust is made just according to our abilities'.

Jane Morris, a member of the diocesan RENEW team, in her presentation noted that the RENEW programme of formation over three years was similar to the time Our Lord had spent with his disciples during His public ministry. She identified the main themes of the five seasons after an initial period of training and preparation, 'travelling together': (1) The Lord's Call: 'we are a people in need; the Lord seeks to answer our need'; (2) Our Response: as 'we turn from our sin and toward the Lord'; (3) Empowerment by the Holy Spirit: 'with the help of the Holy Spirit we try to live justly' and can renew the face of the earth; the consideration of 'justice issues and the need for systemic change'; (4) Discipleship: 'we form ourselves for mission to others'; our own personal spiritual life and development; and (5) Evangelization: 'we reach out to bring the Good News to all'. She then outlined the many options available, 'something for every need', including suggestions for the Sunday liturgies, take-home materials, large group activities, and 'faith-sharing opportunities' in small groups, 'sharing prayer and growing together'.

In her presentation Sister Mary Richards, the third member of the diocesan team, noted that 'RENEW is built on a firm balance of prayer and organization'. She outlined the available resource materials and training provisions, including the forthcoming overnights which would explore the message of RENEW and provide an impetus for personal renewal and hope for parish renewal. The decision whether or not to take up RENEW would be made in the parishes after the overnights. She claimed that RENEW could motivate more people, train leaders, prepare discussion group leaders, and interest parishioners in serving on parish organizations, welcoming committees, liturgy committees, parish councils, prayer and devotional service, and 'serving the larger community'. RENEW would be 'a coordinated effort' involving all the diocesan and parish agencies, 'all united in an effort to avoid competition for parish time and attention'. RENEW was faith-based: 'Christ must be allowed to renew our own personal lives.' There were no short cuts to personal conversion and spiritual growth.

Bishop Patrick then noted that he had listened to priests and people both formally and informally. There had been 'a general request for formation and renewal of faith'. We were all called to 'renew our faith in Jesus Christ and in doing so reach out to the world about'. This task was 'the work of the Holy Spirit' and it was necessary to open ourselves to it. In the lively discussion which followed, a priest suggested that RENEW would clash with ecumenical programmes. Bishop Patrick responded that he had spoken to the local Anglican bishops to explain the priority which RENEW would have for Catholics during the programme. In response to questions from lay people who asked what would happen if the parish priest was not keen on RENEW, the bishop responded that 91 per cent of the priests had said they did want to adopt it and that where they did not, there 'needs to be dialogue'. He emphasized that he would not 'mandate every parish [to do RENEW] but expect each parish to consider it'. To the observation that RENEW placed an impossible burden upon priests who were already busy people, the bishop responded that 'a burden shared is a burden lightened', a hint, perhaps, that he favoured notions of a participative laity and collaborative ministries. He concluded that it was 'time for stepping out and trusting in the Holy Spirit'.

The final part of the evening was spent in parish groups considering the question: 'what value do you think RENEW might be for your parish?' It might be noted that the consideration of RENEW as against alternative pastoral strategies was not on the agenda. In one parish group the view that the focus of RENEW was not clear enough on transforming the world found no other supporters and one member pointed out that Our Lord had started out with a small group of friends first, not with the idea of transforming the world.

Another participant thought 'the whole thing was a lot of hot air and simply repeating previous attempts' such as the *Person-to-Person* programme, a recently completed evangelically-inspired promotion of mission. But the overwhelming majority stressed the need for spiritual renewal first, before being open to the Holy Spirit taking over and transforming the world. By focusing on the widely-expressed need for spiritual renewal in general rather than comparisons between RENEW and alternative responses to the needs of the diocese, there was a 'mobilization of bias' in favour of 'renewal'. Not surprisingly, parish activists were well and truly co-opted into the RENEW programme. In the words of one parish co-ordinator:

I was in favour from the beginning. I felt that a process of personal renewal which was going to reach out to every member of the parish and beyond, including the 'lapsed', couldn't be bad, no matter how much renewal people have had already.   (Interview, 24 Oct. 1988)

4.2   The Emergence of the Core Team

It is probable that the core teams were selected in a variety of different ways in the 120 or so parishes in the diocese. We do not have comprehensive data about this. The likelihood is that in most parishes the core team was appointed by the parish priest rather than elected by lay people. Even so, there may well have been elements of ambiguity in the terms of reference of the lay people originally invited to attend the overnights, and they may not have been aware that it was anticipated that with their parish priest they would subsequently constitute the parish core team with responsibility for running and co-ordinating the 2½-year programme.

This was the case in one of our research parishes, St Cyril's, where one of the participants in the overnight reported that it only became clear to him towards the end of the overnight how important the key role of parish co-ordinator was, a sort of religious managing director expected to be gifted with both tact and drive. Neither he nor the other lay representative felt capable or sufficiently available to take on the task of parish co-ordinator. It also became clear that neither of the priests from his parish had realized that finding, asking, and appointing such a person for the whole period of RENEW had been expected.

This informant regarded the overnight as a demonstration of the techniques of modern marketing and business management to the 'religious enterprise'. These features were to annoy other active parishioners, especially in the early stages of RENEW. The hard-sell approach experienced at the overnight was to reappear in the 'sign-up' techniques before each season of RENEW, in the advertising of events and the distribution of literature for home consumption, and in the telephoning of parishioners and door-to-door calling on people to encourage their involvement in anything from private prayer to active participation in the programme. 'Organic' management styles of organizational revitalization, to bring people with complementary skills together and find leaders to subvert old ways of doing things, were also in evidence.

One of the first tasks of the core group after their return from the overnight was to appoint a parish RENEW co-ordinator, a lay person whose task it was to oversee the general organization of RENEW and bring committee leaders together to prepare activities and evaluate their effectiveness afterwards. The co-ordinator was supposed to pay 'special attention to communication with the Priest(s) and with the committees' (Resource Sheet A). Not only was it necessary to choose a person who was known to be reliable, committed, affable, and a good organizer, it was also necessary that the person had the time and imagination to devote to liaising with others and motivating them, promoting imaginative responses, and co-ordinating them into a coherent parish programme. The typical English parish has no full-time, paid pastoral assistants. It was only by scaling down the level of commitments that a part-time, unpaid appointment became a realistic alternative.

In St Cyril's parish, a key parish activist who worked part-time in the caring services was approached. Though it was not generally known, she had been invited to attend a meeting of diocesan laity at which the bishop had first mooted the possibility of adopting RENEW in the diocese. Her wish that the parish take up RENEW, as it promised so much for positive change in the parish, was known to one of the original core group. On being approached by the parish priest she welcomed the proposal and agreed to become co-ordinator. The core group, however, remained four in number as the assistant priest was moved to another parish at about this time.

Ann Potter, later to become a replacement member of the diocesan RENEW team, described the meeting at St Winifred's well before RENEW started. About sixty lay people were taken to the pastoral centre for an overnight. None of them knew why they were there and it became the joke of the evening that they were all people who had never sent Bishop Patrick a birthday card. There seemed to be no common thread though they learned at the end of the overnight that they had been mentioned by someone or some group as people with presentation skills who ultimately might be useful during RENEW to supplement the diocesan team and assist with pre-RENEW training (Interview, 2 Dec. 1992).

A similar process of soundings and negotiation took place in our main research parish, St Matthew's where the role of co-ordinator was operated as a duo. One member was the chairperson of the Parish Council who saw her role as selling the idea of RENEW and getting it off the ground. She was involved in setting up the RENEW team. She approached various people and there was a general appeal from the parish priest from the pulpit in the weekend liturgies and in the weekly parish newsletters. A number of people declined to take on the leadership role until she asked an elderly but active and busy widow who

was already enthusiastic, committed and had the dynamism to sell it . . . I was willing to work with [her] . . . We drifted into it together, only a few people expressing any interest . . . [She] then coordinated and I would help. I felt that my role would be administrative and [hers] doing the selling and inspiring role I can't do.   (Interview, 24 Oct. 1988)

In the Sacred Heart parish there was no parish council or any formal arrangements for consultation between the priest and lay people so there was no mechanism for obtaining a parish decision on whether or not to take up RENEW. An informant described the outcome of the poorly attended parish meeting at which the parish priest reported that he had already told the bishop that the parish would do RENEW.

And because nobody really knew what it was about and because there is an enormous amount of loyalty to the parish priest—he is a man who is greatly loved—. . . I think the people said: 'well, if he has decided we shall do it then we will do it because we support him and we are loyal.'   (Interview, 9 Nov. 1988)

In this parish where people had had little opportunity for leadership, 'there was a certain amount of relief' when people volunteered for the core group or other roles in the parish RENEW team.

These three examples suggest that the selection of the parish core groups was by no means a simple task and was likely to have involved a certain amount of negotiation and persuasion in many cases. In general it seems likely that the parish priest either selected or sponsored somebody known to be involved in the life of the parish and willing, for whatever reason, to encourage participation in the bishop's RENEW programme. Sociologically, the selection of the core group marked another step on the road to lay co-optation in the diocese and in the parishes. The observation of the new chairperson of the Parish Council in St Matthew's parish that they 'did feel coerced ... the bishop said we should do it, and being a good parish, we did' (Interview, 15 Sept. 1989), was probably fairly typical and does emphasize the top-down nature of RENEW.

4.3 The Emergence of the Parish Team

We have seen that when the initial core groups returned to their parishes after the overnight they were

responsible for feeding back as widely as possible the understanding they have gained of RENEW and of its possibilities for the Parish, so that a Parish decision can be made. If the decision is positive, they are then responsible for initiating the process that will enable the Parish RENEW Team to be set up. (*Planning for RENEW in Your Parish*, paper distributed to participants at the overnights)

This constituted the second of the nine stages in planning for RENEW. It was to be followed by 'decision on RENEW' (Stage 3), 'preparing to set up the Parish RENEW Team' (Stage 4), and 'the Parish RENEW Team is chosen' (Stage 5). In practice these stages were often conflated as can be seen from the following accounts.

The first task of the core group was to prepare lists of parishioners who might be prepared to take on the responsibility of leadership of the ten key committees. The *Leadership Handbook* counselled drawing up a list of perhaps thirty candidates before refining it by assigning qualities each would bring, praying before determining the number needed and priorities of selection, and finally deciding on the method of recruitment (Martin, 1982: 7). In St Cyril's parish about fifteen names were agreed on; others were excluded either on the grounds of overwork or of the likelihood of opposition or coolness towards the programme. Those on the short-list were approached briefly by the parish priest or another member of the core group. A number turned down the invitation leaving ten, including the original two lay people who had attended the overnight, who were prepared tentatively to lead one of the committees.

This task was completed within three weeks of the overnight. The prospective leaders or committee chairs were given details of two meetings they were expected to attend: one with the rest of the leaders of the parish together with RENEW committee leaders from other local parishes, and the second for leaders of specific committees from different parishes at diocesan centres for the purpose of receiving training appropriate for their specific function. Each committee leader proceeded to gather committee members over a period of several weeks. Before this work was completed a two-hour evening meeting for all committee members was arranged. For most participants this was their first real contact with RENEW.

At this meeting, the core group had to persuade the RENEW team of the desirability of the parish's committed participation in the diocesan programme of RENEW. About twenty-five people attended, most of whom were well-known in the parish. They included two or three from the five or six activists in the St Vincent de Paul Society, three or four women who decorated the church, some from the Union of Catholic Mothers, two or three from those involved with the children's liturgy, two from the folk choir, two or three from the main choir, others from the 'One Hundred Club' which raised extra funds for the parish from a regular sweepstake, and others who helped with the church liturgy and parish events. There were also about five unfamiliar faces or new recruits.

After singing hymns, praying, and reflecting on scripture, three presentations of various aspects of RENEW—its content, timing and aims, organization, and the small groups—were made. Participants were generally enthusiastic though some fears about the responsibilities entailed and whether individuals would have the time to fulfil them were expressed. Members of the core group responded that people could only do what they had time to do, reflecting remarks made by the diocesan RENEW team at the overnights. The hidden message was that if those attending did not co-operate, the whole RENEW programme would be stillborn and that some kind of RENEW was better than none at all. A principal focus of the meeting was the importance of setting up small groups. Though stress was laid on the formal structure of these groups—praying and meditating on a set theme each week, using appropriate scripture readings—it was clear that some aimed to use the occasion to pursue their own agenda. In spite of the disapproval of the parish priest, a rosary prayer group became established in this way.

Shortly after this meeting members of some of the committees, especially those whose work had to be completed before the start of the first RENEW season, met to discuss their role and plan their work. But before Season 1 commenced two of the ten committee leaders had withdrawn on the grounds of overcommitment and had to be replaced. Other leaders adapted the high expectations implied in the *Leadership Book* to the reality of their own lives and parish responsibilities. It might be noted that in this parish there was no evidence that parishioners were given a realistic choice about whether or not to take up RENEW.

Similar processes of negotiation and adaptation were reported in other parishes. In St Matthew's parish, the meeting to introduce RENEW had been given only a brief notice in the weekly newsletter and the parish priest had mentioned it only casually along with other notices during the weekend liturgies. One informant noted:

Does he do this consciously? He never seems to push anything or specific-ally urge attendance at anything. Yet he is the religious leader of the parish and this diocesan-wide programme in principle is the most important element in our pastoral strategy for the next three or four years. Strange—but for lay people also incredibly frustrating. (Fieldnotes, 22 Mar. 1988)

In the event about seventy people turned up to consider for which of the ten groups they would volunteer. One of the co-ordinators exuded confidence: 'I am bubbling over with excitement.... The Lord is calling to us tonight.... We're still not getting closer to God and each other.' There was a need to develop their spirituality and get closer to the Lord. 'We're all a little fearful.' Even so, a number voiced their doubts: 'it is meant for "dead" parishes; it should have started where people are; it seemed crazy putting so much emphasis on administration before anyone had any [RENEW] materials on the actual programme.' The two co-ordinators had been informed that the RENEW materials would not be available for inspection until the training day for parish teams the following month.

A member of the core team described how haphazard the selec-tion of the parish team had been at this meeting:

We had this big open meeting where everyone was asked to come along if they wished to hear more about RENEW and to form the St Matthew's team. And the culmination of this evening . . . was to be a commissioning of the RENEW team leaders. And we got to the commissioning bit and I said: 'hang on a bit! We haven't got anybody volunteered! Who are we going to commission?' Because nobody, at that stage, had come forward to actually take on a team apart from [one person]. And so, panic stations! And quick rush around, quick twisting of arms, and I think before they knew what had happened, we had a team. Now whether they've lived to regret it, I don't know. But it really was as dramatic as that. Five minutes to the prayer we hadn't got a leader, literally . . . And there and then, in the last five minutes before we went into the prayer . . . over coffee . . . in St Matthew's parish hall . . . It really was as close as that. (Interview, 24 Oct. 1988)

Once again, it is absolutely clear from this account that there was no meaningful sense in which the parish made a conscious decision for or against adopting the RENEW programme. By this stage the decision had been taken and it was a question of fulfilling the requirements as best as the parish could. Here again is another example of the gap between the theory of the RENEW planners and the realities of parochial life.

The ways in which one parish freely adapted RENEW was described by a member of the Sacred Heart parish team. She observed how, in a parish with little previous record of active lay leadership, people 'who had a track record of some kind', people who were seen to be 'loyal supporters of the parish', who had run stalls at parish functions, were on the Finance Committee, or were willing to be involved in the life of the parish, were co-opted onto the parish team. But 'it would be extremely low key', because

very few people had any enthusiasm about it whatsoever ... So it was clear to me that, if the RENEW team, as it was being formed, could be seen in terms of a parish council in embryo, which had been vetoed by the parish priest, then perhaps RENEW was not such a bad thing after all. That ... by the back door, parishes that were reluctant or unwilling to do some of the more formal things that the bishop had been asking for a very long time, could in fact embrace them under the umbrella of RENEW. (Interview, 9 Nov. 1988)

What this final extract indicates is that some active laity also had their own agendas (such as getting a parish council where previously there had been none) and so were prepared to negotiate and adapt the RENEW programme in the pursuit of their goals. In this parish, as in a number throughout the diocese, the daily scripture reading booklet was distributed free (at the parish's expense) to every known Catholic in the parish.

We have reached the stage where the parish teams and committees were in place to a greater or lesser extent some time during the summer of 1988. It was the task of these committees to mobilize the bulk of Catholic laity in each parish throughout the diocese for the start of Season 1 of RENEW which was scheduled for the autumn/fall of 1988.

4.4   Mobilizing the Parishioners

Our ethnographic data for this stage of the RENEW process again comes mainly from the same three parishes. Our informant in St Cyril's parish noted that most of the organizing work of the core group was limited to the first few months and it only met on a further two occasions and before Season 2, and then mainly for prayer and reflection. Most of the organization from then on was done by the RENEW co-ordinator and the chairs of each committee, who together made up the parish RENEW team.

Several committees were particularly involved in the recruitment of as many parishioners as possible for the RENEW programme in each season. In St Cyril's parish a minimalist approach to sign-up was adopted throughout the five seasons. Registration cards for the RENEW small groups were distributed and collected at each of the four Sunday Masses, usually two weeks before the start of each season. It seemed to the parish team that the duties listed in the handbook amounted to a form of 'overkill' and that 'common sense' dictated that unnecessary additional work should be avoided because active people already had busy lives.

The Small Group Committee attempted to group people who had signed the registration forms so as to avoid clashes of personality. The idea of small groups was viewed with considerable suspicion by many regular parishioners. 'It's just not me' was a common reaction. The RENEW team pointed out that even a rosary group was a small group and that while sharing one's faith was to be encouraged, people should be made to feel at home in a fairly relaxed atmosphere. In this parish, as also in St Matthew's, there were criticisms of inadequate training for small group leaders. People were expected to cope with groups, not to guide too much, and to be well-informed, after only a couple of afternoons' preparation.

Difficulties were also experienced in recruiting people for the other committees. It was felt that the scale of operations recommended in the RENEW literature for a Telephone Committee was unrealistic for a small English parish with under 700 Mass attenders. The idea of telephoning people to invite their participation in RENEW was regarded as alien to the religious culture of English Catholics. 'Who would undertake such a thing? People will think there is something wrong with you! It just is not done.' There was also little success in forming a Home Visiting Committee to encourage maximum participation in the programme. It was felt that visiting all members listed on the parish card files would not be appreciated by parishioners and there were fears of canvassing in the evenings after dark. After a number of members had dropped out, the leaders of the Telephone Committee, a professional social worker, and the Home Visiting Committee, a woman who was inexperienced but delighted to have been invited by the parish priest to undertake the task, combined and aimed to undertake about forty home visits of the sick, aged, and housebound in a different area of the parish each season.

A Prayer Network Committee was responsible for setting up the Prayer Commitment Sunday two weeks before the start of each season of RENEW. Collectors distributed prayer commitment cards around the church and after his homily, the parish priest invited people to complete them and place them on supplementary collection plates. About three-quarters of those attending committed themselves to read scripture, spend time in meditation, or attend an additional Mass during RENEW. The Liturgy Committee was constructed by invitation from the appointed chair. It consisted of the Master of Ceremonies, who oversaw the altar boys, three members from the senior and folk choirs, the organizer of the children's liturgy group, one other lay person, and the parish priest. In this sense it institutionalized the liturgical interest groups in the parish but replaced the previous liturgy group, whose main arguments had centred around hymn choices, with one which had relatively new blood and changed priorities, with prayer, preaching, and liturgical innovation as its focal points.

In this parish a Publicity Committee of three people was set up but it found it difficult to effect more than a few of the duties recommended in the *Leadership Handbook* (Martin, 1982). Despite good will and effort and some measure of skill (since one member of the group was a professional communicator), it was difficult to get articles published in the local secular press. A number of parish advertisements were produced and a banner to hang at the front of the church was commissioned. But most of the advertising came from other RENEW groups. One of the walls in the church entrance was usually covered with RENEW material and a tableau of photographs of the RENEW leaders was prominently displayed. Regular information about the RENEW seasons appeared on the parish noticeboard and the parish weekly newsletter began to include a paragraph or more on RENEW. It was suggested that these more unstructured aspects of publicity seemed to have been more effective than the formal committee. This probably reflects a difference in style and expertise in the small parish structures in England where there are no full-time parish staff other than the parish priest.

A perusal of the minutes of the Pastoral Council of St Matthew's Parish and of the weekly newsletters for 1987–8 throws some light on the process of decision-making by parishioners and of the various stages in the mobilization process. Our starting-point is the 'overnight' in early January 1988 attended by the parish priest, the co-ordinator and deputy co-ordinator. It seems that at this meeting they committed themselves to obtaining a decision from the parish on whether or not to adopt RENEW before the end of February.

Shortly after their overnight, the two lay co-ordinators reported back to the parish at all weekend Masses. The purpose of this talk was clearly to mobilize parishioners in support of RENEW. Thus the notes of the deputy co-ordinator indicate that after briefly outlining the background to RENEW she added 'and why I feel it is important to the growth of the parish'. She reported that 'after much prayer and discussion, Bishop Patrick has decided to offer the RENEW process to all parishes in the diocese'. Drawing attention to the RENEW prayer card which the congregation had been given on entering the church and which outlined the themes of each of the five seasons, she stressed that 'there is something for everyone. The housebound and the more "fringe" members of the parish community will all be encouraged to take part; this I feel is one of the most important, positive features of RENEW.' She proceeded to describe the symbolism of the oak tree logo adopted by the diocese, 'with its roots firmly in the tradition and teaching of the Church, putting out new growth which surely will bear fruit'. Parishioners were asked to read carefully the explanatory leaflet about RENEW which they were to be given on leaving the church, to consult with the two lay co-ordinators and to pray that when the parish responded at the end of February, 'the Holy Spirit will guide us to make the right decision'.

On the weekend of the first Sunday of Lent the parish newsletter asked: 'Do you want our Parish to take part in this diocesan process? Please pray for our decision and mark the form with a tick or cross and place it in the collection plate' for the offertory procession. The newsletter of 28 February reported the result: 'Many thanks to all who took part in our decision last Sunday. There were 215 in favour, 25 against and 21 blank papers. So our parish will be taking part in this diocesan process.' A later notice indicated that 'as our parish is now committed to RENEW' there would be a meeting on 22 March 1988 'for all those people in the parish young and old who would like to offer their time and talents in any way to make this process a spiritual success. *The parish needs you, you have so much to give.*'

The clerical leadership of the diocese no doubt interpret this process of voting, as in the case of the priests voting at an earlier stage, as a form of 'consultation'. We would suggest that it is a very impoverished form of consultation which in effect simply invites 'the People of God' to say whether or not they agree with the decision arrived at over many months by their bishop. There was no substantial consideration of alternatives and there had been no opportunity to evaluate the RENEW materials. We therefore suggest that in spite of a nominal vote on the matter, the process can best be seen as the co-optation of ordinary lay people in the diocese by sponsored lay activists who had themselves been co-opted by the clerical leadership at an earlier stage.

This interpretation is supported by an analysis of the minutes of the Parish Pastoral Council (PPC). As early as 2 September 1986 there is a reference to RENEW and it was decided to seek further information from the Downlands Christian Education Centre (DCEC) or the Redemptorist bookshop. On 7 October it was reported that this was 'very difficult and expensive to obtain' but that the bishop 'would be discussing this publication' and one member of the PPC would follow it up. On 4 November it was noted that this member of the PPC would be attending a meeting about RENEW at St Richard's seminary. (This was the DPC meeting addressed by Mgr. John Carroll from Newark). The minute of the next meeting of the PPC on 2 December 1986 records the report of the parish priest and the lay members who had attended Mgr. Carroll's presentations. It notes the 'strong sales presentation' by the Americans and their claim that 'RENEW held the answer to all or any parishes' problems'. It reported that 'Bishop Patrick had not yet decided whether he would introduce this programme but may wish to use it as an answer to the call for renewal in the diocese but it would involve Fr. Gerry [the parish priest] and a steering committee in many hours of meetings'.

Interestingly, the PPC 'generally felt that we should not get involved in a programme that was solely for Catholics but would prefer a more ecumenical scheme. [The member of the PPC] would write to the bishop with the Council's opinion and ask if [he/she] could possibly have a sample copy of RENEW' materials. A tape of the presentations at St Richard's was circulated round the members of the PPC for several months. By 7 April the Liturgy Committee was reporting to the PPC that 'it was generally agreed that although they were not in favour of an American product they would support the diocese if Bishop Patrick decided to implement it'. A PPC minute for 5 May 1987 bluntly recorded that 'the RENEW programme is to go ahead in the diocese'. It might be noted that this was nine months before the parish 'vote' and 'decision'.

The PPC meeting on 2 June 1987 considered a suggestion originating from a well-known Catholic psychiatrist for a three-year programme of Pastoral Care of Marriage and Family Life. The parish priest was reported as saying that 'we could not instigate this as the diocese intended running the RENEW programme and we could not manage both'. The parish AGM in July 1987 was more concerned with the forthcoming *Person-to-Person* promotion of evangelization in ecumenical house groups in the autumn of 1987, to which reference has already been made, than with RENEW. But at the October 1987 meeting of the PPC the parish priest was drawing attention to the deanery information evening and the RE-NEW 'overnights', and it was recorded that 'the housegroup leaders may also be asked to help launch and orchestrate the programme'. The import of these reflections is that the PPC expected decisions about RENEW to be taken by the diocese and were prepared to conform loyally whatever local plans there might have been.

RENEW did not loom large in the minutes of the PPC in the first nine months of 1988 before the start of Season 1. January's meeting reports feedback from the parish priest and two lay co-ordinators after their overnight and anticipated their short explanations at the following Sunday's Masses. Reference is made in February to a deanery meeting. The March meeting recorded the vote for RE-NEW and plans for the parish meeting later in the month, and the April meeting reported that approximately seventy-two parishioners had attended it. A training day for RENEW team leaders took place in mid-April and a further one was planned for mid-May to check areas of responsibility and action. The minutes of the May meeting noted that 'we are allowing £1,000 per year in the budget for the expenses of RENEW, although any information of the actual cost to the parish is very vague'. It also noted that a letter would go out by hand to all parishioners with the next parish magazine to advise them of the beginning of the RENEW programme. In June there was a meeting of the whole RENEW team and it was reported that the morning session of the DPC meeting had been devoted to RENEW, 'all very encouraging'. The September meeting reported that plans were in hand for sign-up Sunday. Finally the November meeting 'pointed out that the RENEW programme would prevent us from participating this year' in the ecumenical Lenten house groups.

The mobilization of parishioners seems to have been more com-prehensive and to have approximated the *Leadership Handbook* guidelines more closely in St Matthew's parish as compared to St Cyril's. The meeting to identify committee leaders and recruit vol-unteer members in March 1988 successfully initiated preparations over the next few months by nine of the ten committees. The ex-ception was the Large Group Committee which was stillborn due to the commitments of its leader. The summer issue of the parish magazine, which was distributed to all known Catholics in the parish, included a letter from the parish priest which called for a return to the qualities of the early Christians which others found so attractive. It was in order to renew this spirit that the RENEW process had been started. The names and telephone numbers of members of the RENEW team and their committee responsibilities were given and parishioners were invited to volunteer their talents. The special RENEW prayer was printed. In due course it was reproduced on prayer cards for distribution to all parishioners and over the next 2½ years was prayed at every Mass in the parish. A sung version was regularly used at Sunday liturgies.

Finally, an informant in the Sacred Heart Parish which had no parish council or tradition of small groups, reported that no telephone committee was ever formed and home visiting was 'played down'. But it seems that the parish priest wrote to every known Catholic, sending them a copy of the daily scripture reading booklet, and inviting them to participate in whatever way they could in RENEW. To the informant's surprise 105 people signed up for the small groups and ten groups were formed in a parish of 350–400 people where there was no history of group activity and 'a lot of people had been expressing nervousness about it'. She observed that the parish priest must have been remarkably persuasive for people to say: 'I don't think I'll like it but I'll give it a go' (Interview, 9 Nov. 1988).

In sum, it appears that the evidence we have from these three parishes supports the view that the ordinary Catholic laity were successfully co-opted to the bishop's RENEW venture between the information nights in the twelve deaneries in October 1987 and the launch of RENEW just under a year later. There is no strong evidence that ordinary Catholics ever had a serious opportunity to reject RENEW or consider alternative proposals. Rather their religious leaders had pre-empted the decision but went through the motions of getting the decision underwritten by lay people in the parishes. We strongly suspect that in very few, if any, parishes was there ever the slightest chance that lay people would resist the proposal. Our data on the experiences of RENEW, which we shall review in Chapters 5 and 6, will indicate that while some parishioners overtly resisted and others covertly resisted, many were conformist loyalists who would respond wholeheartedly to any request from the bishop or parish priest. The second point which can be made is that our evidence points strongly to the conclusion that individual parishes, priests, and/or lay people interpreted the programme to suit their own purposes and that there was a considerable degree of divergence from the recommended patterns and procedures in the formal programme literature.

The stage was set, then, for the launch of RENEW. Sign-up Sunday was early in September 1988. In St Matthew's parish a special introductory talk was given by the headteacher of the local Catholic comprehensive school. On entering the church, people were given an envelope which they were invited to open. Inside was a slip of paper indicating one of a number of 'gifts' (such as 'comforter') and it was suggested that everyone in the Church had a gift or talent which they were invited to contribute to the Church. Later the deputy co-ordinator reflected that while the homily had dealt with talents and the building of community, it had made no reference to the small faith-sharing groups which were seen as the core of the RENEW process. While members of the RENEW teams at every level (international, diocesan, and parish) repeatedly stressed that parishioners could participate in the RENEW process in a variety of legitimate ways, *the* measure of the success of RENEW was taken to be the level of recruitment to the small faith-sharing groups. This was clearly the case with the diocese's own 'evaluations' at the end of Season 1. The parish newsletter the following week reported that 190 people had signed up to join the small 'faith sharing' groups.

'Prayer Commitment Sunday' was the following weekend. All Mass attenders were asked to pray for the success of RENEW by committing themselves to one or more of nine alternative forms of prayer by completing a card during Mass. These were collected and taken up in an offertory procession. The weekly newsletter reported the following week that 300 had signed up for one or more of the suggestions.

One week later, in late September 1988, an estimated 18,500 Catholics converged on the soccer stadium of Southlands Athletic to celebrate the launching of the RENEW process in the diocese (*DT* Oct./Nov. 1988). The organizers no doubt saw this as a great diocesan celebration and demonstration of priest–lay collaboration. This was not how it was experienced by some who attended. For example, the deputy co-ordinator in St Matthew's parish noted that there had been problems with the venue and with the unloading of coaches and lack of direction from the stewards. More significantly, the metal fencing designed to prevent pitch invasions by soccer fans constituted a psychological barrier for the liturgy. The bishop and priests and the liturgical action were very distant from the lay people who were not allowed to go onto the turf. Nevertheless the celebration and singing had been good and it had been 'great to be part of such a great gathering'.

Another informant reported that 150 had attended the launch from St Luke's Parish. Coaches had left Riverton promptly at noon and taken two hours to get to the ground. There had been no special placings so that parish groups were not kept together. An hour's singing had been followed by Mass. But the proceedings had not ended until 6p.m. by which time people were tired having stood in a dry but cold and windy venue for several hours. One family with a child of five had waited until 8p.m. before their coach had been called and did not arrive home until 10p.m.

With the official start of RENEW, the mobilization of people in the diocese to participate in a diocesan-wide venture at the invitation of the bishop was completed. The evidence shows clearly that at no stage were lay people involved in making a genuine decision to participate or not, or to select RENEW as against alternative renewal programmes. The top-down nature of the organizational structure of RENEW was symbolized by the segregation of clergy and lay people at the opening ceremony.

4.5   First Impressions of RENEW

Our earliest fieldnotes point to some of the concerns of the RENEW team in St Matthew's Parish in the month before the start of Season 1. The Take-Home Committee had selected materials for printing but they were not ready for distribution. 'It was all a great muddle' and 'we are trying to run before we can walk'. Several of the people involved were worried about the expense even if none of the volunteers asked for travelling expenses and the costs of telephoning and postage. Unexpectedly the diocesan RENEW team were not assisting in any inter-parochial administration, for example in promoting the distribution of material through the pupils of the local Catholic comprehensive school. The recommended book for the prayer team members was considered to be too expensive and members of the Telephone Committee reported that when they had followed the recommended procedures for contacting parishioners, 'the results had been disastrous'.

The Telephone Committee, whose efficiency did not impress the Take-Home Committee, claimed to have telephoned between 150 and 200 people who had expressed interest in receiving the take-home material. But by the time the latter committee had deleted the 'silliest' names, people who were known to attend Mass regularly and people living well outside the parish, only fourteen additional people were identified who would not otherwise be reached by the regular distribution of the parish magazine. It was reported that 'core activists were working themselves unmercifully' at this time and that the composition of the RENEW small groups was not posted under its leaders on the Sunday prior to the start of Season 1 for fear 'that there would be an avalanche of people wanting to change'.

The unanticipated cost of RENEW to the parish and to participating individuals was the subject of conversation in the parish in the first week of Season 1 when it was said that the parish priest was proposing to ask the parish at the end of Season 1 to contribute to the cost of the materials. The parish newsletter reported in the final week of this season that RENEW had cost the parish around £1,100. This included the daily scripture booklets, which had been distributed free, and the booklets for the members and leaders of the small groups, prayer cards and take-home leaflets, publicity, and photocopying. An informant noted that 'nobody thought it was going to cost individuals anything when it was voted on'.

With the end of Season 1 we have seen the mobilization of large numbers of ordinary Catholics in the Diocese of Downlands in the RENEW process. We have noted that a sometimes bewildered core of activist Catholics in the parishes had struggled to interpret the spirit and intentions of the programme which they had been persuaded to accept by the bishop and the diocesan RENEW team. To a greater or lesser extent, and with a good measure of 'common sense', innovation in the interpretation of the standardized procedures of the *Leadership Handbook*, and with judicious doses of improvisation and tolerance of deviance, the RENEW programme got under way in the Autumn of 1988.

There were several distinct stages in this process. First of all there were meetings in October 1987 in each of the deaneries which were addressed by the bishop and each member of the already-appointed diocesan RENEW team. We have suggested that there was a very effective 'mobilization of bias' at these meetings which were attended by around 2,000–3,000 of the most active parishioners in the diocese. Secondly, parish priests appointed two or more lay people to constitute with them the parish core groups. These were invited to spend an overnight at a diocesan pastoral centre and were comprehensively co-opted by the bishop and the diocesan team to commit themselves to promote RENEW in their own parishes. Thirdly, this core team in turn co-opted a team of collaborators in their own parishes in the early part of 1988. Leaders of the ten parish committees required by the RENEW programme were sought and to a greater or lesser extent found. Fourthly, often before they knew what they had committed themselves to, these various leaders and their committee members attempted, with more-or-less success, to follow the recommended procedures for Season 1. Finally, the ordinary Catholics in the Diocese of Downlands were bemused by the unfamiliar activities. Some were totally alienated and distanced themselves from what they regarded as a foreign intrusion into their expectations of Catholicism in England. Others were cynical and saw RENEW as yet another in a long line of renewal programmes over the past two decades. For them it was a case of *déjà vu*. But a substantial proportion of the Catholic population did loyally attempt to participate to some extent in the RENEW programme.

In Chapters 3 and 4 we have shown that the adoption of RE-NEW in the Diocese of Downlands was hierarchical and top-down in execution. In terms of the cultural dimension of spirituality, we would suggest that there was a certain amount of ambiguity and contradiction in the eclecticism of the influences which could be detected in the genesis of RENEW. Thus one can detect elements of the thinking found in community development, liberation Christianity and notions of empowerment, group dynamics and non-directive counselling, as well as charismatic Christianity, traditional devotionalism, and scriptural emphases. In terms of the model we derived in Chapter 2, it would seem that there are elements of both traditional and modern styles of spirituality in RENEW.

We turn next to a consideration of the experiences of ordinary Catholics in the diocese over the five seasons of RENEW in order to illustrate the utility of the classification of spiritualities which we derived in Chapter 2. In Chapter 5 we will report some of our earliest qualitative data collected from a wide range of participants throughout the diocese, particularly in Seasons 1 and 2. Chapter 6 will then report some of the more quantitative data we collected from a number of parishes over the five seasons of RENEW. In this chapter we will also draw on the rich variety of data about the actual experiences of ordinary Catholics which we obtained in our parish field work and which we believe were not adequately reflected in the diocesan 'evaluation' procedures at the end of each season of RENEW.

5

An Assessment of the Diocesan Experience

5.1 The Evaluation of the RENEW Programme

In this and the following chapter we commence the analysis of the experience of the five RENEW seasons in the diocese as a whole and in the parishes. We will report a wide range of findings, using a variety of data collection methods, about the actual experiences of Catholics, whether they were actively involved as members of parish core teams or committees, or as participants in the small groups, or simply as regular Mass attenders. We will also refer to the reported findings from the official diocesan 'evaluation' reports at the end of each season of RENEW and point to some inconsistencies and biases in these. We wish to stress the complexity of the experiences of RENEW and suggest that they did not conform to an easily summarized, coherent, and consistent pattern. Rather, in reality, there was a great deal of contradiction, ambiguity, and conflict.

Our focus in this chapter will be the experience of RENEW in the diocese as a whole and we shall draw, in particular, from the large amount of qualitative data we collected from a wide range of respondents, published sources, and our systematic observations at every level in the diocese. In Chapter 6 we will report on the data we collected in a number of parishes and especially on the more quantitative findings from our surveys of parishioners and members of small groups.

We indicated at the beginning of this study that we did not initially set out to *evaluate*, in any social scientific sense of the term, the RENEW programme in the Diocese of Downlands. Rather our purpose was to offer a descriptive and analytical account of it, as experienced by people in the diocese, though with the eventual aim of understanding it in relation to the history and sociology of spiritualities generally within Roman Catholicism. Nevertheless, built into the whole RENEW programme is an 'evaluation' process at the end of each season. The sponsors of RENEW see 'developmental evaluation' as a form of organizational feedback to take 'corrective action' in the case of 'misdirected effort' (Martin, 1982: 79). We commence by outlining the results of the diocesan evaluations at the end of each season of RENEW and the way in which they were interpreted by the RENEW team. We then offer a critique of this version which takes into account the many critical observations of Catholics at all levels in the diocese and in the light of the general sociological framework adopted in this book.

During the course of our research we used a wide variety of data collection procedures. These included the content analysis of RENEW publications, reports in the diocesan newspaper and parish newsletter, field notes of meetings at diocesan, deanery, and parish levels, including our participation in the Evaluation Committees of two parishes, tape-recorded interviews with informants at all levels in the diocese, and observations made and conversations overheard throughout the whole RENEW programme. Such data collected in the first two seasons of RENEW were then subjected to 'soft data' analysis, as developed by Norris (1981) when researching a community-development project. We have employed it in this study to distinguish which of the four types of spirituality identified in Chapter 2 appeared to be dominant and which others also appeared relevant.

The *Leadership Book* for RENEW specifies that the role of the parish Evaluation Committee is to

assist renewal efforts by providing on-going evaluation of progress and growth. This committee stays in touch with all the activities of RENEW to insure that the program is remaining true to its purpose. It keeps in close and frequent contact with every committee to indicate where change and adaptation are needed or *to reinforce what seems to be working well.* (Martin, 1982: 7; emphasis added)

One might note here the use of the word 'program[me]' to indicate the structured nature of RENEW. More often than not the RENEW literature preferred the more ideologically loaded term 'process'.

In the Information Packet for parish evaluators some general thoughts on evaluation are offered:

There are two kinds of evaluation. *One is evaluation at the end of an effort or project* to determine whether it did what it was supposed to do, was worth the cost, should have been done better, or perhaps should not have been undertaken at all. *The second kind of evaluation is that conducted while an effort is in progress,* to make sure that it is on the right track and is being well executed, in order to correct the situation while the project is still in progress.

The latter we can term developmental evaluation, and it is this which is the responsibility of the Evaluation Committee.   (Martin, 1982: 79; emphases in original)

At the end of each season of RENEW, each parish was required to submit an evaluation to the diocesan team. In a *Summary of Parish Evaluations* based on returns from 97 of the 112 participating parishes at the end of the first season, while both strengths and weaknesses in the various areas—liturgy, take-home materials, small groups, large group activities—were noted, the general tenor was congratulatory and enthusiastic:

70 parishes returned figures revealing that 13,956 in their parishes made a prayer commitment.
Scripture Reflection booklets very popular—some 20,000 distributed.
Small Groups: An excellent *beginning* has been made: *12,421 participating across the Diocese!*
Those parishes where (there were home visiting and/or telephone groups, about 44% of all parishes) . . . report that 1,220 people across the Diocese have become involved as a result.
(*DT* Apr./May 1989: 16; emphases in original)

Another measure reported was the distribution of materials from the RENEW Office—'a staggering amount' including: 'just under 16,000 Small Group Participant books; and 7,500 Children's Take Home leaflet packs' (*Downlands Times*, Feb./Mar. 1989).

Writing in the diocesan paper, the Director of RENEW particularly noted that there was general agreement about the success of the small groups: 'Many of you expressed delight (and surprise!) that it had been such a good experience' (*DT* Feb./Mar. 1989) and this was supported by a selection of comments from small group members:

— The people in our group are so friendly and supportive.
— It took us some time to feel comfortable together, but I was amazed how quickly we came to trust one another.
— I have really longed to be able to talk about my faith with others.
— It helps me feel I really belong to the parish.

In the next issue Fr. Liam O'Brien wrote:

Even more significant than numbers are the conclusions of the Parish RENEW Teams about their parish efforts: 'change of atmosphere', 'friendliness', 'getting to know strangers', 'work as a team', 'creative', and so on. We have made a good beginning but there is no ground for complacency. There are too many in our parishes not involved.   (*DT* Apr./May 1989)

5.2   Limitations of the RENEW Evaluations

The testimonies summarized in the previous section reflect some part of the reality that was RENEW. But they are not the whole story. In spite of the generally favourable interpretation of the parish evaluation returns by the diocesan leadership, there are good grounds for treating them with some caution. First of all the diocesan 'evaluation' exercise was systematically biased in favour of the existing programme by the requirement to 'be positive'. For example, the above figures suggest that around two-fifths of adult Mass attenders did *not* make even the least demanding commitment of RENEW to pray regularly in one way or another. And, remarkable as it was that so many people were reported to have signed up to participate in the small groups, nearly 70 per cent of adult Mass attenders (or 90 per cent of all known Catholics) did not. Furthermore, well over half the parishes had no home visiting or telephone committees which could be said to reflect the greatest commitment to 'searching out the lost sheep' in the parishes. The diocesan methods of 'evaluation' did not adequately reflect the views of the large majority of ordinary Catholics who did *not* actively participate in RENEW.

As we noted above, parish evaluators were instructed to 'reinforce what seems to be working well' or to always 'think positive'. There were some obvious flaws in the 'evaluation' instruments recommended in the information package (Martin, 1982). These included 'leading' questions ('What did you find most exciting in Season 1 of RENEW?') and fixed choice responses with little provision for negative comment. Respondents were often asked to comment on positive outcomes only ('Which goals do you feel have been achieved to an expected or better than expected degree?'). Complex issues were over-simplified with only 'Yes/No' responses allowed ('Were [small group] leaders well prepared [did they understand their role as facilitator, have awareness of basic group dynamics, understand the material, etc.]?'). Respondents were required to judge to what extent the aims of RENEW had been achieved though no allowance was made for different starting points and no criteria for judging success were offered. The problem of representativeness of samples of parishioners or small group members was not addressed and during a public meeting, a diocesan team member asked to explain random sampling—a method suggested in the information package—in fact described chance encounters.

There was also pressure on the parish Evaluation Committees to report their findings very quickly after the end of each season, partly for the benefit of the parish core team, but also to provide information requested by the diocese. A deanery meeting called to discuss results after the first season was very professionally led by the diocesan RENEW team, employing 'buzz' sessions. However, the ensuing discussion was conducted on the lines of a carefully planned publicity promotion, encouraging positive statements and giving little time or credence to criticism. A serious exercise in action research would have concentrated on criticisms made and discussed possible changes to be adopted as a result. Indicators of success would have been more clearly defined.

Evaluators in other parishes mentioned other factors which discourage reliance on the credibility of the diocesan evaluation. Some had been asked by their core team for 'a favourable evaluation' and were 'not allowed independence'. Some were unsure whether they were expected 'to produce a report which urged people on to greater efforts by stressing success' or 'to ruthlessly expose shortcomings'. Lack of objectivity was not regarded as a problem. The use made of results was also disquieting. Some respondents were disappointed that criticisms, made with the intention of promoting constructive change, appeared to be disregarded. 'The programme seems to be immutable', said one. The diocesan team publicly discounted frequent criticism that the programme was American and made little or no concessions to British culture. One evaluator, who wrote a long critique, tempered with some tactful praise of success, was indignant to find the few approving comments reprinted in RENEW publicity literature, with no reference to the adverse criticisms.

A second criticism of the official parish 'evaluations' was that they sometimes simply reflected the views of one individual and not necessarily those of the parish team. Several reports were described as being the personal opinions of the chief evaluator and were sometimes strongly criticized by others in the parish who held different views. It was reported that one parish priest had rewritten the evaluator's report to give a better impression to the diocese. A member of the diocesan team who was concerned that our own evaluations might give a misleading interpretation of a parish's response to RENEW observed that it was extremely dependent:

on who you talk to in the parish and how well the whole process was handled within that parish. In some parishes the whole process worked in spite of the co-ordinator, in spite of the priest, ... and it didn't work in some parishes because of personalities ... I don't think that it was a fair profile of [my own] parish ... There were two people concerned in the parish who were quite antagonistic, very strong and very able to articulate their reservations. A number of people who were gaining a tremendous amount out of what was going on didn't have the same voice ... That parish has blossomed and grown and perhaps it needed time to grow. (Interview, 2 Dec. 1992)

In this case the informant was concerned that the 'evaluation' was not as favourable as the RENEW team would have liked. But it is even more likely that the biases in the evaluations worked in the opposite direction and that members of parish teams wished to emphasize what they had achieved and draw a veil over what had not been successful. It was for this reason that, as we will report in the following chapter, we devised methods of evaluation which encouraged the widest possible response to the RENEW programme, including from non-participants. Our own concept of evaluation was much stricter than that employed by the diocese as was admitted by the member of the diocesan team:

I accept the bias of only looking for the positive, but you know as well as I do, that if you ask people what's not going right that's all you get ... Because the main idea of the evaluations was not so much to evaluate what had happened but to point people in the direction of what might happen.   (Interview, 2 Dec. 1992)

This well illustrates a third criticism of the parish evaluations: that they were collected for a specific purpose other than to monitor progress over the whole RENEW programme. Such a purpose was apparent in the decision by the diocesan team to distribute the parish-by-parish summary returns to all parishes at the end of Season 1. This was described by one senior priest as being 'just a little bit naughty', but he added that 'a diocese like ours needs a kick in the arse ... to move it'. Through the publication of these 'evaluation' returns it was hoped that parishes with lower than average involvement, for example in numbers in small groups or undertaking home visiting, would be shamed into greater efforts in the later seasons. Such techniques are familiar in marketing campaigns to increase competition amongst sales representatives. In the case of parish clergy, a priest informant reported rather more heated deanery meetings than usual as numbers in small groups and the ways in which leaders were promoted were compared (Interview, 4 Sep. 1989).

This use of the parish evaluation returns to encourage commitment to the RENEW programme did not appear to be repeated after Season 1 and there were no comparable summary reports distributed round the parishes. It seems that the comparative analysis was a 'one-off' initiative and that the diocesan RENEW team did not devote the same energies to the compilation of full parish returns after subsequent seasons. Some records were kept but in inconsistent ways which did not allow of the analysis of trends, for example diocesan aggregate numbers in small groups through all five seasons. Some returns listed total numbers in small groups while others distinguished between on-going groups which pre-dated RENEW and RENEW groups. Other returns recorded purchases of the small group booklets but there were numerous inconsistencies between the numbers of purchases and numbers reported in the groups (Interview with member of diocesan team, 2 Dec. 1992).

Finally, a full evaluation of RENEW would have to take into account any disruptions to the work of on-going diocesan agencies by the implanting of the RENEW team with two newcomers unfamiliar with the diocese. One informant who was involved with the development of adult education in the diocese (Interview, 1 Feb. 1989) suggested that the Downlands Christian Education Centre was completely marginalized by the RENEW team, a marginalization which was aggravated by the fact of their physical separation in another part of the diocese as the bishop had acknowledged (Interview, 7/10/92). There also seems to be evidence that the DCEC was unpopular with a number of clergy within the diocese. Whatever the reasons, little attempt appears to have been made to co-opt them into the training programmes for parish leaders or to build on the substantial training courses which were already in place. Apparently, existing agencies resented the fact that resources were made available for RENEW which had long been denied them. There also appeared to have been conflicts over the model of Church which was being promoted. Our informant felt that the parish-based model of RENEW was a sophisticated way of incorporating the laity, whereas the model which the DCEC had been promoting for some time was more concerned to empower the laity and this was seen as a threat by some clergy.

5.3 'Soft Data' Analysis

For reasons such as those we have indicated, we did not consider that the official evaluation procedures in the diocese were designed to give an accurate picture of the range of experiences of the RENEW programme with respect to ordinary Catholics. Accordingly, from a very early stage in our research, we began to collect, as systematically as we could, a wide range of materials for more intensive analysis. These included the log notes which we made of our observations of, and records of comments on RENEW in diocesan, deanery, or parish meetings, or in other formal or informal contexts; transcripts or notes of interviews; correspondence with a wide range of informants and respondents at all levels in the diocese; the voluminous RENEW literature and publicity material, including the *Leadership Book*; public statements recorded in the *Downlands Times*; and so on. It was on the basis of a content analysis of these materials that we began to compile a list of constantly recurring themes and concepts. We refer to these materials as 'soft data'. One approach which we found particularly helpful in the 'grounded' (Glaser and Strauss, 1973) construction of the theoretical framework for our study was the analysis of soft data.

Soft data analysis was originally developed in the late seventies (Norris, 1981) to investigate a community-development project which used small group techniques to change the attitudes and behaviour of participants. Changes in that project, in small groups, in participants, in the sponsoring organization, and in the community at large, were evaluated using both quantitative and qualitative methods (Norris, 1979; 1982). A range of alternative theoretical approaches to community development were detected and it was suggested then that soft data analysis of qualitative materials could be used in evaluating other community projects. RENEW appeared to be permeated with the ideas of community development and with notions of individual change prompted by work in small groups. We therefore considered that the use of soft data analysis was one appropriate strategy for the study of the RENEW programme. The findings we report in this chapter have been based on this form of analysis. (A more extended analysis is given in Norris, Hornsby-Smith, and Fulton, 1995.)

Detailed content analysis of the materials collected before the commencement of the third season of RENEW generated a list of constantly recurring concepts. While a number of these concepts were found to be similar to those in the community-development project, a notable difference, as might have been expected, was RENEW's stress on spiritual matters. The four-cell typology of spiritualities shown in Figure 5.1 provided the theoretical framework for the analysis of our soft data and is an elaboration of the general historical and comparative classification outlined in Figure 2.3.

The first axis for the promotion of RENEW is concerned with organizational means which could either be *hierarchical* or stress *mutual responsibility*. A hierarchical Church manifests a traditionally directive or 'mechanistic' organizational style. This is efficient, bureaucratic, and uses a pyramid structure to provide expert skills, train selected delegates, and distribute resources, in order to ensure that people pursue a preconceived plan. The rationale for directive

CULTURE	ORGANIZATION	
	Mechanistic	Organic
MODERN	Type A	Type B
Communal group commitment	Group supervised from above (programme)	Group develops under its own impetus (process)
Globally and societally conscious mission (political conscience)	Global and societal agenda provided (only certain issues politicized e.g. abortion)	Global and societal agenda self-initiated
Commitment involves justice	Justice issues prescribed, social concern encouraged	Justice from below (conscientization)
Reading 'the signs of the times'	Change orderly, relayed from above	System-disturbing and prophet-like initiatives
Change anticipated/ principles dominate	Lay leaders introduced but chosen from above and carefully monitored	Leaders emerge from group according to need
TRADITIONAL	Type C	Type D
Private and personal salvation-oriented	Priests and people focus on personal sanctity and proselytism, while leadership supervises society (seeks cultural monopoly) or seeks to protect 'faithful' (in a separate denominational culture)	Groups centre on changing the individual and renewing traditional practices
Love is charity-oriented	Individual 'resolutions' to action encouraged	'Social concern' rather than social justice developed
Traditions maintained/ rule-governed	Rules authoritatively stated, laity in subordinate roles, seen as passive/ wilful and needing control, always directed	Rules 'obvious', consensual change paramount, others trusted to share responsibility

FIG. 5.1 An Elaborated Typology of Spiritualities

techniques (Burns and Stalker, 1966) places responsibility for achieving goals firmly with experts or leaders, and tends to assume that the average person is naturally rather lazy, dislikes responsibility, is selfish and resistant to change, and may also be gullible and easily led.

Alternatively, a more 'organic' Church envisages a style embracing 'mutual responsibility' which is more unconventional and non-directive (and, in religious parlance, 'collaborative'), where participants decide what form the organization should take and what their needs are, and one which permits a faster and more appropriate response to the changing world of today. The task of experts and leaders is to arrange operations so that people can formulate and achieve their goals. Advocates of this approach tend to think people are only self-centred, passive, and resistant to change because their experience in traditional institutions has made them so. However, this more fluid system may appear less efficient to those accustomed to a conventional model.

These organizational approaches may not be without theological implications. For example, it might be suggested that the first type assumes that people are basically 'bad', sinful, or ignorant, and will go astray unless carefully led. The second model, on the other hand, tends to assume that people are 'good' and are capable of achieving right ends.

The second axis is concerned with two alternative views of a renewed Church spirituality. On the one hand, there is a 'communal, this-worldly, mission-oriented', more modern cultural style. This assumes that traditional views are open to reinterpretation, that social justice concerns are more important than individual piety, that prayer is a powerhouse for promoting active mission for justice and peace, and that evangelization is promoted by witness and example. This view of spirituality assumes that participants embrace challenge and conflict as a means of growth and fruitful development.

On the other hand, there is a 'private, other-worldly, salvation-oriented', more traditional cultural style, which regards prayer as a private act, religion and politics as separate issues, justice to be achieved by personal acts of charity or in the life hereafter, rules as immutable, and aggressive evangelization as justified. In general this cultural style assumes participants avoid conflict within the Church, regarding harmonious agreement and obedience as most likely to promote their aims.

As with all typologies which provide a framework for comparative analysis, it is unlikely that any participant or programme will adopt these organizational means or have these religious aims in a pure and undiluted form. In other words they are likely to be located at least partially in more than one cell.

Statements and activities which emphasize working within the existing arrangements will be placed in cell C. Participants in this style will work in a bureaucratic manner, in a hierarchical structure where experts or leaders persuade or coerce others in order to achieve the existing goals. This assumes a consensual definition of norms, of what is 'right' or 'obvious'. This is the most traditional type.

In cell A, the same directive working style will be used to promote a new goal seen by experts or leaders, also probably in a hierarchical structure, as 'right' and 'proper', although it may differ from some norms held by participants. Such conventional norms may be regarded as those of only one section of the Church, perhaps a powerful minority or a misguided majority. Thus in group work, participants may be urged by leaders to pursue innovative activities designed to promote a particular style of personal growth but which may differ from the prevailing norm. More usually pastoral strategies are intended to achieve higher standards in a consensual norm in order to benefit individuals, groups, and eventually the whole community (i.e. type C).

In cells B and D mutual responsibility and collaborative decision-making are favoured. Processes rather than projects or programmes are sponsored. Experts or leaders express confidence in the ability of the community to make its own decisions. They offer, without imposing, expertise or help and aim to avoid creating dependency on expert skills. Here leaders or experts may be given responsibility for organizing the project but potential for achievement is believed to be present in all participants. In community or group work, members are regarded in an egalitarian manner, and personal growth or community goals are pursued according to the wishes of the participants, even when, as in type B, their goals may not conform to those traditionally regarded as appropriate. Type B is the most innovative form of spirituality. Alternatively, however, the means of change may be innovative, for example using lay rather than hierarchical initiatives, but renewal of traditional forms of spirituality may be promoted (type D).

It should be noted that almost all statements and activities of participants are likely to require attribution to two cells since, for example, communal or private forms of spirituality may be clearly expressed but without any specification of the organizational approach to be adopted. Similarly, manifestly directive organizational means may be adopted in pastoral renewal without any clear indication of the cultural content of spirituality which is to be promoted.

In our soft data analysis, recurring statements and activities of both participants and non-participants were allocated to six main categories, each with seventeen subcategories. We have seen that the first four categories, traditional and modern *statements* and traditional and modern *activities*, were used to generate the four types of spirituality which constituted the initial formulation of our theoretical framework in Figure 5.1. The remaining two categories included activities (and a few statements) which impeded the achievement of, respectively, traditional or modern aims specified by the first four categories. These *hindering activities* contribute to the explanation of why some aims but not others were achieved by the RENEW programme. Illustrations of the six main categories, each with seventeen subcategories, taken from our soft data have been given in Appendix 1. While there is a certain symmetry about the conceptual content of all seventeen subcategories, which usefully aids comprehension and analysis, this is not a logical necessity and in a few instances symmetry is not complete.

The issues of the reliability and validity of our data need to be considered if we are to avoid the objection that counting categories of qualitative data merely gives a spurious gloss to subjectively selected material. Some indication of the reliability of our data is the evidence that material collected quite independently and in different settings by the three authors of this study yielded similar distributions among the main categories and subcategories. Soft data analysis must be regarded as 'illuminative' and needs to be validated by prediction or its face value for participants in analysing their own experiences or in recognizing explanations of past events. In the current study, a variety of complementary research methods were employed (and the results reported in later chapters in this book). It is to be expected that respondents to parishioners' questionnaires, for example, will be more involved in and favourably disposed to RENEW, than critical non-participants in the programme whose views are more likely to be reflected in the log notes of participant observers. The inclusion of the latter, we would suggest, gives a more rounded interpretation of the RENEW experience than the rather partial and selectively positive views which were reported in the diocesan 'evaluations' from the parishes at the end of each season.

5.4   The Spirituality of RENEW

In Seasons 1 and 2 of the RENEW programme we recorded a total of 1,190 statements and activities (i.e. data 'events' other than hindering events). For the reasons we noted above, each of these can be allocated to two cells of the typology in Figure 5.1. The total number of attributions from all sources was, therefore, 2,380 which were coded according to the classifications given in Appendix 1. When these attributions were distributed between the four cells of Figure 5.1, roughly one-third were found to lie in each of cells A and C, one-fifth in cell B, and one-sixth in cell D (Table 5.1). Expressed differently, nearly two-thirds of all attributions imply a traditional, mechanistic methodology (styles A and C) and only one-third a participatory approach stressing lay responsibility (styles B and D), while attributions of the aims of Church spirituality were split almost equally between traditional (C and D) and modern (A and B) styles.

In order to understand something of the dynamic reality of RENEW it is also necessary to take into account hindering events attributable to any style which may hamper or retard the implementation of aims appropriate to that style. In this calculus, actions are arguably more effective than statements (Norris, 1981) and the differential influence or authority of different participants is also likely to affect specific outcomes. A total of 663 hindering 'events', in addition to the 1,190 positive statements and activities, were recorded in the diocese in the first two seasons of RENEW. Roughly equal numbers of traditional and modern positive statements were recorded. But on the other hand, nearly four times as many traditional compared to modern activities were noted. Overall, far more traditional events, both positive and negative, than innovative events were noted. The data suggest that the RENEW programme in the diocese tended to promote traditional practice in terms of organizational means and managerial style rather than in terms of the culture of spirituality encouraged.

When the analysis distinguished between different categories of respondent, informant, or other information source, some interesting variations emerged. Seven categories of participant were distinguished in this analysis which was confined to the first two seasons of RENEW:

(a) the diocesan RENEW team, including a diocesan priest and consultants from the International RENEW team;

(b) members of parish core teams, usually a parish priest and a small number of laity whom he invited to join him;

(c) members of parish committees (whose leaders were usually selected by the core team but who invited or persuaded others to join them);

TABLE 5.1 *Renewal Styles in the Diocese of Downlands—Seasons 1 and 2*

Religious Culture	Power in the Organizational Church	
	Mechanistic (Traditional)	Organic (Modern)
Modern	(A) TS 1–4, 6, 8–10, 12, 14 = 246 MS 11, 13, 15–17 = 151 TA 1–4, 6, 8–10, 12–14 = 347 MA 11, 13, 15–17 = 43 TOTAL = 787 (Few modern activities) (33% of +ve attributions)	(B) TS = 0 MS 1–17 = 331 TA = 0 MA 1–17 = 111 TOTAL = 442 (Fewer acts than statements) (19% of +ve attributions)
Traditional	(C) TS 1–17 = 364 MS = 0 TA 1–17 = 384 MA = 0 TOTAL = 748 (No modern data) (31% of +ve attributions)	(D) TS 5, 7, 11, 13, 15–17 = 118 MS 1–10, 12, 14 = 180 TA 5, 7, 11, 13, 15–17 = 37 MA 1–10, 12, 14 = 68 TOTAL = 403 (Fewer acts than statements) (17% of +ve attributions)

BRIEF SUB-CATEGORY KEY—for fuller details see Appendix 1

(S)tatements and (A)ctivities favouring:

(T)radition

1 Predetermined tasks
2 Reliance on experts
3 Bureaucratic procedures
4 Hierarchical authority
5 Co-operation, unproblematic
6 Leaders responsible
7 'Rules' unproblematic
8 Resources administered from above
9 Confidentiality, censorship
10 Benefits conferred by leaders
11 Maintenance of *status quo*
12 Participation defined
13 Conflict suppressed
14 Evaluation benefits organization
15 Private piety
16 Proselytism
17 Other-worldliness

(M)odernity

1 'Process'
2 Confidence in all
3 All partake in decisions/execution of policy
4 Negotiated authority
5 Co-operation, sometimes problematic
6 Mutual responsibility
7 'Rules' problematic
8 Resources raised and distributed by all
9 Undistorted information, freely communicated
10 Mutual benefits
11 *Status quo* challenged
12 Participation negotiated
13 Conflict effects change
14 Evaluation benefits all
15 Shared worship, mission
16 Open evangelism
17 This-worldliness

TABLE 5.2   Renewal Styles by Group (Seasons 1 and 2): Percentage Distribution of Positive Attributions

Group	% of Positive Attributions within Renewal Styles			
	(A)	(B)	(C)	(D)
Whole Diocese (N = 2380)	33	19	31	17
a: The diocesan RENEW team (N = 912)	32	18	32	18
b: Members of parish core teams (N = 504)	35	17	33	15
c: Members of parish committees (N = 244)	41	9	41	8
d: Clergy other than bishops (N = 142)	33	18	32	16
e: Bishops (UK and elsewhere) (N = 148)	33	18	32	17
f: Parishioners not in other categories (N = 362)	28	27	23	22
g: Laity in official or semi-official diocesan posts (N = 68)	28	25	25	22

(d) clergy other than bishops;

(e) bishops from Great Britain and overseas, not necessarily involved in the diocesan programme, but whose activities or statements were publicized during or just before the programme commenced;

(f) lay parishioners not in the preceding categories, excepting a small subset of (g);

(g) laity in official or semi-official diocesan posts.

In Table 5.2 the distributions of renewal styles for each of these seven categories of participants and for the diocese as a whole have been presented. It might be noted that similar distributions were found for members of the parish core teams (b), priests (d), and bishops (e). From these findings it might be inferred that in the first two seasons of RENEW, people hoping for organizational changes (for example, a shift to greater lay involvement in pastoral practice) would have found RENEW disappointing.

However, interesting variations emerged when considering the remaining three groups. In particular, lay members of the parish committees (*c*), whose leaders were mainly selected or sponsored by members of the parish core teams (*b*), in turn advised by the diocesan RENEW team (*a*), were noticeably the group most oriented towards traditional 'mechanistic' organization. Almost all the positive activities of lay members of parish committees comprised tasks delegated to them by groups (*a*) and (*b*). By contrast, the patterns for groups (*f*) and (*g*), ordinary parishioners and those laity whose particular qualifications made them influential in other ways in the diocese, were noticeably less oriented towards traditional organizational means. The percentage of activities in the 'organic' cells B and D for these two groups was greater than for other groups. However, the sheer weight of numbers of parishioners, reflected in the numerous 'modern' activities and statements recorded, may prove influential in the long-term effect of the RENEW programme. In a community development study of change over a five-year period (Norris, 1981; 1982) it was 'innovative' activity among the more numerous ordinary participants that gradually shifted the whole project towards an innovative pattern. There, too, activities of a traditional kind were observed more frequently amongst experts and managers despite statements supporting innovation.

In the community development study hindering activities were almost as frequent as positive events and considerably impeded change. In our RENEW study the number of hindering events (663) was about one-half of the number of positive events (1,190) and the ratio was roughly the same for both traditional and modern styles. However, the ratio varied between subcategories and groups. Nevertheless, there is sufficient symmetry among the subcategories across all six main categories (traditional and modern statements and activities, and activities and statements hindering traditional and modern aims) to draw some interesting conclusions from our data.

The balance between positive and hindering events is likely to determine whether change occurs, and the direction of change on the ratio of modern to traditional positive events. For example, in subcategory 8, problems with resources far outweighed positive events. Evidence from participant observation and interviews suggested that the RENEW team were in fact inclined to be dismissive of criticisms about the materials provided. There was little opportunity for radical alterations during the programme in response to the evaluations at the end of each season.

The soft data analysis was also helpful in the interpretation of occasions of conflict. In the RENEW programme conflict was rarely seen as an opportunity for fruitful outcome and was therefore usually suppressed. For example, people left groups or went to Mass elsewhere (occasionally in another diocese) rather than cause offence by criticism. Consequently, few attempts were made to resolve conflict by constructive criticism. Unresolved conflict predictably (Coleman, 1957) became personalized, degenerating from rational disagreement about the programme to criticisms of people in it. This was very likely to happen when management styles suppressing conflict or criticism were used by the same people who were proposing 'modern' forms of lay participation. Sometimes information, for example that collected as a result of the inbuilt 'evaluation', seemed to be manipulated in well-meaning attempts to avoid conflict or to suppress evidence of it.

Reclassifying hindering events in terms of some kind of resistance to the programme, on the one hand, or inept attempts to implement it, on the other, was also illuminating. Overall, instances of resistance accounted for three-fifths of recorded hindrances, but whereas there were as many cases of resistance as ineptness in the case of traditional aims, there were more than three times as many cases of resistance recorded, relative to cases of ineptness, in respect of modern aims. The five subcategories with the largest numbers of recorded hindrances were agreed or delegated tasks not fulfilled; lack of confidence expressed in participants, or experts demonstrated incompetence; RENEW process, plan, or tasks unsuccessfully explained; unanticipated tasks imposed, or authority for delegating tasks questioned; inadequate or inappropriate resources, sometimes distributed incompetently, and resulting in overwork for some participants.

Summarizing the results of these various analyses of data collected in the first two seasons of RENEW, it seemed that the traditional delegation of tasks was successfully implemented (subcategory 3 with 19 per cent of all data events), with activities outweighing hindrances. Furthermore, traditional authority was affirmed (subcategory 6 with 6 per cent of all recorded events) since despite frequent modern statements, actions strongly reinforced traditional practice. In the domain of religious culture, statements were more frequently recorded than actions and were confusingly likely to advocate both modern–communal and traditional–private forms of spirituality (subcategory 15, 12 per cent of all events) but modern activities were relatively frequently recorded. Elsewhere modern statements about more open evangelism and more this-worldly political activities were made but there was little evidence of action. However, during the first two seasons of RENEW there was also little resistance recorded to these statements which suggested the possibility of an enhanced concern for issues of social justice. Conflicts over this issue will be considered further in Chapter 7.

Differences between the seven groups of participants, whose orientations were reported in Table 5.2, might be noted here. During the first two seasons, the RENEW team was responsible for most statements about RENEW policy. The issues most frequently addressed by the team were those which described hierarchical organizational procedures to be adopted (subcategory 3; N = 56) and gave detailed instructions for delegating activities (subcategory 1; N = 51). However, while their individual statements about the spiritual orientation of RENEW were clear, they were split between those which stressed a 'modern' spirituality (N = 87) and those which reinforced a more traditional view (N = 53). Similar ambiguities were recorded when the diocesan team's explanations of the RENEW process were examined. One-third of these statements clearly described a plan, another third clearly described a process. An almost similar number of team statements were confusing enough to hinder the plan apparently intended. Problems with resources were frequently attributed to the team (N = 37).

The diocesan team's statements tended to be echoed to the parishes by the core teams. Delegated tasks accounted for the relatively high proportion of traditional activities in which parish committees engaged. The high proportion of hindering activities amongst parish committee members mostly reflected delegated tasks not completed, often due to inadequate resources, and some resistance to details of the programme, for example small group leaders in particular being inclined to 'do their own thing'.

Laity in official or semi-official positions in the diocese, for whom a small number of events were recorded, were relatively more likely to make modern statements than parishioners and more likely than other groups, except parishioners, to engage in modern activities. Their traditional activities, usually delegated tasks, were often implemented as a result of loyalty to the bishop, expressions of which also accounted for their traditional statements.

The core committees were recorded as being engaged in many positive events and seem to have been efficient, having a low proportion of recorded hindering events and very few impeding innovation. Bishops, the RENEW team, and the more influential laity also had relatively low proportions of hindering activities. The RENEW team and parish core committee members also showed low levels of hindrance to innovation. Other groups showed more signs of resistance to implementing activities or accepting ideas and more internal conflict, since resistance was recorded, both to innovation and to tradition.

Parishioners were less likely to implement delegated tasks than members of parish committees, though tasks were the most frequently recorded traditional activity. Parishioners were more often engaged in innovative activities than any other group, but the high proportion of parishioner activities hindering innovation indicated a conflict of opinions amongst parishioners about this. There were similar indications of conflicts of opinion amongst clergy. Conflict may lead to an impasse, perhaps of particular significance for the parishioner group. Otherwise, their numbers and activity levels might, in the absence of strong traditional control, shift the overall pattern for the diocese.

The results of this innovative soft data analysis during the first two seasons of RENEW appear to indicate a reinforcement of the traditional hierarchical and bureaucratic styles of diocesan organization whilst involving the laity in numerous delegated tasks. This managerial style appeared on balance to be intended by the RENEW team to achieve a modern spiritual development, and parishioners, in particular, engaged in activities which indicated a modern spiritual orientation. However, there were also strong indications of conflicts of opinion amongst parishioners, and their resistance, and that of some members of parish committees, to delegated tasks and to spiritual innovation are likely to have reduced the impact of innovative efforts.

At the same time the traditional organizational style may have reassured many participants who perhaps engaged in innovative delegated tasks only out of a sense of loyalty to authority. Recorded comments on loyalty to the hierarchy as the prime motivation for some activities supports this interpretation. However, this must undermine aspects of any process aiming to wean participants from dependence on experts and leaders and may result in the abandonment of innovation after the end of RENEW. We will return to such considerations in Chapter 8.

5.5   Hidden Critics

We argued earlier in this chapter that the official diocesan evaluation procedures were flawed in the sense that they gave a misleadingly enthusiastic picture of the response to the RENEW programme and failed adequately to reflect the numerous criticisms and grumbles expressed by ordinary Catholics in the parishes. In our soft data analysis we reported on the scale of conflict expressed and on 663 hindering events recorded by us in the course of our fieldwork in the first two seasons of RENEW. The objections of three of these hidden critics will be presented briefly in order to illustrate something of the flavour of the opposition. Further evidence will be presented in the following chapter.

An elderly lady in her eighties complained about the 'gimmicky' nature of RENEW and all the 'American razzmatazz'. She disliked the posters in the church, the 'childish' literature, the 'banal' RENEW hymn which 'nearly drives me mad', 'all those pieces of paper [and] form-filling', for example, used for making the prayer commitments before the start of each season of RENEW. 'Then there's the cost . . . several of us said: "oh, what a waste of money for a rather futile effort".' She did not see any value in the symbolism of the stones intended to signify hardness of heart at the beginning of Season 2. A young oak tree intended to represent the diocesan logo unfortunately died and so provided her with the opportunity to ask the parish priest: 'What does that dead oak tree symbolize? The death of St Matthew's?' She favoured the reforms of the Second Vatican Council but did not like 'the Mass so broken up with trivial things'. She saw no evidence that young people or non-Catholics were being attracted and added:

I think it's putting a great burden on people, which doesn't seem to be of any benefit . . . working hard going to meetings, study groups, conferences, prayer groups . . . They are all rushing round frantically and saying: 'Oh I shall be glad when the season's over', all taking on too much.   (Interview, 18 Sept. 1989)

Finally she quoted her son's observation that 'it's like rearranging deckchairs on the sinking *Titanic*'. The implication was that fundamental issues (unspecified) needing reform were not being addressed. In protest she had moved to the adjacent parish where the liturgies seemed to her to be more restrained and dignified.

In another parish a middle-aged man challenged the rather optimistic evaluations prepared by the RENEW team on the grounds that they were unrepresentative of all the parishioners since the response rates to questionnaires had been low and mainly from active participants. He complained that the diocesan team appeared to be doing the same:

They seem not to listen to criticism from within RENEW and to ignore those who chose not to join; furthermore, by indulging in self-praise . . . they are not helping RENEW or making it possible for others to join.   (Letter, 17 Apr. 1989)

In *A Personal View* (12 Apr. 1989) appended to his parish's evaluation report after Season 2 he made similar criticisms as the woman above: 'Americanisms', 'dismal', 'off-putting, unnerving and . . .

childish', and 'silly'. The advice that small groups should remain together throughout the five seasons was regarded as 'misconceived'. RENEW might have been an appropriate 'American Catholic answer to the Jimmy Bakkers of this world' but 'it will not work here'.

A year later he was writing to the bishop about the financial implications of RENEW. As a member of the parish Finance Committee he noted that for the first time the number of new and superseding covenants was the lowest since their introduction some years ago. He 'detected a certain malaise amongst parishioners regarding the amount of expenditure reported to have been incurred by the diocese with RENEW' which he estimated would amount to £180,000 (Letter, 25 June 1990). In his reply Bishop Patrick did not think that the RENEW expenditure was as much as this and asked the Financial Secretary 'to give you details of this expenditure which, of course, everybody has a right to know' (Letter, 28 June 1990).

In a *Notebook* piece in *The Tablet* (9 June 1990) before the final season, a rather glowing account of RENEW was given. This quoted liberally from the diocesan director of RENEW and the 'convert' Mgr. Bob Reilly who was later to be seconded to work for the International RENEW team. It prompted a response from one parishioner who observed tartly that since the programme was not yet completed and the evaluations adequately undertaken it was premature to judge its success. She noted that

some doubts have certainly been voiced . . . about the real effect of the great investment of time, effort and money in RENEW. An increase in community spirit, in caring, in understanding each other's different needs, and in participation in parish affairs has been apparent to some of us, but the style of the programme has alienated others . . . in order to inspire us to greater efforts, published extracts from the RENEW evaluation process . . . mainly report success and omit adverse comments which we know are sometimes made. Some of us feel that criticism is not taken seriously. We have heard little from people who feel unhappy with the programme, or excluded from participation in it—more than half of parishioners? It has been suggested that this may result in divisions, not community building. (*The Tablet*, 22 June 1990)

Finally she noted that it 'has been difficult to sustain efforts throughout the programme—progressively harder to find people with time and energy to act as group leaders'.

These three examples illustrate that there were hidden critics of RENEW who very often had no voice in the relentless progress through the five seasons of RENEW. In assessing the programme it is important to ensure that due weight is given to their views. We believe the official accounts of RENEW failed adequately to reflect this reality and it is our hope that the extracts from our data which we have presented will go some way to providing a more balanced and rounded version of the RENEW experience.

5.6 Towards a more Balanced Account

In this chapter we first outlined the RENEW evaluation procedures at the end of each season. These were designed to 'be positive' and to 'reinforce what seems to be working well', 'not so much to evaluate what had happened but to point people in the direction of what might happen'. In the light of such instructions to parish evaluators, it is not surprising that the reported results of RENEW were glowing. However, from a social scientific perspective, such evaluations were likely to have been seriously biased and to have systematically ignored the many criticisms of RENEW which were voiced by ordinary Catholics throughout the diocese.

Our earliest attempts to seek a more balanced assessment of RENEW led to the use of soft data analysis, a technique originally developed in the study of a community-development project. From content analysis of RENEW literature and field notes taken during our ethnographic work in the first two seasons of RENEW we identified a total of 1,190 statements and activities and a further 663 hindering events. These were classified in terms of the axes of spiritualities outlined in Chapter 2.

The results demonstrated a clear preponderance of traditional mechanistic forms of organization but an equal balance of traditional (pietistic) and modern (and more communally-oriented) forms of spirituality. When the results for seven different groups of participants were compared it was noted that there were significant similarities between the diocesan RENEW team, members of parish core teams, clergy, and bishops. Members of parish committees were significantly more likely than these groups to be directive and hierarchical. The most 'organic' or participative group consisted of those laity in official or semi-official diocesan posts. It was argued that the long-term impact of RENEW was likely to depend on the balance between positive and hindering events and the ratio of innovative to traditional positive events in each of a range of seventeen different subcategories identified.

A traditional mechanistic organizational style was all too apparent in the pained objections of one of the diocesan team when asked if there had been any people who had decided that they did not wish to be constrained by the RENEW programme:

Yes, there have been, you see, and I fight against that . . . I feel we all need to . . . RENEW is a particular process we have taken on (throughout the whole diocese) . . . But you find here, there and everywhere people come into leadership . . . then they impose their own limitations on everyone else in the parish. It's not with consultation; all they're doing there . . . we're exchanging some aging, bumbling, somewhat incompetent cleric who is quite loveable for some unloveable oligarchy.   (Interview, 4 Oct. 1989)

In other words, parish leadership is fine provided that it conforms to the delegated tasks given to it by the diocesan team. This interview extract clearly demonstrates the hierarchical, directive, and top-down nature of the organizational style employed by RENEW.

In spite of all the rhetoric about lay empowerment, in fact, RENEW was imposed by the religious leadership in the diocese from the top down. In earlier chapters we showed that this was the case as far as the decision to adopt the RENEW programme was concerned. In this chapter we have demonstrated that a similar directiveness applied to the actual operation of the programme. Once the decision to follow the RENEW programme had been taken, strong pressure was applied to co-opt practically all the parishes in the diocese, to ensure the maximum level of conformity to the stipulated procedures of the programme, and to meet its expectations in terms of the specified criteria such as small group participation and home visiting. Hierarchical control was also apparent in the sequencing of themes, the priority to be accorded to RENEW small groups over pre-existing ecumenical house groups, the insistence that participants faithfully follow the instructions in the small group booklets, the encouragement not to change groups between seasons, and so on.

Our soft data analysis also provided a basis for the interpretation of conflicts which existed in the parishes as a result of the RENEW programme. We have noted that the official evaluation exercise tended to discount the existence of such conflicts and of criticisms of the programme. We concluded the chapter by reporting the objections of some of the hidden critics. In the following chapter we will continue our investigation into the experience of RENEW at parish level and provide further evidence that the official diocesan version of RENEW was not the whole story.

6

The Experience of RENEW in the Parishes

6.1 Parish Evaluations

At the end of Chapter 4 we had arrived at the point where the RENEW programme was about to start at the beginning of Season 1. All the preparations had been made and the programme was launched with a Mass concelebrated by Bishop Patrick and his priests in the soccer stadium of Southlands Athletic. At the end of Season 1 a diocesan evaluation exercise was undertaken. In the previous chapter we showed that its results were systematically biased in favour of the positive outcomes of the programme and that many of the criticisms expressed about the programme in the diocese tended to be discounted. We also offered an analysis of a very large amount of soft data which we collected from a wide variety of different sources and levels in the diocese during the first two seasons of RENEW. We documented a substantial amount of conflict and hindrances which, we suggested, indicated a considerable amount of both manifest but more often latent resistance to the RENEW programme.

In this chapter we will provide further evidence of the actual experiences of RENEW in the parishes, and especially in the small groups. In particular we will report the findings of questionnaire surveys of both adult parishioners and members of small groups at the end of each of the five RENEW seasons in St Matthew's parish. In this way we will be able to note trends in participation and emphasis across the whole programme over a 2½-year period. We will supplement these survey findings with data from a number of interviews with participants in this parish as well as a considerable amount of data obtained from our own observations and as participants in the Evaluation Committee of this parish. In effect we conducted a parish case study within the diocesan case study. It should be noted that this parish was one of the most committed to the RENEW programme, in the sense that its reported participation rate in the small groups in Season 1 was the thirteenth highest out of 113 parishes for whom data were available. If anything, therefore, the results from this parish are likely to be more favourable towards RENEW than in the diocese as a whole.

In order to demonstrate that our main research parish was not unusual, we are able to report some comparable survey data from six other parishes. Although data from these parishes were obtained opportunistically, through the co-operation of the parish priests and/ or key members of their Evaluation Committees, one of these parishes had reported small group participation rates in the top quintile of parishes in the diocese, one in the bottom two quintiles and the remaining four from the middle two quintiles. By this criterion, the seven parishes from which we have obtained some survey data represent a good cross-section of the parishes in the diocese. Our data go beyond what was obtained from the diocesan evaluations at the end of each season in terms of both comprehensiveness and representativeness.

A summary of the available data from parishioner and small group questionnaires has been given in Table 6.1. A total of 1,177 parishioner questionnaires were completed over the five seasons in St Matthew's parish (Parish 1) and 1,202 were obtained from four other parishes. About half the adult Mass attenders completed them in three parishes but the response rates were lower in the two other parishes. The table also reports several measures of participation in small groups. In St Matthew's parish there was an average of eighteen small groups in each of the five seasons of RENEW. In three other parishes the average was eight. Two measures of group participation are given. Reported sign-up for small groups before the start of each season averaged just under one-third in the five parishes for which we have data, ranging from one-half of adult Mass attenders in St Matthew's parish to only one-eighth in another. Actual attendances were somewhat lower but averaged just under one-third of adult Mass attenders in four of the five parishes for which we have data. In the fifth parish only around one in fifteen adult Mass attenders were reported to have been in small groups. A total of 971 questionnaires were completed by around two-thirds of the members of small groups surveyed in five parishes; in St Matthew's parish the response rate was as high as 84 per cent. Three measures of prayer activity have been reported. Over two-thirds of those responding to the parishioner questionnaires in the first three seasons said they had committed themselves to say the RENEW prayer daily. The estimates made by parish evaluators were very similar but the proportion of respondents to the parish

TABLE 6.1 *Summary of Data from Seven Parishes across Five Seasons*

Variable	Parish						
	1	2	3	4	5	6	7
Q'naires for seasons[1]	1–5	3–5	4–5	3–5	none	none	3
Mass attendance (1988)[2]	521	464	364	310	765	630	739
Est. adult Mass att. (AMA)[3]	384	380	298	254	626	515	605
Av. parishioner q'naires (N)	235	180[4]	157	59	n/a	n/a	173
Response rate (% AMA)	61	47	53[5]	23	n/a	n/a	29
No. small groups	18	7	9	n/a	n/a	n/a	9
Reported sign-up (N)	187	n/a	114	n/a	176	221	72
(% AMA)	49	n/a	38	n/a	28	43	12
Reported gp. attendance (N)	165	91	97	81	n/a	n/a	40
(% AMA)	43	24	33	32	n/a	n/a	7
Av. small gp. q'naires (N)	138	52	54	51	n/a	n/a	20
Response rate (% SGA)	84	57	56	63	n/a	n/a	50
Prayer commitments made:							
In parishioner q'naires (N)	166	169	n/a	22	n/a	n/a	117
As % respondents (% PQs)	71	63	n/a	22	n/a	n/a	68
In parish eval. reports (N)	285	n/a	n/a	n/a	320	420	390
(% AMA)	74	n/a	n/a	n/a	51	82	64
Reported prayed more (N)	130	125	61	43	n/a	n/a	100
As % respondents (% PQs)	55	69	39	73	n/a	n/a	58
Number of committees (N)	9	n/a	5	n/a	7	n/a	n/a
As % maximum (% max)	90	n/a	50	n/a	70	n/a	n/a

[1] There were no small group questionnaires in Season 4 from Parish 2, and in Seasons 3 and 4 from Parish 4.

[2] Diocesan Directory, 1990.

[3] AMA is the estimated number of adult Mass attenders in 1988 at the start of the RENEW programme. For Parishes 2–7 it has been calculated as 81.8% of the reported Mass attendance figures given in the Diocesan Directory. The estimated proportion of children and young people under the age of 16 has been based on the population distribution in the 1991 census. In Parish 1 (St Matthew's) only, for which a March 1993 church attendance census distribution is available, the proportion has been taken to be 73.7%.

[4] Some low rates for Parish 2 result from the fact that there was co-operation from only one church of three in the parish in two of the three seasons. Demographic data supports the view that responses were still representative.

[5] In Seasons 4 and 5, Parish 3 counted 149 and 184 adult Mass attenders on the days that parishioner questionnaires were completed. These figures would give a response rate of 94%.

questionnaires who reported that they had prayed more during the RENEW seasons was very much lower at just over one-half. Finally, in none of the parishes for which we have data was there a full complement of ten RENEW committees.

In the analyses which follow we will mainly be concerned with the results from St Matthew's parish which is the only parish for which we have comprehensive survey data from both Mass attending parishioners and small group participants for all five seasons. In this parish we obtained data from 61 per cent of the estimated adult Mass attenders (the parishioner questionnaires) and 84 per cent of the estimated small group members. The results obtained can, therefore, be regarded as reasonably representative, particularly in the case of the small group members. However, there are good grounds for suspecting that those who responded to the parishioner questionnaires were more committed and involved than the average parishioner. For example, a higher proportion of them were members of the RENEW small groups.

A summary of the demographic characteristics of the adult Mass attenders and small group members in St Matthew's parish has been given in Table 6.2 and comparisons made with those obtained from a nationally representative sample of Roman Catholics in England and Wales in the late 1970s (Hornsby-Smith and Lee, 1979: 163). Thus it appears that men, young people aged 35 or under, and those in religiously mixed marriages are under-represented and married people are over-represented among the parishioners in St Matthew's parish. The lower proportion in full-time and the higher proportion in part-time employment might simply reflect the economic restructuring processes of recent years. When we compare small group members with parishioners it is clear that men and the younger age groups, especially those with children under school age, and those in part-time employment, were under-represented in the RENEW small groups. These appeared to be particularly attractive to housewives and retired people, the middle-aged (36–65 years) and married people, particularly those without very young children.

The surveys carried out in the other six parishes were not as comprehensive as those in St Matthew's parish and the lower response rates achieved suggest that they were less representative of both parishioners generally and the members of the small groups. The results from these parishes, however, offer useful, if patchy, comparative data where response rates are reasonably satisfactory. This would seem to be the case especially in the case of Parishes 2 and 3 as far as the parishioner surveys are concerned, and in the case of the small group members' surveys in Parishes 2, 3, and 4.

TABLE 6.2 *Demographic Data for Parishioners and Small Group Members across Five Seasons, St Matthew's Parish (%)*

Variable	Seasons	Adult Mass Attenders	Small Gp. Members[1]		All Catholics (1979)[2]
			PQ	SGL	
Sex:					
Male		34	28	25	44
Female	1–5	66	71	75	56
N = 100%	1–5	1,114	566	818	1,023
Age:					
16–20		4	3	3	11
21–35		13	9	16	31
36–50	1–5	39	41	35	29
51–65		27	32	29	18
over 65		17	16	16	10
N = 100%	1–5	1,131	580	775	1,023
Marital Status:					
Married		72	75	75	68
Single		15	12	15	19
Divorced/Sep.	1–5	5	6	3	4
Widowed		7	8	7	9
N = 100%	1–5	1,119	632	765	1,023
Employment Status:					
Full-time		39	41	46	45
Part-time	PQ = 1	20	6	6	16
Retired	SGL = 1–5	11	16	13	10
Housewife		25	36	30	22
Other/Student		4	1	4	6
N = 100%		236	113	657	987
Other:					
Non-Cath. spouse	2	39	37	n/a	44
Children school age or under	3	48	46	n/a	n/a
Children pre-school age	4	12	7	n/a	n/a

[1] Two estimates for small group members are available: from small group respondents to parishioner questionnaires (PQ) and from questionnaires completed by small group leaders (SGL).

[2] Data for all Catholics in England and Wales have been taken from Hornsby–Smith and Lee (1979). Age distributions have been estimated by interpolation.

Our main results relate to the case study of St Matthew's (Parish 1) but we have some very useful comparative data from several other parishes which lend strength to our analysis and provide strong evidence that St Matthew's was in no obvious way atypical of the parishes in the diocese.

We begin our review by reporting the results of our questionnaire surveys of parishioners across the five seasons and, to a limited extent, across different parishes. These data are then supplemented by other data from interviews with informants or from our particip- ant observation. Since the small 'faith-sharing' groups represented the core of the RENEW programme (however much the RENEW organizers stressed that parishioners could participate in RENEW in a multiplicity of ways), we next report the findings from our surveys of small group members in St Matthew's parish across the five seasons, and again, to a limited extent, comparatively across several parishes. Of particular importance is the interpretation of the weekly 'action-response' requirement and the salience of 'social concerns'. Our analysis concludes by commenting on variations in the experi- ences across the different age groups and between the sexes, and in the seven parishes from which we obtained some data.

6.2   *The Experiences of Parishioners*

At the end of each season of RENEW in St Matthew's parish, the parish priest agreed with the proposal of the Evaluation Committee that the best way to ensure a representative response of Mass at- tenders was to survey them using self-completion questionnaires during Saturday night/Sunday morning Masses. The results obtained after Season 1 were used to construct the more structured questions which were used after the end of each of the remaining seasons. A copy of the parishioner questionnaire used in these later seasons has been given in Appendix 2. The parish priest led the congregation through the questionnaire question by question and the whole ex- ercise was completed within five to ten minutes. It must be admitted that in spite of repeated pleas from the evaluation team not to risk biasing responses by elaborating or suggesting typical answers, the parish priest could not avoid the temptation on occasions. The purist researcher would cringe but we were just grateful to have been allowed to survey a captive congregation in a Catholic church at all. For all its limitations we believe the results over the five seasons indicate a good measure of reliability and face validity and are of considerable interest. In our submission they add consider- ably to the evaluation reports prepared for the diocesan team.

In a census of the 373 Mass attenders in St Matthew's parish in the town of Riverton in March 1993 about 26 per cent were children or young people under the age of sixteen. It appears, therefore that this parish has a younger profile than that of the general population in the town of Riverton (19 per cent according to the 1991 national census). There was the expected gender distribution with 61 per cent of attenders being female (compared to 51 per cent in Riverton). Since respondents to parishioner questionnaires were predominantly female (66 per cent) and 44 per cent were aged 50 or over (compared to 39 per cent in Riverton), this provides additional evidence that there was a slight underrepresentation of males and younger adults in the parishioner surveys.

The main results obtained in our main research parish, St Matthew's, over the five seasons are given in Table 6.3. We noted above that around 70 per cent of the respondents to the parishioner questionnaires (in the first three seasons) claimed to have made a prayer commitment before the start of each season. Rather fewer claimed to have prayed more during the season. The proportion peaked at 68 per cent of respondents at the end of Season 2 which had as its theme the participant's response to the Lord's call. Thereafter it declined steadily to only two-fifths of respondents after the final season. It is possible that this decline reflects a generally heightened level of prayer as a result of RENEW so that each season it became more difficult to pray more. It is also possible that the decline is a real trend and reflects a growing weariness over the $2^{1}/_{2}$ years of the programme. One measure of involvement in RENEW is an indication of an awareness of the main theme of each season. By this criterion RENEW did not score highly. The largest proportion of respondents able to name the main theme of each season was under one-third in Season 3 which aimed to raise issues of social concern under the umbrella theme of 'empowerment by the Spirit'; the proportion fell to under one-eighth after Season 4.

One of the main aims of RENEW was to encourage a higher level of reading of scripture. We asked respondents to indicate how frequently they had read scripture during the RENEW seasons. Again the proportions peaked during Season 2, when over one-third claimed to have done so daily or most days, and declined to one-quarter during the final season. Correspondingly, the proportion who admitted never to have read scripture during RENEW increased from just over one-quarter in the first two seasons to over two-fifths in the last three seasons.

On the basis of responses after Season 1, parishioners were asked after the remaining seasons to indicate which of a range of activities had most helped them take part in RENEW. The two most

TABLE 6.3 Summary of Parishioner Surveys after Five Seasons, St Matthew's Parish

Responses to RENEW	Season									
	1		2		3		4		5	
N = 100%	248		245		220		220		244	
	N	%	N	%	N	%	N	%	N	%
Made a prayer commitment	169	68	169	69	160	73	–	–	–	–
Prayed more	154	62	166	68	122	55	114	52	96	39
Could name season's theme	–	–	44	18	68	31	27	12	53	22
Read scripture:										
Daily/most days	81	33	87	36	61	28	59	27	60	24
Sometimes	89	36	87	36	66	30	59	27	70	29
Never	68	27	66	27	89	41	88	40	104	43
Helped to take part in RENEW this Season most by:										
Belonging to small group	–	–	129	53	110	50	106	48	102	42
Attending Sunday Mass	–	–	101	41	121	55	104	47	114	47
Attending other Masses	–	–	26	11	26	12	16	7	24	10
The altar posters	–	–	18	7	35	16	17	7	26	11
The scripture booklet	–	–	82	33	47	21	46	21	45	18
Weekly take-home leaflets	–	–	34	14	16	7	41	19	25	10
Attending large gp event	–	–	5	2	3	1	4	2	6	2

Responses to RENEW		Season								
	1		2		3		4		5	
N = 100%	248		245		220		220		244	
	N	%	N	%	N	%	N	%	N	%
Made difference to life (S.1&2), Did something different (S.3&4), Changed life (S.5):										
Yes	143	58	126	51	85	39	32	14	94	39
Helped to take part in Mass most by:										
The homily	–	–	80	33	109	50	69	31	90	37
The congregation	–	–	33	13	19	9	16	7	23	9
The singing	–	–	38	16	49	22	32	15	25	10
The symbols	–	–	56	23	6	3	18	8	10	4
Extended exch. peace (S.4&5)	–	–	–	–	–	–	49	22	59	24

frequently selected options were belonging to a small group and attending Sunday Mass. After Season 2, over half of parishioner respondents mentioned small groups but the proportion declined steadily to just over two-fifths after the final season. Similarly, whereas one-third of respondents had mentioned the daily scripture readings in a special booklet distributed free in this parish in Season 1 (though contributions to defray the cost were invited in subsequent seasons), after Season 2 the proportion declined steadily to under one-fifth after Season 5. Correspondingly, there was a gradual increase in the numbers mentioning attendance at Sunday Mass from two-fifths after Season 1 to around one-half after the remaining seasons. It might be inferred from these figures that over the nearly three years of the RENEW programme there was a steady decline in commitment and extra endeavour and a regression to the known and familiar.

This inference seems to be given support from the questions which asked parishioners whether RENEW had made any difference to their lives. The precise wording was altered twice over the course of the five seasons so that care is necessary in the interpretation of the results. They do, however, appear to indicate a decline in the proportion who admitted that RENEW had made a difference and an increase in the proportion who said it had not. After Season 5, two-fifths of parishioners reported that RENEW had changed their lives in some general way; almost all of them claimed they had been 'deepened spiritually'. Just under one-third of respondents reported in addition to spiritual change, some change concerning their involvement in parish life generally, or in the areas of social justice or evangelism. This may be regarded as evidence of the achievement of the more communal aims of RENEW. Another question asked parishioners what had most helped them to take part in Mass. The homily was mentioned most frequently in all seasons though special symbols, such as 'dead' stones, were helpful in Season 2 and an extended exchange of peace in the last two seasons was mentioned by over one-fifth of the respondents.

At the end of Season 4, Mass attending parishioners were asked which of a range of possible prayer commitments they had actually fulfilled. Only just under one-third said they had prayed the RENEW prayer daily but between one-quarter and one-third had attended at least one weekday Mass. Around one-fifth had prayed before the Blessed Sacrament at least weekly and a similar proportion had read the scripture selections. Smaller proportions had said the rosary, made a day of prayer and fasting, prayed as a family, or prayerfully prepared the Sunday Mass readings. At the end of the final season, over one-third of the parishioner respondents felt RENEW had deepened their spirituality, one in eight said they were more involved in the parish, one in twelve respondents said they were involved in social justice and a similar proportion in evangelism.

We have previously noted the lower response rates to the parishioner questionnaire surveys in four other parishes in one or more of Seasons 3 to 5. However, when due account has been taken of the possible skewing of the results due to non-response, the comparative data obtained from these other parishes using the same questionnaires offer considerable support to the view that the results obtained in St Matthew's parish were by no means atypical in the diocese. A summary of comparative results has been given in Table 6.4. The results from Parish 4 need to be treated with some caution since it appears that the bulk of respondents were small group members and that an adequate representation of other Mass attenders was not achieved. This is reflected in the consistently higher levels of prayer, commitment to regular scripture reading, awareness of the main theme, and sadness at the end of the RENEW programme than in other parishes. Parish 7 is also unusual in that some disruption was caused when the parish priest died during the RENEW programme and a key member of the Evaluation Committee was ill or absent abroad for much of the time. The most reliable data, therefore, are those for Parishes 1, 2, and 3.

In all three parishes there was a decline in the proportions praying more and attending a small group between Seasons 4 and 5. In two of the parishes there was also a decline in scripture reading. The results for naming the main theme of the season were more variable between parishes and seasons and appear to reflect different priorities and historical legacies specific to the individual parishes. Around one-third of the respondents in the three parishes said that RENEW had changed their lives and the types of changes they mentioned were very similar. Between one-quarter and one-fifth said RENEW had given them a deepened spirituality and between one-eighth and one-fifth had got involved more in their parishes. Smaller proportions in all three parishes had got involved in either social justice or evangelism. Responses on aspects it was hoped would continue after RENEW and feelings at the end of the final season of RENEW were remarkably consistent between the parishes while nevertheless being indicative of different historical traditions and probably interest groups. The low level of support for a continuing Liturgy Committee in St Matthew's parish is strange, given that the parish had had such a committee for a decade or more before the commencement of RENEW. Our evidence suggests that

TABLE 6.4 *Comparative Data for Five Parishes across Seasons 3–5 (% Respondents to Parishioner Questionnaires)*

Responses to RENEW	Season	Parish 1	2	3	4	7
Prayed more	3	55	56	–	68	58
	4	52	65	45	77	–
	5	39	55	34	63	–
Attended small group	3	51	40	–	87	23
	4	48	50	43	70	–
	5	46	42	38	100	–
Read scripture daily or most days	3	28	25	–	71	16
	4	27	20	24	48	–
	5	24	32	16	60	–
Named season's theme	3	31	12	–	42	11
	4	12	8	7	14	–
	5	22	20	11	30	–
RENEW had changed life	5	39	35	31	65	–
Type of change:						
Deepened spirituality	5	35	31	26	65	–
Involved in parish	5	13	19	20	31	–
Involved in social justice	5	8	7	5	9	–
Involved in evangelism	5	8	9	9	22	–
Aspects to be continued after RENEW:						
Small groups	4	34	29	35	39	–
Liturgy committee	4	8	12	20	11	–
Social concern	4	22	26	48	30	–
Another RENEW programme	4	29	11	45	43	–
Feelings after end of RENEW:						
Very or a little sad	5	32	35	22	70	–
A little or very relieved	5	27	17	23	8	–
Indifferent or mixed feelings	5	36	25	41	11	–
Visitor to parish	5	4	6	18	2	–
Attend regularly but do not live in parish	5	22	19	42	0	–
Have attended Mass here less than 5 years	5	40	17	31	22	–
Average N parish questionnaires (= 100%)	3–5	235	180	157	59	173

this was a protest vote embodying a distaste for some aspects of RENEW and, in particular, for a perceived low level of aesthetic symbolism and visual impact. The death of oak trees, which were intended to symbolize potential strength and vitality, was regarded with wry amusement by the critics, some of whom moved to an adjacent parish. Similarly, the low support in Parish 2 for another programme like RENEW after its completion, taken along with some of our ethnographic data, also suggests a protest: 'enough is enough.' Even allowing for such parish idiosyncrasies, the general pattern of feelings at the end of RENEW was remarkably consistent. Between one-fifth and one-third were sad when RENEW ended while between one-sixth and one-quarter were relieved.

Finally, some indication of the different social environments of these three parishes can be judged from the characteristics of their Mass attenders. In two of the parishes around one in twenty were visitors on the day of the survey but in Parish 3 the proportion was very nearly one-fifth. This parish also had over two-fifths of its regular attenders living outside the geographical boundaries, twice as many as in the other two parishes. One measure of the mobility of parish congregations is given by the proportions which have attended Mass for under five years. St Matthew's parish has a number of large new estates which are popular with young mobile families and this is reflected in the fact that two-fifths of the respondents have attended for under five years. The general pattern of these comparative results, using the same research instruments in several parishes over several seasons, provides strong support for the conclusion that the results from our main parish case study are reliable and have wider validity. Since this is clearly the case with the more quantitative data, there are no grounds for doubting that the analysis of the processes taking place in this parish and explored in our ethnographic work will also apply to a very considerable extent to the other parishes in the diocese.

6.3   Parish Ethnographies

It is important to note that while the RENEW machine rolled unstoppably through Season 1 and involved very large numbers of parishioners, its course was not uniformly welcomed. As early as the first week in October 1988 there was evidence of resistance from some regular Mass attenders. Because RENEW had originated from and been legitimated by the bishop and had co-opted large numbers of active parishioners, such indications of dissent were not often publically voiced. But they were shared in small friendship groups and we have numerous examples which the diocesan evaluation procedures did not, we believe, adequately reflect.

Thus two men and a woman, all regular Mass attenders in St Matthew's parish, middle class and aged about 60, exchanged the following observations at this time. The woman asked what the others thought of RENEW and replies included such remarks as: 'what's it supposed to do?'; 'all this silly kindergarten stuff'; 'patronizing'; 'childish'; 'nothing to get one's teeth into'; 'we've done all this before'; 'silly to have groups without any prior selection'; 'what's it all going to cost?' and 'who is going to pay?'; 'refuse to participate'; 'resent all this pressuring, arm-twisting'. On being asked how they avoided becoming involved, the answers included: 'oh, easily, it's a laugh ... it's a joke ... You return blank sheets of paper, or pseudonyms'; 'you can put your name down for a time ... when no one else can attend'; 'if pressure is immorally applied, it is justifiable to adopt strategems which will not make you conspicuous; ... some priests are doing the same'.

These remarks were laced with a strong antagonism to modern liturgical developments: 'it's enough to make one turn to Lefebvre.' Whereas previously the parishioners could vote with their feet and choose a church with a style with which the worshipper was comfortable, RENEW was like the national curriculum: people could only acquiesce, however reluctantly, or abandon practice altogether. A few people even migrated to the neighbouring diocese in order to avoid the RENEW process. The general consensus among the three was that RENEW would alienate the moderates and might mean that Mass attendance would drop in the long run. A few weeks later, an elderly parishioner informed us that 'all this American razzmatazz' was 'like selling soap-powder'. She commented adversely on the expense and the 'ridiculousness of having to sell T-shirts and balloons to offset this'. There is clear evidence in these remarks of a high level of antagonism towards RENEW and of a substantial measure of covert resistance and dissent at least among some non-participants.

As part of the process of reinforcing commitment and enhancing the preparations for Season 2 of RENEW which was due to commence early in February 1989, a number of training evenings for parish RENEW teams were held in the deaneries. The presentation in the Riverton deanery was highly professional and the audience quietly attentive. They were encouraged to see the task of the parish RENEW team as creating the right atmosphere by growing in their experience of faith-sharing in community. They were urged to revitalize their role by enhanced commitment, comprehension, and conviction but warned of the danger of 'burn out'. Finally, the tasks of each of the parish committees in preparation for Season 2 were outlined. For example, the small group leaders were urged to ensure that groups stayed together to build on the faith-sharing and trust that had been cultivated in Season 1. The materials had been deliberately structured and the groups were not Bible-study groups or problem-solving groups; the action-response was not trivial or childish but an integral part of the RENEW process.

The presenter suggested that the image of the parish and Church as hierarchical and pyramidical was not appropriate to RENEW which envisaged a cluster of small faith-communities around the core. The core team was not a task force but a growing cell, a model for the rest of the parish in showing the need to reset sights, a source of learning for the rest of the parish, and an expression of their convictions as a 'faith-community'. RENEW was a 'process', open to the Holy Spirit as a means of effecting growth in the parish. This view of RENEW suggests that it derived its inspiration from the processual community-development movement of the 1970s, adapted for religious rather than political purposes, and drawing on notions of personal growth engendered by sensitivity or T-group dynamics. (Both aspects have been well-researched and are now regarded with rather more scepticism than previously.)

Not everyone appreciated the presentation. One person observed: 'I'm here under false pretences. It's not my idea of what these groups are for at all and I find this quite alarming.' Such observations, which were rarely recorded by the official diocesan evaluators because they were negative rather than positive and constructive, tended to be made informally and between friends. We believe that our account of the RENEW process as it was actually experienced, and recorded systematically in our ethnographic field notes, gives a more rounded and complete assessment than the official versions of what happened.

A month after the end of Season 1 there was a meeting for the parish RENEW teams in the Riverton deanery. The meeting started twenty minutes late but ended on time at 10p.m. About seventy-four people, mostly in the older age groups, attended; twenty-nine of these were men and there were five priests and three nuns. Sister Mary of the diocesan team invited contributions from the floor of the 'positive results' from Season 1. These included getting to know people; a friendlier atmosphere in the parish; a deeper prayer life; a greater measure of mutual support; more reading and discussion of scripture; greater commitment and the discovery of new leaders; spiritual fellowship; and so on.

Sister Mary then asked about 'concerns', that is 'things we still have in mind to improve'. It might be noted here that this is a clear example of the 'mobilization of bias'; there is no mention of 'negative' outcomes or of criticisms. Among the points raised were the lack of involvement of youth and men; a fear of élitism or exclusivity; the need to involve those not yet involved; contradictory views of sharing and the need to clarify its meaning; 'keeping the doors open' and finding ways of inviting people; the fact that some have been 'put off' by RENEW; the need to involve more people in preparing the liturgy.

Participants next split into groups to discuss what had worked and what had not in Season 1 and to refine plans for Season 2. Evaluators from four parishes exchanged notes. In St Augustine's, the chief evaluator was abroad much of the time. His colleague wanted to know whether evaluation was an aid to encourage greater efforts or more ruthlessly evaluate shortcomings. The evaluator from St Catherine's distinguished two distinct geographical areas in his parish, 'one particularly hidebound'. This evaluator reported that he was under great pressure to produce a report which met the requirements of the core team that the evaluation should be favourable; he did not think they were allowed to be at all independent.

We also recorded a report from the evaluator in St Thomas's parish that the parish priest had prevented the use of our questionnaires after they had been reproduced by the evaluation team. The evaluator from St Cyril's parish complained repeatedly that there was no helpful feedback from the diocesan team in response to the parish evaluation returns. 'We were filling in details which suited their purposes but not ours.' In reality the diocesan team did not have the staff resources to do this and in any case, the shortness of the gaps between Seasons 1 and 2, and between 3 and 4 were such that plans were usually too far advanced to permit any significant changes from what was already in hand. As the same evaluator noted: 'the materials for the next season of RENEW were already printed, and nothing could be changed, so what was the point' other than the provision of a set of 'statistics for the "league tables" of parish activities' which 'place invidious pressure both on priest and lay people'.

Our ethnographic field notes from St Cyril's parish also recorded the various ways in which the relatively small number of activist laity 'took ownership' of the RENEW programme and attempted to implement it by adapting it to their own particular circumstances. Among the weaknesses noted after Season 1 were: the need to target youth whose participation was low; the small numbers of people involved in the various committees and the danger, therefore, of over-burdening the few; the shortage of small group leaders and the need for better training; and the difficulty of involving existing parish organizations. At the end of Season 2, further problems were identified including 'the need for material more acceptable to the wide intellectual capabilities of parishioners ... and for this to arrive *much* earlier to allow for realistic forward planning'. At the end of the following season fears were expressed that 'RENEW people' might become a status group 'above' other parishioners. But there was also evidence of innovation, for example when the Liturgy Group chose readings for the Sunday Mass which corresponded more closely to the RENEW theme. When the much-loved parish priest died in Season 4, the cadre of three or four lay activists ensured that the RENEW programme was 'kept on track'. Our informant attributed the 'empowerment' of this small group of activists in part to the former parish priest who had regarded them very much as collaborative ministers, but also to RENEW 'and the delegation of powers it involved'.

Interviews with participants in a number of parishes threw some light on the actual experiences of ordinary Catholics of the RENEW programme (or 'course' as one co-ordinator tellingly described it). The head of the Telephone Committee in one parish described how the parish priest used to enjoy hugely the references to his 'parish call girls'. The co-ordinator from St Joan's parish in Beachcliff, objected strongly to 'this feeling of competitiveness there always was' about the programme and how it was stoked up by frequent visits from Fr. Liam O'Brien, the Diocesan Director, who was always telling them about what other parishes were doing and what percentages were involved, for example in small groups. She told how her parish priest used to tell them:

'Well, you can get the numbers up' by what the target was. It was all very American, you had a target ... Milwaukee could do it, let's see if we can do it ... I wasn't really happy about this, didn't really take to this. It was like [selling] double glazing or something, all these unwanted calls. 'Have you ever thought of having a porch built? of joining a small group?'

The same co-ordinator continued with some frank admissions about the evaluation process.

I've a sinking feeling that we rather fiddled the numbers ... At the core meetings we all had to sit and give progress reports, so we were all quite good at making it sound good, really rather good, especially when Liam was there.

Later, talking generally about people's reactions to RENEW, she distinguished 'two levels of feedback':

There was what you heard in the local supermarket. 'Are you still going to your group?' 'Yes, well, you know, they're so nice.' And then there was 'Thank goodness it's nearly over', true of leaders too. 'Well, the evenings are going to be my own again.' Then [on the other hand] you got the pious hopes ... 'Oh yes, it was wonderful; yes, we really shared.' And really, people said what they thought people wanted to hear ... There is a tendency, when there is much time and energy invested in this, the temptation to say it fulfilled your expectations is enormous. That's a danger, winding everything up ... after all these sessions, after all this training, after all these committee meetings, who's going to say that what was really achieved was questionnable?

This informant also raised the matter of the expense of some aspects of the RENEW programme and the tacit assumption that many of these costs would be carried by individual committee members. Many people in the Diocese of Downlands are among the most affluent in the country but this is not necessarily true of individual Catholics. Our informant observed of the activities of the Telephone Committee in St Joan's:

We made all these calls, and the expense of it! ... I said: 'Look, it's OK in America where those local calls are free, but they are far from free here.' All sorts of ideas were suggested, like making calls from the presbytery, but the girls wanted to do it in their own time ... so in the event they, well a lot of them were very good and just quietly footed the bill themselves.

She proceeded to explain that she had insisted that this was wrong and would inhibit people volunteering for anything if they could not afford it. Finally, she was sceptical about the value of all the efforts:

There were positive things, like the girls and I enjoyed our little meets and got to know each other, but it bore relatively little in the way of real results, but it all sounds good.   (Interview, 16 Dec. 1992)

There are at least three very interesting admissions in these observations. Firstly, in spite of the sense of fun and the jokiness which was sometimes found, the competitive aspects of the comparative evaluations were often disliked. They were not infrequently attributed to American forms of high-pressure salesmanship which were regarded as distasteful and inappropriate in the context of a pastoral renewal programme. Secondly, there were strong pressures to present unduly favourable evaluations, not least in defence of one's own efforts, but also so as not to 'let the side down' or offend hardworking and dedicated people. But thirdly, in the private talk between friends and 'off the record', people often groaned about their regular RENEW commitments.

6.4 *Small Group Experiences*

We noted earlier that on the basis of the parish evaluations at the end of Season 1, it was estimated by the diocesan team that 12, 421 people had participated in small groups (*DT* Apr./May 1989). This represents about 28 per cent of adult Mass attenders or 10 per cent of the estimated adult Catholic population. The majority of those attending the small groups would have been doing so for the first time and would have had no previous experience of faith-sharing. The sheer numbers involved in these new experiences is impressive. We endeavoured to find out what group members thought of their experiences by surveying them at the end of each season. Responses to questions asked of small group participants after Season 1 in St Matthew's parish were included as alternative categories in the more structured questionnaires used after the remaining four seasons. A copy of the resulting small group members' questionnaire has been given in Appendix 3. Apart from the questionnaires completed by small group members, group leaders also completed a further questionnaire. This included an alternative source of information on average attendances as well as some additional information about the occupational backgrounds of their members. As in the case of the parishioners, we first report the results of our surveys in St Matthew's parish and then review some comparative data from a number of other parishes which used our instruments in some of the later seasons.

In St Matthew's parish, weekly attendance at the small group meetings peaked in Season 2 with just under one-half of adult Mass attenders going. In subsequent seasons there was a steady fall to just over two-fifths. Our research suggested that around 8–9 per cent of those who signed up before each season to attend a small group in fact failed to attend a single meeting. We have reported two measures of attendances at the six small group meetings each season. Questionnaire respondents consistently reported higher attendances than the group leaders but this may simply indicate that respondents were the most active members. Group leaders reported a steady decline of attendance rates across the five seasons. The results showed that even in this parish, which had had a long tradition of small groups for well over a decade, over two-fifths of those attending the small groups in Season 1 were doing so for the first time. In aggregate over the five seasons around 133 parishioners, or over one-third of the Mass attenders, were introduced to them. In this parish, in accordance with the RENEW emphasis on retaining the same group membership throughout the five seasons in order to develop

TABLE 6.5 *Small Group Participation by Season, St Matthew's Parish*

Small Group Participation	1		2		Season 3[3]		4		5	
	N	%	N	%	N	%	N	%	N	%
Estim. particip. (% AMA)[1]	173	45	190	49	158	41	149	39	157	41
Reported drop-outs (% sign-up)	18	13	17	13	n/a	n/a	17	n/a	6	n/a
Previous sg. exper. (% SGA)[2]:										
Belonged to gp. previously	82	57	133	78	106	91	122	90	109	90
New to small groups	62	43	35	21	10	9	14	10	12	10
Composition of sg.s (% SGA):										
All or some same	38	27	114	87	84	87	106	91	–	–
All new people	105	73	17	13	13	13	10	9	–	–
Programme followed (% Leaders):										
Yes	11	55	11	61	5	56	10	67	8	42
More or less	5	25	2	11	3	33	2	13	7	37
No	4	20	5	28	1	11	3	20	4	21
RENEW material (% SGA):										
Very good or good	73	53	66	39	53	46	–	–	–	–
Fairly good	57	40	85	50	54	47	–	–	–	–
Not very good	7	5	12	7	2	2	–	–	–	–
Mean attendance at meetings:										
Reported by sg. respondents	5.07		5.02		5.00		4.85		5.10	
Reported by sg. leaders	4.89		4.81		4.70		4.65		4.18	

[1] AMA = Adult Mass Attenders (estimated to be 384)
[2] SGA = Respondents to small group members' questionnaire
[3] In S3 some regular group members did not re-sign and there was no sign-up in Seasons 4 and 5. Problems with the distribution of small group members' questionnaires resulted in a lower response rate in S3.

trust through faith-sharing and then building on that and growing as a small faith-community, the large majority of groups retained a largely unchanged membership. Rather more than one-half of the small group leaders claimed to follow the RENEW programme exactly and a further one-quarter said they did so 'more or less'. However, as many as one leader in five admitted that s/he did *not* do so. Of thirty-two leaders from other parishes who told us about their approach, eighteen (56%) did not follow the programme at all. Most people thought the small group booklets were reasonably satisfactory though the strength of this view did vary; members were less satisfied with the Season 2 materials than with those in Seasons 1 and 3.

Small group members were asked which two of the offered categories 'were most important to you personally this Season?'. A mirror image of the same question invited them to indicate the two least important aspects of RENEW. They were also invited to indicate to which of seven alternative aspects they would like their group to pay more attention during the following season (or, after Season 5, if they joined a small group after RENEW); multiple responses were allowed to this question. The responses have been given in Table 6.6.

The results are of considerable interest and tell us a great deal about the cultural dimension of RENEW spirituality as it was interpreted by the small group members. In Seasons 2, 4, and 5, the most important aspect of RENEW was said to be the opportunities it provided for faith-sharing, though it is important to recognize that there were widely differing interpretations of what this meant in the small groups. Related aspects, such as making new friends and stimulated discussion were also strongly reflected in these seasons. The least important aspect of RENEW, given in response to the mirror-image question, was awareness of the worldwide community. Yet this aspect was the most strongly identified in Season 3 which aimed to raise awareness of justice issues. What is very noticeable, however, is that the consciousness of social concerns raised in Season 3 did not persist through to the later seasons once the special focus of 'empowerment by the Spirit' to act in the pursuit of social justice was removed. We shall discuss this further in the following chapter.

Given the intention of the proponents of RENEW to increase the level of scriptural awareness among Catholics, the relatively slight emphasis placed on this aspect by the small group members, declining steadily from Season 2 to Season 5, must have been disappointing. After Season 2 one-fifth of small group respondents considered

TABLE 6.6 Summary of Small Group Members' Responses after Five Seasons, St Matthew's Parish

Responses to RENEW	Season									
	1 144		2 170		3 116		4 138		5 121	
N = 100%	N	%	N	%	N	%	N	%	N	%
Most important aspects of RENEW:										
Prayed more or better	5	3	45	26	25	22	42	30	32	26
Personal development	11	8	28	16	15	13	29	21	24	20
Aware of worldwide community	–	–	9	5	41	35	12	9	16	13
Better communic. family/friends	–	–	16	9	14	12	15	11	8	7
Stimulated discussion	–	–	47	28	38	33	34	25	29	24
Made new friends	14	10	55	32	12	10	36	26	30	25
More interest in scripture	7	5	33	19	15	13	18	13	20	17
Take part in parish/local comm.	–	–	6	3	17	15	9	7	9	7
Open to faith-sharing	30	21	82	48	32	28	57	41	54	45
More attention required in next season:										
Prayer	–	–	45	26	23	20	34	25	38	31
Personal/group development	–	–	62	36	47	41	48	35	50	41
Scripture reading	–	–	24	14	21	18	27	20	40	33
Discussion	–	–	52	31	27	23	43	31	45	37
Action response—home	–	–	24	14	15	13	13	9	8	7
Action response—parish	–	–	25	15	21	18	28	20	23	19
Action response—wider comm.	–	–	28	16	29	25	30	22	27	22

it one of the two most important aspects of RENEW but this proportion had been halved by the end of the RENEW programme.
Another aim of RENEW was to increase participation in parish life
and to increase the number of leaders. Again the results are disappointing in that apart from the raising of such domestic concerns in
Season 3, this aspect was considered of least importance by respondents after Season 5.

The responses to the question asking group members to which
aspects of RENEW they wished a greater emphasis to be given in
the following season throw further light on the impact of RENEW.
A steady proportion of about one-fifth of group members appeared
to consider that there were deficiencies in the concern for action in
the wider community and a similar proportion also thought there
should be more attention paid to action in the parish and locality.
Action-responses in the home, however, which appeared to be the
easiest way of achieving a concrete outcome to the challenge of
RENEW, seemed to have been met to the extent that concern in this
area was seen as of declining significance over the course of RENEW.

What is particularly interesting is that in all four seasons for
which we have data, personal or group development was regarded
as the aspect to which group members wanted more attention to be
paid. This suggests that the low ranking of this item in the previous
question is to be interpreted as a judgement of the concrete experience of RENEW rather than as an unimportant aspect. In other
words, RENEW was seen as doing little for personal development
and it should give more attention to it. In the same way it could be
suggested that in spite of the intentions of the promoters of RE-
NEW, scripture was seen as having a relatively low and declining
emphasis in the programme. Conversely, members expressed the
view increasingly from one season to the next that more attention
should be paid to scripture reading.

We have a limited amount of comparative data from four other
parishes. After Season 3 we have some completed questionnaires
from St Cyril's small group members and after Season 4 from the
Sacred Heart parish. At the end of the fifth and final season we
obtained comparable data from three parishes. In order to report
these data we have aggregated the responses over all seasons. Three
distinct emphases may be discerned in the spirituality cultures:

(*a*) openness to faith-sharing, stimulated discussion, and made
new friends have been regarded as *communal* aspects of the spirituality of RENEW, at least to the extent that they involved some
specific interaction with others;

TABLE 6.7   *Spirituality Cultures: Most Important Aspects of RENEW (% Responses Small Group Members, Seasons 2 to 5)*

Aspects of Spirituality Culture	St Matthew's Parish	Other Parishes	All Parishes
COMMUNAL			
Faith-sharing	22	21	22
Stimulated discussion	15	16	15
Made new friends	13	11	13
All communal	50	48	50
INDIVIDUAL			
Personal development	10	7	9
Prayed more or better	14	14	14
Interest in scripture	9	12	9
All individual	32	33	33
ACTION-ORIENTED			
Family and friends	5	6	5
Parish community	4	8	5
World community	8	6	7
All action-oriented	17	20	18
N = 100%	1,004	391	1,395

(*b*) personal development, praying more or better, and more interest in scripture have been regarded as *individual* aspects of the spirituality of RENEW; and

(*c*) better communications with family and friends, taking part in the parish and local community, and awareness of the worldwide community have been regarded as *action-oriented* aspects of the RENEW spirituality.

The results from all available parishes have been classified in this way in Table 6.7. From these it can be seen that the results from the four other parishes are broadly similar to those for St Matthew's parish. These confirm our view that the results we have reported for St Matthew's parish are not unusual and are reflected in other parishes. There was also an enhanced action-orientation in St Cyril's parish in Season 3 as we had noted in St Matthew's parish and a regression to a lower concern in subsequent seasons was also reflected.

When all the 1395 responses over all seasons are aggregated, it seems that one-half of the responses reflect a 'communal' emphasis in the sense of stressing relationships and discussion with others.

We will develop further our analysis of the communal aspects of spirituality in the following chapter. There is also a strong emphasis, expressed in one-third of the responses, on personal piety, including private prayer and scripture reading. In general the evidence suggests that RENEW was interpreted by participants as encouraging a fairly traditional view of spirituality. There does not seem to have been much evidence of a shift to innovative forms of spirituality. In particular, it does not seem to have developed a strong action orientation. Even a very wide definition, which includes a concern to improve relationships in the domestic home and with friends and neighbours, was only mentioned in one-sixth of all responses. It seems clear that the interest expressed after Season 3 was short-lived and declined by one-half by the end of the RENEW programme. In terms of our typology of spiritualities, it seems that while RENEW promoted some aspects of a modern communal form of religious culture, strong traditional elements persisted. There was little evidence of the emergence of an action-oriented religious culture.

Finally, our data indicated that over the five RENEW seasons there was a general attrition of participation, a decline in the number of groups and mean attendance of regular members. Around one person in eight who had sampled a group earlier in the programme no longer belonged to a group in Season 5. We also noted an increase in the expression of negative responses, such as the proportion never reading the scripture booklet.

6.5 Small Group Ethnographies

In our field work we interviewed a number of people about their experiences as leaders or members of the RENEW small groups. These helped to put some flesh on the bones of the findings from the end-of-season questionnaire surveys. Six members of RENEW groups in St Matthew's parish were interviewed in September and October 1989, that is just before and during Season 3. The following themes were among those raised:

(1) People new to groups were at first apprehensive and felt incompetent and ill-equipped to discuss their faith, but they were reassured and grew in confidence to such an extent that they felt able, sometimes for the first time in their lives, to talk quite openly about religion to other people.

I think to start with I was terribly apprehensive about it: 'this isn't me; I shall dry up; I don't know what to say.' I didn't think I should be able to take part properly. Then when it actually started, obviously at the first meeting, just meeting the people, I felt so reassured. They were just the same as me; it was wonderful; it was great; and I was so enthusiastic. All the people I talked to, even with people who weren't in the Church, just friends, I was able to share it a bit because there was something that people were so positive about . . . I felt the Holy Spirit was there; we have something special. (Interview, 16 Oct. 1989)

(2) For some people RENEW provided a golden opportunity to get to know other parishioners. This was especially the case for converts or those whose spouses were not also Catholics. This sometimes meant a preference for changing groups between seasons though this clashed with the RENEW aim of developing faith-sharing communities.

I was new in the Catholic Church. During that time I haven't grown as a Catholic. I want to know and understand more . . . make it more relevant . . . I was most anxious to get to know as many people in the parish as possible. If I stayed in the same group I couldn't do that. I started in a house group; this changed to a RENEW group, so I wanted to move and change every season. But I've since realised that this is not practical. RENEW calls for a greater commitment and revealing oneself and [one's] inner feelings. So I am staying where I am. (Interview, 15 Sept. 1989)

Another convert in the same group acknowledged that she had not got the 'background knowledge that cradle Catholics have' and wished to 'learn more about basic Catholicism, meet people, and extend [her] knowledge of the parish'. Though she felt diffident about speaking freely in the group she found that she was now bringing religion out in conversation with friends. 'RENEW is great; it's wonderful.' (Interview, 14 Sept. 1989)

One man for whom RENEW was 'a welcome chore', observed of a woman in the parish, that although he had worked with her before over a period of thirty years, he 'only got to know her through being in the [RENEW] meetings with her . . . I knew her more in the two seasons we've been together . . . in the same group'. (Interview, 19 Sept. 1989)

(3) There were variations between groups as leaders tried, with varying degrees of success, to reconcile the often conflicting expectations of their members.

As I was going to lead a group I felt terribly responsible for the people who were going, that they should be relaxed and get something out of it. I was used to being in a small group . . . but I do know that for some it was their first experience, and to bring eight people together who knew each other only by sight . . . it's a difficult thing to do . . . It's up to the Lord to make it gel . . . I was quite upset when that young lady dropped out after the first time. I didn't think she'd given it a chance at all.   (Interview, 9 Sept. 1989)

Everybody is very understanding, charitable, and when people mention a problem they have, people might be too forgiving . . . makes us put the person at ease. Is that the right way to go about it? Are we just salving their conscience (rather than offering) a good and practical cure? . . . Sometimes we haven't covered things properly [and] have [just] prattled [on]. (Interview, 15 Sept. 1989)

The first group was a bit of a disaster because there were only five of us and most of them . . . were all my age group, and we knew each other too well. There was no interaction and I found it really hard work, nothing coming back . . . It fizzled out . . . In the second season . . . I joined Mary's group . . . Mary is one for silences. And I think silences are fine if people are gelled together and know what silences are about. But quite honestly, if you have silences in a group which had not gelled, then you are wasting your time . . . I didn't feel that it really worked. We weren't doing what we should have been doing . . . We could have gone into scripture reading a lot more.   (Interview, 19 Sept. 1989)

[My group in the second season] was more friendly; the first was rather more official, neat. This one was maybe not so deep in faith, but it was run on more human lines.   (Interview, 18 Sept. 1989)

(4) Some people were disappointed with the *content* of RENEW and wanted a stronger *teaching* element. Thus one convert felt she needed 'to go on a course' (Interview, 15 Sept. 1989). Another parishioner

felt I didn't get any more than I already had . . . I expect greater teaching . . . The parish is desperate for spiritual food, refreshment . . . We're missing the vital thing, stimulation for deepening spirituality.   (Interview, 19 Sept. 1989)

We also have useful data on the operation of small groups in other parishes. Thus one leader in the Sacred Heart parish who had had considerable experience of small groups, originally expressed her astonishment and dismay when the leader of her RENEW group announced: 'I'm the leader of the group and there are two things: (1) I'm not going to go by the book, and (2) I don't want any sharing.' She described in some detail how the chairman excluded some matters from open discussions and this led to some 'head-to-head confrontation'. In this first tentative experience of sharing some men were saying: 'I've got my family, my work; I go to Mass on Sunday [but] I've never seen a connecting thread like this before. Life [is] a series of compartments. Of course I'm a Catholic [but I] couldn't see it had anything to do with how I behave at work.' Our informant described in glowing terms the changes she observed over the six weeks of the RENEW season. In that time she saw 'the barriers coming down'. People who were originally silent could not stop talking, and people who six weeks previously were 'cold strangers and acquaintances' were showing 'love, friendship, and warmth'. The chairman who had originally said he would run the group his way was now saying 'I don't know what I'm going to do between seasons'. Things would 'never be quite the same again' (Interview, 9 Nov. 1988). Having said that, this chairman remained a very vocal critic throughout the whole RENEW programme.

There was evidence from other informants in the same parish that there was a deep rift between those who wished to pursue the RENEW aims of faith-sharing and those who 'will go along with it but have no intention of following the exact format laid down by RENEW in groups, evangelizing, or encouraging extempore prayer'. The leader of the small group committee in this parish reported that her group was 'resistant to action or public prayer . . . concentrating on reading scripture and discussing that'. She claimed that in response to questions on the matter they had received contradictory advice from Sister Josephine, a member of the Newark international team, who allowed that the small group booklet consisted of 'guidelines only', while Sister Mary Richards, from the diocesan RENEW team, had been emphatic that the book had to be followed closely (Conversation, 15 May 1989).

A small group leader from St Joan's parish gave a vivid portrait of her RENEW small group:

They were an interesting group . . . We had two very different sorts of couples . . . One couple was very traditional, one couple was very devout, very spiritual, but . . . much more tolerant. Then we had (a foreign) lady who sort of came and went; we had a very nice teacher . . . who . . . was very busy, didn't come regularly . . . a young man who also came periodically [and] a woman—very regular attender . . . We had a very old lady. I think she just liked coming out for a cup of tea! I don't know how successful our group was. To be honest, I think a lot of people came because they felt they should—and Catholics are very dutiful, aren't they? . . . What did I get out of it? . . . I remember as we went through the material, which was very patchy in terms of quality . . . I remember listening to the experiences, for instance, of the very devout couple, and I was very moved by them in the way that one is when one comes into contact with a very deep and genuine spirituality . . . They were very humble people . . . That was what I got out of RENEW, actually, just listening to them, . . . because this is how I renew my faith, by being with other people who are like that. Having said that, that's really it. There were some magic[al] moments . . . How [people] felt about it seems to range enormously according to who else was in the group at the time, who was group leader. Some people had to grit their teeth to get through . . . I had a friend who said: 'I sit round the table and sometimes I could absolutely scream at some of the things' . . . she . . . had a group leader who was conspicuously ignoring all the guidelines about how to lead a group . . . I met people in the street who said: 'Oh, my God', and I felt rather the same . . . My own feeling was it was hyped up . . . It was a huge sort of public relations exercise with teams and I just felt it was over the top . . . I'm not sure . . . that anyone changed at all, you know. My very traditional couple remained fixed in their views, about what religion is about: a vague set of rules, and if you do that, that's all right, and if you don't, look out for eternity! . . . My lovely, lovely couple would have been wonderful, like they were; it wasn't RENEW that made them like that. (Interview, 16 Dec. 1992)

Later in the interview she pointed out that in her parish not many groups stayed together throughout the five seasons, the exceptions being the 'lovely old ducks who like to meet each other, have a cup of tea and a bun'. While up to a point this was valuable, there was a danger that the Church 'can become a jolly, closed, smug club, where everything is fine for the members.' Lay empowerment, to 'strengthen people in their faith and then they go forth . . . honestly doesn't seem to happen . . . Rather than deepening spirituality . . . there is a danger that this kind of socializing can become exclusive and cosy and, in a sense, cushions people against the harsh realities . . . [in the world] around them.'

These various extracts from interviews with small group leaders have thrown up a number of themes which recurred in comments made by informants in several different parishes. First, group members were often very heterogeneous and this created problems of leadership for which the training was often inadequate. Secondly, people attended for a variety of reasons including the opportunity for lonely people to meet others. We have a great deal of data which suggests that the RENEW groups were very successful at introducing fellow parishioners to each other and providing social support. Thirdly, another prominent reason was the loyal and obedient response of many dutiful Catholics to the call to participate from their bishop; to some extent this might be seen as evidence of a continuing sense of belonging to a distinctive subculture. Fourthly, not infrequently some of the faith-sharing among small group members was deeply moving. There was evidence of a rich variety of lay spiritualities. Fifthly, on the other hand, it was not unusual for small groups to depart from the recommendations of the RENEW organizers. In particular, some, perhaps many, small groups were run as discussion groups and the sharing of faith-experiences was strongly discouraged by some authoritarian leaders who limited the scope of their groups. Groups often changed their membership and this limited the possibilities of their developing into small base communities. Sixthly, there were dangers that the success of the groups at the level of socializing might in fact divert members from wider concerns. Far from being 'empowered' to act purposively in the wider society, small groups might induce a cosy complacency and introspectiveness.

It seems that the younger parishioners were, perhaps surprisingly, less enthusiastic participants in the small groups and more likely to be relieved when RENEW ended. The elderly were slower to become participants but seem to have enjoyed groups, though it has to be said that, judging by comments made, some groups were very undemanding and provided light entertainment rather than group work. After five seasons and despite the stress on training, some leaders were still unable to control groups and some group interaction was reported to be 'more like a coffee morning', gossipy, and occasionally uncharitable. There was a shortage of leaders and the predicted increase in lay leadership did not seem to materialize. Responses to questions asking what sort of changes RENEW had effected were sometimes extraordinarily trivial. Inviting other Mass attenders to join their group in Season 5 was regarded as an acceptable form of evangelization.

6.6   Emergent Themes

In this chapter we have drawn on a wide range of data to convey something of the actual experience of RENEW in the parishes. Our survey data have enabled us to tap the experiences of a more representative cross-section of participants than was possible in the more subjective evaluations submitted by each parish at the end of each season to the diocesan team. We have drawn on a rich variety of data using several different research methods. We were also able to reflect some of the popular criticisms of RENEW which tended to be omitted from the official evaluations for reasons of loyalty to the bishop, or the parish priest, or the parish activists who had worked so hard to make the programme a success. In sum, our data are both more representative and more comprehensive than those previously reported and they allow us to convey more of the rich variety of experiences of RENEW.

Our parish surveys confirm the expected under-representation of men and young adults at Mass and indicate that this was even more pronounced in the membership of the RENEW small groups. There also tended to be a significant under-representation in these groups of those with pre-school children. By using the same research instrument over several seasons it was possible to detect a steady decline in participation beyond Season 2.

An analysis of the type of spiritual culture favoured by RENEW, as judged from the responses of small group members, suggested that while there was a dominant emphasis on communal aspects of spirituality, traditional personal piety was also very prominent, and an emphasis on an action-response, even when using a very broad definition, was very much a minority concern. Our survey data show a significant rise in interest in the 'worldwide community' in Season 3 but this was not retained after the remaining two seasons. We wish to elaborate on this interpretation in the following chapter. For present purposes, we will simply note that it is necessary to distinguish between the communal forms of encouragement given to the development of individual sanctity, on the one hand, and the communal promotion of a 'social project', such as a just society, on the other. The data we have reported provide evidence of the former but very little of the latter.

While our survey findings are valuable in tracing the broad pattern of changes during the course of the RENEW programme, a greater sense of what RENEW meant for the participants was derived from our interview material and our field work notes of informal conversations and overheard remarks made between friends. These indicated a subterranean antagonism towards, and sometimes latent resistance to, what were widely perceived as alien 'American' characteristics and styles of promotion, such as the use made of comparative rates of small group involvement and the sale of T-shirts. On the other hand, it was obvious that a great deal of participation reflected a sense of duty and an obligation to support the bishop (or parish priest) once the programme was inevitable. Similarly, formal evaluations were regarded as an aspect of public relations and there was a desire not to offend those who had worked hard to make RENEW a success. Thus it was clear that not all the forms of spirituality and activity reported in the diocesan evaluations were directly attributed to RENEW. Regular prayer and some scripture reading had been features of the everyday lives of many Catholics. Several parishes had had small groups and Liturgy Committees long before RENEW and some large group events would have taken place in any case under some other name. We suggest that for reasons such as these, the formal diocesan evaluation procedures tended to be unduly positive. In reality there was a considerable amount of grumbling and private jokiness about how awful and time-consuming RENEW was.

Finally, we have reported some evidence of the actual workings of the RENEW small groups. There is no doubt that for many these provided a welcome opportunity to meet and befriend other parishioners previously known only by sight. This seemed to be particularly important to some converts and people in religiously 'mixed' marriages, but also to traditional Catholics for whom religion was a differentiated element in their highly segmented lives. On occasion there was also evidence of rich faith-sharing experiences. But there was also evidence that the small group experiences were very uneven. Some leaders were authoritarian; some refused to follow the official instructions and created their own agenda which often attenuated the aims of faith-sharing. There was evidence that not everyone appreciated the aims of remaining in the same groups in order to build on the trust and rapport developed in the early seasons. Groups varied in the degree to which they shared a common spirituality, and leaders, often with limited training, varied in their skills at reconciling conflicting purposes. Some were little more than discussion groups.

In this chapter and the previous one we have endeavoured to convey something of the experience of RENEW both in the diocese and in the parishes and small groups. We have noted that an action-oriented spirituality briefly emerged during Season 3 but did not appear to persist. In the following chapter we will explore the struggles in the diocese to promote a more socially concerned form of Catholicism.

7

The Politics of Social Concern

7.1 A Justice Spirituality

We have suggested (Figure 5.1) that the analysis of types of spirituality needs to take into account two separate dimensions: (a) the organizational matter of who it is who controls the spirituality, and (b) the cultural dimension concerned with its content. In our case study of both the introduction of RENEW (Chapters 3 and 4) and its implementation in the diocese (Chapter 5) and the parishes (Chapter 6), we have sought to demonstrate that in spite of some rhetoric about lay participation and empowerment, there is little doubt that the decision to follow the RENEW programme in the Diocese of Downlands was originally taken by the bishop and his closest advisers who then proceeded systematically to co-opt the priests, lay leaders, and parish activists. Although each of these groups originally had some reservations about the programme, all were successfully co-opted into the parish planning and execution of the five RENEW seasons and, on the whole, all participated loyally and conscientiously. While we found some evidence that ordinary Catholics deviated from the prescribed routines and constructed their own meanings and imposed their own purposes in the small groups and other parish activities, in general there is no doubt that the control of the RENEW programme was top down. One looked in vain for signs of an innovative, grass-roots, 'bottom-up' spirituality encouraged by an organic, empowerment model of the local Church.

As far as the second dimension of spirituality was concerned, the situation was more complex and required further investigation and elaboration. Our soft data analyses and our survey data from small group participants have shown that while a communal form of spirituality was promoted, so also were traditional forms of personal piety while there was very little stress on an action-oriented spirituality (Table 6.7). We suggest that it is necessary to distinguish between those forms of spirituality which promote a 'social project' (such as the achievement of a just society by political means), and those which do not. Thus it is possible for some communal forms

Spirituality Culture	Promotion of Social Project	
	No	Yes
Communal	(Type 1) e.g. Post-Vatican Piety	(Type 2) Social Catholicism
Privatized	(Type 3) e.g. Tridentine Piety	(Type 4) e.g. Catholic Action

FIG. 7.1   A Typology of Social Projects and Spirituality Cultures

of spirituality, such as post-Vatican, participative liturgies or charismatic prayer groups, to have no concern for a social project but to have as their aim the development of the personal sanctity of their members. This would be a weak form of communal spirituality concerned to promote individual salvation and piety. A strong version would correspond to notions of community development and the active promotion of a social project. The possibilities have been summarized in Figure 7.1.

What we have taken into account here is the evidence that in the modern world, it is possible to promote a communal form of spirituality which nevertheless remains relatively cut off from the wider world and its problems. Most mainstream religion in Britain today is of this type and has no significant engagement with the world. If we refer back to our main classification of spiritualities in Figure 5.1, communal forms of religion can be found in all four cells. However, the dominant form in the Roman Catholic Church since the Middle Ages has been the privatized and non-communal version which was reinforced by the Tridentine Mass and associated reforms and by the devotional renewal of the nineteenth century. This did not prevent communal groups, such as sodalities, developing which combined a concern to restore the medieval Catholic world (type 4) with the promotion of individual sanctity (type 3). In other words, the communal lay associations of the Tridentine reforms privatized spirituality while at the same time they pursued a political religion to guarantee Catholic order in society. This was a premodern or traditional project. The RENEW small groups, on the other hand, might be said to have encouraged social interaction and mutual help in the development of a spirituality which was more shared, partly influenced by the charismatic movement and relatively free from clerical control, but without a manifest social project. In terms of our typology they were more likely to be located in Cell 1 than Cell 2.

In this chapter we wish to consider further the treatment of matters of social justice by RENEW and the extent to which it promoted a communal spiritual culture and set out to engage with the modern world by means of an appropriate social project. Such a social project would be likely to be political as it sought to develop a spirituality and morality appropriate to modern needs of democracy, justice, and peace. It would be communal because it expects to achieve its goals only in collaboration with others. It would be unlikely for a privatized religion to deal with modernity itself, since it would only be interested in creating religious groups and spiritualities which survive in the modern world but without making a difference to it. Social Catholicism (type 2) would endeavour to translate the message of love and justice at the centre of the Gospel message into actions appropriate to that message.

In the Church generally, there is much rhetoric that matters of justice are at the heart of the Gospel message. Thus, the third basic theme of the RENEW programme was 'establishing justice formation and action' (Martin, 1982: iv). In a short leaflet *A Way to Revitalise the Spiritual Life of Your Parish* published by the diocesan team in the Diocese of Downlands at the beginning of the RENEW programme, the third of four objectives of RENEW claimed that 'RENEW helps people connect their faith to concern for social justice'. The third season on the theme 'Empowerment by the Spirit' was largely devoted to the consideration of justice concerns and appropriate responses to them. In this chapter, therefore, we will offer an analysis of the treatment of issues of social justice during and after the RENEW programme in an endeavour to elaborate on the analysis of the dimensions of spirituality which we have so far developed.

In effect this chapter constitutes a case study of the treatment by the RENEW programme of the challenges which issues of social justice present to Christians. Such matters are extremely controversial within the Christian community. They are inevitably political in that they involve decisions about proper relationships between those who differ in terms of power or resources in the light of a set of values which purport to inform those decisions. But Christians are also deeply divided between those who believe that religion and politics should be clearly differentiated, on the one hand, and those who reject such a separation, on the other. We wished, therefore, to investigate the way in which the RENEW programme tackled this matter and observe how Catholics in the diocese interpreted the programme and responded to it. We aimed to explore further the nature of control employed in the diocese and the extent to which it was prepared to encourage a social-action orientation. We also wished to assess the extent to which any impact of RENEW in this area might be temporary or more permanent.

Our analysis will focus on four matters in particular. First, within the existing justice and peace movement in the diocese there was initially a great deal of resistance to what was perceived as the imposition of RENEW and the priority it claimed over diocesan activities, resources, and energies during the course of the programme. This focused on the promotion by the diocesan team of the concept of 'social concern' rather than 'social justice'. Activists generally felt that the stress on the former term was a device for domesticating more prophetic challenges in terms of justice. Secondly, in the light of such suspicion, there was a serious consideration of whether or not to participate in RENEW or rather to continue with existing activities independently. Thirdly, we will return to the impact of Season 3 in the parishes to which we drew attention in the previous chapter. We have shown that the initial impact of efforts made during Season 3 largely dissolved away in subsequent seasons though a number of social action initiatives in the area of homelessness did emerge in the parishes around this time. Fourthly, we will consider the struggle over the allocation of resources to the justice and peace movement in the diocese, particularly after the end of the RENEW programme.

7.2 *Justice or Concern?*

It was well known, as a result of experiences in the United States and elsewhere, that Season 3 would give rise to some tensions because of its treatment of the relationship between religious beliefs and social justice commitments. Perhaps in consequence, a greater amount of effort went into the preparation of this season than any other. The diocesan director observed that some people had wanted the justice emphasis to be dropped: 'They thought there should be something more charismatic ... without seeing that what the Holy Spirit does is to give us the courage ... the empowerment we're talking about' (Interview, 17 Nov. 1992). Encouragement for justice concerns were reported in various issues of *Downlands Times* before and during Season 3. In the summer of 1989 the Director of RENEW in a Scottish diocese wrote in the diocesan newspaper:

Justice ... is the concern which obsesses God. It is about His unswerving fidelity to the world He has made. The justice story begins with God hearing the groans of His people ... The prophets constantly complain about the lack of justice. There are two reasons for lack of justice: a pre-occupation with false gods and a dependence on ritual observance . . . During Season Three we focus on the Holy Spirit for the Spirit of God is the spirit of Justice, restoring and renewing relationships, establishing right relationships. This is the heart of renewal and therefore the core of RENEW. (*DT* June/July 1989)

These themes were developed by Mgr. John Carroll, the originator of RENEW in Newark, in the next issue of the diocesan newspaper. He noted the growing appreciation of the Holy Spirit in the lives of Catholics since the Second Vatican Council and commented:

Two areas that often seem to arise as weaknesses are our relationship with the Holy Spirit and our ability to make activity for justice an essential part of our spirituality . . . In very concrete ways the Holy Spirit helps us to be more loving and to relate well to others. This ability to relate extends from our most personal relationships, to neighbour and people we work with, to the poor and needy who may be quite removed from us and to the very creation of better relationships in the world order of our human family. (*DT* Aug./Sept. 1989)

A similar position was taken by a Scottish bishop writing in the same issue and referring to Matt. 25 : 40.

In his pastoral message for Sign-Up Sunday for Season 3 Bishop Patrick quoted the well-known passage from the prophet Micah (6 : 8) which he felt 'expresses so well the theme of the third Season of RENEW'. He continued:

As Christians, called to follow Jesus, we have choices to make that affect our way of living. Are we willing to follow Jesus on His way, enabling us to live justly so as to build a better world? . . . What practical steps can we take to bring about a more just society and how do we balance our own legitimate interests with serving the needs of others? (*DT* Oct./Nov. 1989)

The same issue of the diocesan paper quoted the radical statement from the 1971 World Synod of Bishops in Rome that

Action on behalf of justice and participation in the transformation of the world fully appear to us as a constitutive dimension of the preaching of the Gospel, or, in other words, of the Church's mission for the redemption of the human race and its liberation from every oppressive situation.

It also reproduced 'The Two Feet of Christian Service', the first labelled 'direct service', helping people survive their present crisis (e.g. by soup kitchens, visiting, and voluntary care) but which must lead to the second foot labelled 'social change', removing the causes of those problems (e.g. by political action and educating the public conscience).

While few Catholics would deny the validity of the first step (the 'corporal acts of mercy'), many, probably most, would reject the second step if it involved political action. It was considerations such as these which has led to a 'softly-softly' approach to these issues by RENEW. Thus Mgr. Carroll noted that on many social issues there was no official Catholic position. This often led to argumentation but this only 'clouds issues, impedes growth and confirms people in defensive positions. Such lack of harmony immediately foils the work of the Spirit' (*DT* Aug./Sept. 1989). This denial of the creative value of conflict permeates the perspective on justice issues taken by RENEW and was the focal point of much debate within the diocesan justice and peace movement. A former member of the diocesan Justice and Peace Commission expressed the prophetic view forcibly:

For us all this 'spiritual renewal bit' is, as Bishop Lebayen said 'icing sugar on top of a mouldy cake.' ... Fussing about the liturgy, about getting people to Mass, about training Readers and encouraging more ministries within the Church whilst disregarding the misery on our doorsteps and remaining silent in the face of every kind of manifest injustice seems to me to have the cart entirely before the horse. And the idea that somehow out of more purely religious activity the rest will follow is nothing more than the 'trickle down' theory in economics applied to our Faith.   (Letter, 11 May 1989)

As one justice and peace activist observed, 'prophetic witness is bound to ruffle feathers' (Letter, 26 Jan. 1992).

One of the most outspoken comments urging the more prophetic stance was made by a priest who felt that not enough was being done to address current injustices and social needs in the diocese. He had been 'disgusted' by the decision to follow the RENEW programme which he regarded as 'insufficiently radical and innocuous', 'introspective and cosy'. In his view the Church in Downlands should 'go out and get hurt ... take risks ... It was time to act ... RENEW was like giving a starving man a spoon of semolina!' At the time he was angry in particular at the lack of support which he felt the diocese and his fellow priests gave for projects for homeless and hungry people though he admitted subsequently that the situation might have changed a little (Conversations, 4 Sept. 1989 and 25 Jan. 1994). Views such as these seemed clearly to be located in Cell 2 (Social Catholicism).

The alternative view was given on 12 April 1989 by Sr. Josephine and Mgr. John Carroll from the International RENEW Office in Newark. They were speaking at a 'day of listening and planning' with the bishop which was attended by around forty priests and sixty laity. Sr. Josephine gently encouraged a softly-softly approach to social concerns. The term 'justice' was seen as a red flag to many people. RENEW was a conversion process which was trying to change hearts and call upon the power of the Holy Spirit to send us out to our families, our parish, into our work, and into the world. It was important to take a gentle approach because we did not wish to alienate anyone. Nor did we wish to use the Bible 'as a weapon'. Fr. Liam O'Brien stressed that it was not a question of watering down the Gospel message so much as developing 'ways of talking' which prevented people from switching off from the message. Sr. Josephine urged that RENEW invited people not into a surface involvement but into a deep spiritual growth process centred in small faith-sharing groups. At the end of Season 3 there would be opportunities for people to sign up for a Social Concerns Committee which would 'do the things which needed to be done'. To the criticism expressed by one activist that 'charity was being substituted for justice', Sr. Josephine replied that this would still be a major development for many people who would participate for the first time. Fr. Liam suggested that there would always be a need for the good Samaritan with concern for the needy. 'Of course we must change structures, but this doesn't mean leaving the ill' (Field Notes, 15 Apr. 1989).

The diocesan director wrote to parish co-ordinators in August 1989 recommending that 'prior to Season III a *contact* person for *social concern* (or whatever other name suits locally) be identified in each parish who would be prepared to channel any interest expressed by parishioners into effective outlets post Season'. The letter had previously noted that

a considerable number of our parishes, of course, have [had] for years groups expressing this social concern in many different ways: S.V.P. (St Vincent de Paul Society), CAFOD (Catholic Fund for Overseas Development), Co-workers of Mother Teresa, Justice and Peace, to mention but a few. RENEW hopes to create a climate in which even more commit themselves to personal service.

It was developments such as these which justice and peace activists found threatening to their on-going activities and regarded as a sophisticated process of domesticating the prophetic call to witness to justice. They seemed to be located in Cell 1 rather than Cell 2.

Mgr. Bob Reilly, the senior priest in the diocese who admitted a late conversion to the RENEW programme, interviewed some time after the end of the programme, claimed that RENEW had significantly promoted justice concerns in the diocese and raised the controversial question of the most appropriate method of doing so. He observed:

J & P [Justice and Peace] has been on the road a long time in this diocese and nothing much has happened, frankly. And this is one of the beauties of RENEW, that it did raise the whole question of justice in the consciousness of 11,000 or 12,000 people. I've been watching J & P in operation in this diocese for the best part of twenty years. And somehow or other, whether it was because it became single-issue orientated, or because of the personalities involved, . . . it never took off, I think because it didn't focus . . . on a teaching role. Because that is what people needed, to find out what is the mind of the Church, what is the teaching of the Church. (Interview, 21 July 1992)

Later in the same interview he elaborated on these remarks and suggested that ever since the Second Vatican Council, and not just in the diocese, J & P 'has had a difficult run'. In spite of the commitment of 'splendid people' in the parishes, and both his and their 'best endeavours', it had never managed to 'take off'. He continued:

I think first of all, that part of the problem was . . . the atmosphere in which they were working. I don't think your average parish community, your average Catholic, is open to justice and peace issues. We don't want to be disturbed, most certainly not in [the Diocese of Downlands] . . . The atmosphere was hostile to justice and peace. I think the second point I would say is that in a number of instances they became single-issue . . . dominated, whether it was nuclear disarmament or whatever . . . Now I don't think that is the right starting point. . . . I think that . . . the challenge facing the teaching Church in [Downlands] is to get the message across, that justice is . . . a constitutive part of preaching the Gospel . . . we've never got that point across through J & P. (Interview, 21 July 1992)

Thus some people who opposed the nuclear deterrence strategy had taken 'direct action', daubing paint on the Ministry of Defence, and so on. Mgr. Reilly argued that that kind of approach

alienates a large segment of people before you've got them on board at all with regard to, that justice is a constitutive part of preaching the Gospel . . . If you start breaking the law of the land before you've got them on board . . . it causes difficulties . . . the whole justice and peace issue had had an image, if you like, which was switching people off. . . . I think . . . RENEW brought that message [of Paul VI that there can be 'no peace without justice'] to 12,000 people. And we've been a long time around this diocese trying to accomplish anything like that. (Interview, 21 July 1992)

There are several revealing assumptions in these remarks, not least the claim that all those who attended the small groups had successfully had their consciousness raised about justice. The evidence we have previously reported shows how little support there is for this claim. There is also a strong expectation of a top-down form of teaching *about* justice issues rather than an expectation of learning inductively *from* the experiences of the oppressed.

A similar defence of the gentle RENEW approach to the issues of justice and peace was given by the initiator of RENEW, Mgr. John Carroll, interviewed in Newark. It was put to him that many in the J & P movement in the diocese felt that the stress on social concerns was actually a dilution of the concept of justice and that basically Jesus did not 'beat about the bush'. He responded that it was great that there was such a debate:

We may just be walking on the other side of the street . . . because I think there's room for both approaches . . . Many . . . justice and peace [groups] . . . are very strong on issues. Oh, it does them a lot of good to get it out and say it as it is . . . And it's beautiful . . . But, I'm not sure it's the only way. . . . What we do is try to get a union of the people who are very strong on the issues . . . with what they might see as this kind of 'milk toast' approach which is much slower, much more gentle, but by heaven, they can be very, very effective.   (Interview, 21 Sept. 1992)

He reminisced about very strong civil rights sermons in the 1960s which resulted in a few people congratulating the priest while many others walked by.

I don't think it changed a person. . . . But I noticed that in the small groups that took the longer time, people would give in and they would turn around, they would change . . . I want to say that I respect the approach of issues . . . but I think there should be respect for the dynamic that allows people to come at their own pace, where you can take bigots into a group and see them turn around. Where we don't just say: 'who's with us and who isn't?' But we let people grow and change and develop, and take on the Gospel and all its implications, and do something about it, not just issue statements. But commit in their daily lives, in the field of politics, in the field of their work world . . . It's a different approach. I think they're complementary. And I think all RENEW wants to do is to bring together all the folks . . . who really care about justice, and to work in unison, but to respect this gentle approach also.   (Interview, 21 Sept. 1992)

In sum, it was claimed that the more aggressive, assertive, and prophetic approaches of justice and peace activists had simply not worked in the past. They had failed to raise the awareness of the bulk of Catholics to the centrality of justice concerns in the way they lived their lives, or to mobilize them in significant numbers either to the first step of social concern and certainly not to the second and more controversial step of political action to eradicate the causes of injustice. Such pragmatic considerations that prophetic witness in fact alienated Catholics and prevented communication were viewed with much suspicion by many activists, and 'there was concern about the proposed formation of social concerns committees after Season Three and their relationship to existing Justice and Peace groups and the commission' (Minutes of Extraordinary Meeting of the Justice and Peace Commission, 11 Dec. 1988).

7.3   Participate or Not?

It will be recalled that the decision to offer RENEW to the diocese was taken in Lourdes in July 1986 and that Mgr. Carroll, from the International RENEW Office in Newark, had faced a rather hostile audience of clergy as late as November 1986, though the laity at the DPC meeting on the following day were more responsive. In the light of this, it is surprising to note that as early as 20 December 1986, the chairman of the diocesan Justice and Peace Commission wrote in his Annual Report that 'we look forward to making positive contributions to the RENEW programme'. Documentary evidence relating to this period before RENEW is limited but there does seem to have been some discussion within the Commission as to whether and to what extent to let RENEW dictate the agenda for J & P groups during the 2½-year span of the programme. The decision to co-operate fully was only taken after some debate and in the light of a pragmatic judgement that the concerns of Justice and Peace activists, such as raising awareness of the centrality of justice to the mission of the Church, might be well served by RENEW. Furthermore, given the emphasis on social concerns in Season 3, RENEW might well be exploited and provide opportunities of reaching a much wider audience, and with much greater diocesan legitimation, resources, and support than would otherwise be the case.

Bishop Patrick attended a meeting of the Justice and Peace Commission in his residence on 7 March 1987 and 'described the importance and significance of RENEW' (Minutes of 32nd meeting). The minutes of the 33rd meeting of the Commission (16 May 1987) report that it was agreed that 'Commission members should involve themselves with RENEW, to give a J & P dimension'. At this time the Commission was mainly concerned with preparing a two-page statement 'The Prospect of a General Election' which was to be held on 11 June 1987. The statement outlined a number of areas of concern about which parliamentary candidates might be questioned, but some people in the diocese angrily protested to the bishop at what they saw as 'blatant left-wing propaganda' (Letter, 1 June 1987).

It was not until his newsletter to Justice and Peace contacts of 20 October 1987 that Fr. Tim Langley, the diocesan J & P co-ordinator, focused attention on the forthcoming RENEW programme. With some exaggeration he wrote that 'the Justice and Peace Commission shares Bishop Patrick's enthusiasm for this programme of spiritual renewal in our Diocese, and it undoubtedly offers many opportunities for creating a more socially aware Christian consciousness among our people'. Two weekend training sessions at a retreat centre in the diocese had been booked for October 1988 and September 1989 and contacts were urged 'meanwhile do please support preparations for RENEW in your parish'.

At the meeting of the Commission on 10 October 1987 Fr. Langley reported on a training course on RENEW which he had attended in his capacity as J & P co-ordinator. He had volunteered that 'the J & P contribution could be important in keeping RENEW on the right lines of lived-out, practical religion'. The minutes of this meeting note that 'an animated discussion followed' with two other members contributing their experiences of various briefings. Some members suspected that RENEW might be a diversion from the hard work of raising awareness of justice issues or might result in its domestication and a dilution of its prophetic challenge. The outcome was that 'a number of reservations were expressed about both the style and content of the programme, but on the whole the Commission felt that RENEW, with its declared aim of increasing the number of committed Christians in each parish, held out some hopes of concomitantly increasing awareness of J & P issues' (Minutes of 35th meeting). It was agreed to ask the diocesan RENEW team how best to help, particularly with the preparations for Season 3 materials, and to use the two planned training weekends to 'brief J & P people on the possibilities open to them in RENEW leadership, and to "beef up" the J & P content' of Season 3.

In spite of such good intentions, the Commission was acutely aware of its lack of resources and the absence of any full-time or part-time staff to service its activities. Accordingly, the chairman wrote at length to the bishop on 22 December 1987 pleading for the appointment of a full-time worker in the diocese since 'we see it as most important that the Commission should have the resources to support the RENEW programme effectively, and also to be able to carry out the tasks you have given it properly', not only during the course of RENEW 'but also in the time of development which it is hoped will follow that programme'. In his end of year report (31 Dec. 1987), the chairman also noted that it was 'hoped to arrange a celebration with the Bishop' at the end of Season 3.

At the next meeting of the Commission, again at the bishop's residence, Fr. Langley reported on his meeting with the diocesan RENEW team who had requested the Commission 'to change its name', presumably to 'Social Concerns' (Minutes of 36th meeting, 30 Jan. 1988). This seemed to confirm the suspicions of the sceptics and at the next meeting of the Commission the minutes were amended to state that 'the Commission members firmly rejected the suggestion that its name be changed' (Minutes of 37th meeting, 23 Apr. 1988). Interestingly, at the January meeting, eight months before the start of RENEW, 'Bishop Patrick expressed a desire to develop a Diocesan Plan which would create an aim and a challenge to Roman Catholics in the country today'. This notion was developed in the post-RENEW period, as we shall see in the next chapter.

At Easter 1988, six months before the start of Season 1 of RE-NEW, Fr. Langley informed justice and peace activists or contacts in the diocese of an 'annual day of contact' with the Commission in July to 'consider how we can best use the opportunities offered by RENEW for ourselves and for others' (Newsletter, 4 Apr. 1988). This day was run by the secretary of the National Liaison Committee of Diocesan Justice and Peace Groups (NLC) and by the fieldworker from an adjacent diocese. Commenting afterwards, the new chairman of the Commission wrote that 'we have something special to offer in ensuring the success of RENEW'. The co-optation of the Justice and Peace Commission, and subsequently the parish groups, followed a similar pattern to that of the parishes generally. But it differed in being far more calculative, the assumption being that activists could *use* RENEW to further the salience of justice concerns in the lives of Christians. Thus Fr. Langley wrote in his Newsletter of 20 September 1988: 'May I remind you that one of the three main objectives of RENEW is to "help people connect their faith to concern for social justice". So there is *something to be gained on the J & P front* in every season of RENEW' (emphasis added).

Before the start of RENEW in October 1988 the chairman had discussed the Commission's contribution with Fr. Liam O'Brien, the diocesan Director of RENEW. As a result the Commission set up two working parties, one to produce a *Justice Resource Book* and another to plan a series of workshops to follow up Season 3 in the autumn of 1989. The *Justice Resource Book* was structured round the questions asked of the King at the Last Judgement (Matthew 25: 31–46):

- When did we see you hungry? When did we see you thirsty? A brief commentary and selections of quotations from scripture and significant writers was followed by listings of both national and local organizations providing food/water for the hungry/ thirsty.
- When did we see you a stranger? Here organizations assisting immigrants, refugees, and ethnic minorities were listed.
- When did we see you naked? A similar framework was followed which listed organizations helping the homeless.
- When did we see you sick? Organizations involved in caring for the sick or handicapped were listed.
- When did we see you in prison? Organizations helping prisoners at home and abroad or seeking penal reform were listed here.

Finally, the names and addresses of organizations helping family life and with general welfare and human rights concerns, and those involved in peace-making and protecting the environment were indicated. The booklet closed with a brief bibliography of readily available books dealing with Christian responses to injustices. The booklet was produced by the RENEW office and distributed to justice and peace activists who attended the annual meeting at a retreat centre in September 1989, and widely throughout the diocese immediately before the start of Season 3 of RENEW.

Some time after the end of Season 2 Bishop Patrick invited a few members of the Justice and Peace Commission to discuss the future of the Commission after RENEW. It seems that he was seeking the best way to co-ordinate the hoped-for 'community of small communities' of social concerns groups which embraced both the existing justice and peace groups and those involved in various forms of care, such as St Vincent de Paul groups. While several members of the Commission feared that 'social concern will colonize J & P after RENEW', as a priest member put it, the bishop indicated that he favoured a smaller executive (and implicitly, more effective) commission with good links with existing groups but charged with investigating 'how J & P concerns could be slotted into parish structures post-RENEW'. The bishop concluded the meeting by joking that 'the aim is vaguely clear!' (Field Notes, 2 May 1989).

Three months later Fr. Langley informed contacts in the justice and peace network of the outcome of the self-examination which the Justice and Peace Commission had been undergoing over the previous year. 'Under Bishop Patrick's guidance we have come to feel that a smaller Commission supported by wide-ranging working-parties, and the whole net-work of parish and deanery J & P contacts might work more efficiently' (J & P Newsletter, 31 July 1989). The implied consensus among members of the Commission was almost certainly exaggerated and some members felt the change was indicative of attempts to constrain and control the work of the Commission which at this stage still had no full-time or part-time secretarial or other support.

The preparations for Season 3 of RENEW commenced nearly a year in advance. Members of the diocesan Justice and Peace Commission were given a preliminary briefing on 25 November 1988, shortly after the end of Season 1. This meeting was organized by the diocesan Director of RENEW and was attended also by members of the RENEW teams from three Scottish dioceses and by Sister Josephine from the International RENEW office. It was observed at the time that 'there seems little doubt that the [Newark] package has to be accepted lock, stock, and barrel. At the end [the Commission members] were still not entirely sure what [they] were being required to prepare' (Field Notes).

In February 1989 a joint letter from the chairman of the J & P Commission and the diocesan Director of RENEW invited parish contacts to an afternoon's briefing from Sr. Josephine on 15 April 1989. Asked in an interview before this meeting about the relationship between responding to problems (e.g. soup kitchens for the hungry) and the search for the underlying causes of those problems, she observed that the Newark experience had indicated that this happened 'very quickly . . . [and] in the third season of RENEW for many, many people' (Interview, 15 Apr. 1989). Later in the meeting with J & P representatives she argued that 'some aren't ready for the Gospel; the soil is not fertile until the appropriate time'. For many people 'justice is a red flag!' Hence the recommendation that a 'gentle approach' be used because 'we don't want to alienate anyone' and the 'Bible mustn't be used as a weapon'.

The argument was repeatedly challenged in the subsequent discussion. When the diocesan Director of RENEW, Fr. Liam O'Brien, argued that 'the slow approach of RENEW "works"' and that '150 dioceses [throughout the world] cannot be wrong', a woman in the audience observed that the 'softly-softly approach didn't work in Germany'. Fr. Liam replied 'never water down the Gospel, but when communicating the Gospel [what is] important is what is heard, not what is said. There are ways of talking which prevent "switching off" from the message'. In other words it was 'a matter of style; not this is the answer . . . [but] starting from the reality of where people are'. This drew forth the response from one man that 'Jesus did harangue!' Finally, Sr. Josephine informed the representatives that at the final meeting of the small groups in Season 3 there would be an opportunity for people to sign up for a Social Concerns Committee 'who do the things which need to be done' because 'J & P didn't say enough!' This led one man to explode: 'Charity is being substituted for justice', in other words there was a 'sidetracking of J & P'. Sr. Josephine suggested that 'this was a major thing these people were doing for the first time' and Fr. Liam added that it was necessary to have 'both first aid and to change society' (Field Notes, 15 Apr. 1989).

These field notes taken from our participant observation indicate clearly that many activists in the justice and peace movement in the diocese were deeply suspicious of the likely impact of RENEW and its softly-softly approach. Nevertheless, they were co-opted into the RENEW process, formally agreed to participate as best they could, given their limited resources, at least partly on the calculative grounds that RENEW offered opportunities and resources to communicate, with diocesan legitimation, with a much wider group of Catholics than would otherwise have been the case.

This process of co-optation was given its final push at a preparatory weekend for justice and peace activists shortly before the start of Season 3. One Commission member observed darkly that 'nobody has been jailed because of RENEW' and suggested that this would be the appropriate criterion of the success of RENEW (Field Notes, 22 Sept. 1989). During the first session on the following day, led by Fr. Liam, a questionnaire *Could We Care Less?*, which was to be distributed in Week 4 of Season 3, was discussed. The parish coordinator from St Matthew's felt this title was unfortunate because it appeared to overlook the fact that 'a lot of people are quietly carrying on caring'. A veteran justice and peace campaigner observed to applause that 'so many Catholics are ready to do good but not seek justice'. Fr. Liam responded by urging activists to 'show people the connections between faith and justice'. In a series of meetings in the diocese before Season 3 he claimed to have addressed over 1,000 people on the theme of 'Justice and Spirituality' (Interview, 4 Oct. 1989). One co-ordinator found these 'a waste of time'. Another participant predicted (accurately, as we noted above in Table 6.6) that Season 3 would 'warm people up only for Season 4 to provide them with an opportunity to retire to gentle discussions of "discipleship"' (Field Notes, 5 Oct. 1989).

A later session led by a senior educationalist from the Catholic Fund for Overseas Development (CAFOD) better fitted the mood of many activists. He urged the need 'to learn about justice by listening to those who experience injustice, being alongside them'. Referring to the 1971 Synod statement that 'action on behalf of justice ... [is] a constitutive dimension of the preaching of the gospel', he urged those present not to be afraid to confront the powerful on behalf of the powerless and despised 'little people'. Changing policies was inevitably political but 'don't shirk it'. While the poor would be the main actors in their liberation, it was the role of J & P activists to accompany and be in solidarity with them, be evangelized by them, raise awareness of their plight 'in a non-threatening way', and 'share hope'. The CAFOD educationalist asked what J & P proposed to *do* as a result of Season 3 and observed that 'in J & P we spend too much time talking at people and instilling guilt' (Field Notes, 23 Sept. 1989).

The weekend had been led by a highly respected and committed resource person, who observed that 'RENEW provides J & P people with as favourable an opportunity as they'll ever get to spread the word and involve people at parish level' (Conversation, 21 Sept. 1989). During the weekend the steady co-optation of the J & P activists in the diocesan RENEW programme was substantially completed. This was in spite of the often fierce challenges made by the activists that RENEW was a diversion from the hard work of raising awareness of justice issues at the parish level. It is interesting to note, as a possible indicator of the diocese's commitment to justice and peace, that it was reported that a first run of only 350 copies of the *Justice Resource Book* had been printed and that it had omitted references to local resource persons and organizations. Even though a second run of 400 copies was being printed, these amounted to only half-a-dozen for each parish in contrast to the thousands of copies of booklets printed for members of the faith-sharing groups.

7.4   Season 3 in the Parishes

What happened in the individual parishes in the preparations for and during Season 3 was often contingent on local factors. This can be illustrated from our field notes of observations made in two parishes.

In a planning meeting of the RENEW team in St Cyril's parish it was noted that the diocesan team (in a letter, 26 Sept. 1989) had recommended that the phrase 'social concern' be substituted for 'social justice' in the list of goals. The consequences of this were probably far-reaching; St Cyril's appears to have been passive in its response to Season 3. The small groups were not encouraged to cover the key dimension of justice formation but to concentrate instead on charitable concern for the poor. Interestingly, a question on justice issues in the parish evaluation was resented by a considerable number of respondents and found irrelevant for the task of 'spiritual renewal'. This seemed to indicate that the hope that justice goals might be pursued in Season 3 did not materialize in this parish. Even the St Vincent de Paul Society was largely unable to extend its recruitment and it remained essentially the same four stalwarts who had made it up for a number of years. The absence through illness during Season 3 of a key member of the parish team and the death of the parish priest in the following season meant that the primary concern of the parish team was simply keeping the programme on track until it had run its course. We suspect that contingent circumstances such as these were of considerable importance in the outcomes of RENEW in the parishes generally.

Our field notes for St Matthew's parish are more comprehensive. Among the early suggestions were large group events in One World Week (to promote awareness of development and overseas aid concerns) in October, Armistice Sunday (focusing on peace issues and the arms race), special Masses and vigils on the First Fridays of October and November on the domestic problem of homelessness and the international problem of refugees and migrant workers, and a shared lunch at which there would be an opportunity to sign up with various justice and peace groupings. In the event few of these materialized and, in spite of posters with seven tongues of fire above the altar labelled with the gifts of the Holy Spirit on the first Sunday of Season 3, the justice theme seemed to be 'incidental to the normal liturgy' and 'pretty low key' (Field Notes, 8 Oct. 1989).

In this parish we have useful observational reflections from two small groups. The leader in the first group had a non-Catholic wife who appeared to resent his involvement in RENEW. Although in a demanding occupation, his leadership evidenced much careful preparation beforehand. In his group of twelve people there were no signs of the overt conflicts over justice issues about which there had been warnings. But participants freely expressed their minds. One, in the first week, said that several of her acquaintances, who had been excited by Season 1, had found that excitement gradually dissipating, so that attendance at the small groups was now a 'chore'. This seemed to be related in part to an increase in the size of the group from 6–8 in Season 1 to 11–12 in Season 3, partly to the more relaxed leadership style of the female group leader in Season 1, and partly to the very full lives of busy and already committed members. Under the action-response part of the meeting, each member agreed to pray for the person on their right during the following week (Field Notes, 11 Oct. 1989 and interview, 13 Oct. 1989).

Field notes from the remaining meetings show a slowly developing attempt to make the weekly action-response more concrete. In the first instance this was concerned with personal relationships: fewer flare-ups with difficult children, and showing compassion to a neighbour whose niece was dying of cancer, and so on. But at the second meeting one member raised the question of group action to help the Cyrenians and led to a general discussion about homelessness (Field Notes, 17 Oct. 1989). The third meeting was again preoccupied with 'coping with difficult relatives' and the question of homelessness was variously attributed to family breakdown and government policies. Several members of the group felt depressed at the enormity of the injustices and asked 'what can we do?' (Field Notes, 25 Oct. 1989). When the evaluation forms were distributed after the fourth meeting, one member observed that she felt 'very negative' over Season 3 and irritated by the 'mess' and lack of coherence of the posters which had been put up in the church during the season. Nevertheless, the group agreed to do something about homelessness and to invite a university researcher, who had lived as a homeless person for nearly two years, to a meeting (Field Notes, 1 Nov. 1989). After this meeting several testified to their consciousness having been raised during Season 3, though one or two (mainly visitors) were unconvinced and felt homelessness was entirely the fault of individuals. Around four or five people in the parish had been following the meetings in the adjacent parish of St Luke's to promote an inter-Church response to the growing and visible problem of homelessness in the town of Riverton (Field Notes, 24 Nov. 1989).

In the second small group our informant told how, in the first meeting, a professional man had reacted very strongly to the comment that 'each individual is created with great human dignity that can be fully realized *only* in community'. Another member of the group, however, testified to the importance of the friendship and support he and his wife had recently received from the RENEW group. A third recounted in horror that there used to be a charismatic prayer group in the parish and 'they used to speak in tongues! I don't believe in all that gibberish!', she said. Later she challenged my informant: 'Do you know the sins against the Holy Ghost? Well I do' (Field Notes, 17 Oct. 1989). At its third meeting this group immediately dismissed the 1971 Synod of Bishops' statement by asserting confidently and dismissively that the Church did not have anything to do with politics (Field Notes, 31 Oct. 1989). Two weeks later our informant felt 'angry', 'bruised', 'frustrated', and 'disturbed' at the many disagreements with traditional Catholics (Field Notes, 15 Nov. 1989).

In contrast, members of another group reported that 'Ours was a lovely group; we didn't have any troublemakers!' Our field notes record tartly: 'In other words, providing it was all undemanding, with no shared prayer to offend the sensitivities of traditional Catholics, and where everyone is agreed that the sun shines in the Thatcherite world, then there is a nice, cosy sense of contentment' (24 Nov. 1989).

In St Matthew's parish, half-way through Season 3, justice and peace activists had organized a shared lunch and exhibition from about a dozen organizations such as CAFOD, Traidcraft, Pax Christi, Catholic Institute for International Relations (CIIR), Amnesty International, a local CARE group, and a parish link in a developing country. A lot of people had taken a lot of trouble putting on probably the biggest display of stalls and posters ever arranged in the parish. Unfortunately, practically nobody other than the organizers came to see it. Numbers attending were well under one-half of those who had attended previous shared lunches after Seasons 1 and 2. The event had been well advertised in the parish newsletter for several weeks. It is possible that its location in a nearby school hall rather than in the adjacent but smaller parish hall was a key determinant but there was also the suspicion that people were afraid of being asked to commit themselves to something (Field Notes, 29 Oct. 1989).

In a letter to parish or deanery J & P representatives at the beginning of Season 3, Fr. Langley informed them of workshops on the theme 'Who Cares?' in five (of the twelve) deaneries. These emerged from the second working party of the Commission and were intended to 'build upon the new interest hopefully created by Season 3' (Letter, 27 Oct. 1989). Some 150 people had attended these meetings and the Commission congratulated itself that participants had generally found them helpful (Minutes, 19 Dec. 1989).

The original title of the questionnaire circulated towards the end of Season 3, *Who Cares?*, was thought by some, for example the RENEW co-ordinators in St Matthew's parish, to be unhelpful and was translated into '*Could We Care Less?*'. It was hoped that as a result of the small group experiences in Season 3 of RENEW, many would wish to be involved in some way in care for those less fortunate. However small these ways may be, they are to be strongly encouraged since they transform what may be a vague, general concern about poverty (spiritual/ material) and justice into personal service and action. (*Could We Care Less?*, 1989)

Individual small group members were invited to identify and name 'Our Local Concerns', to find out 'about social pressures, problems and needs' in their parish and 'what is being done'. Members were invited to indicate in what areas of parish life they had a general interest, whether they could offer car transport to those who needed it, whether they could offer expert advice in a number of areas (financial, plumbing, electrical, etc.) and presented with a check-list of ways in which they could offer help (from 'take a dog for a walk' to 'advise on right to social benefits').

This check-list was very much at the 'social concerns' end of the spectrum and represented 'the first step' in raising awareness of needs at the local level. In order to prompt 'the second step', that is raise a consciousness of the underlying causes of social injustices and prompt a corresponding 'action-response', justice and peace activists in the deanery of Riverton, in response to Season Three, planned a series of three public meetings under the broad theme of 'Living by the Spirit'. These each attracted around 50–65 people, over one-third of whom came from St Matthew's parish where J & P activists had been strongly involved in the planning of the series. The first talk on 'Renewing the Face of the Earth' was given by a specialist on development education from CAFOD, who raised issues about international debt and the notion of stewardship in creation and contemporary environmental concerns. The second was given by a feminist theologian on the theme 'Redeeming the Dream of Creation'. Finally, a Catholic Member of Parliament talked about 'The Christian Response to the Spirit' and political responses to injustices.

In spite of attempts such as these, there were early signs of tension between the diocesan RENEW team and the Justice and Peace Commission. One member of the Commission recalled how the diocesan Director of RENEW had said that he was 'fed up with these J & P people'. He wished they would 'get their act together' because they were 'discrediting RENEW'. It seems that this remark arose out of a meeting addressed by the regional CAFOD representative but attended by only seven people. All the same, this remark was interpreted as an ominous indication of the diocese's antagonism to J & P which they wished to see converted into 'Social Concern' (Field Notes, 2 Nov. 1989). Shortly after the end of Season 3 another member of the Commission observed that there seemed to be strong indications that the diocesan RENEW office was distancing itself from J & P and was unwilling to facilitate publicity for either the planned workshops or the Riverton deanery series in January 1990. The contrast was drawn between the follow-up programmes in the deaneries after Seasons 1 and 2, which had been arranged by the full-time, paid staff of the diocesan Adult Education team, and the efforts of the Justice and Peace Commission, whose priest co-ordinator had recently resigned and which had, at that time, no full-time or part-time paid staff (Field Notes, 13 Nov. 1989).

In Riverton it seems that while a Council of Churches' project to provide overnight shelter for homeless people was the brainchild of the vicar of a central Anglican church and was being discussed before RENEW, a project to provide a drop-in centre certainly had its origins in RENEW groups in St Luke's parish. One of the initiators had been shocked on returning from abroad to see homeless people on the streets of Riverton and had begun to make enquiries about various voluntary groups. Some time after Season 2 of RENEW there was a large group meeting of people who felt the need 'to *do* something' in response to 'the Lord's call'. For one key member who was aware of homelessness, it was the action-response element in the small group meetings which was the initiating factor. A large group meeting in 1989 was 'hijacked' by those with a growing concern for homelessness. A local councillor was challenged about the evidence of local homelessness and an invited speaker told of her experiences of starting a project with no resources in London. Within a short time the police reaction had changed from regarding the homeless as the 'true degenerates of society', who ought not to be attracted to the area by offering them food and shelter, to one of seeking advice as to how best to help the homeless when local by-laws were tightened. One member of the group provided a direct link to the parallel town centre Churches' initiative to provide an overnight shelter. Another insisted that

we're not going to be another of these little churchy groups where middle-class people with loads of money and nice jobs sit around in someone's nice lounge and talk about how dreadful it is for other people to have no homes or to be starving or whatever it is. We're going to *act*. The key thing is to do something by next week and come back next week [to the RENEW small group] and tell people . . . not just sit around.   (Interview, 15 Oct. 1992)

When challenged that their social concern was not tackling the underlying cause, they responded that this was a political issue and their concern was with practical things and 'what you do to the least of my brethren you do to Me' or like the Good Samaritan, you 'don't just cross over [the road]'. 'I can't just turn away my face from those who need it.' When they first opened the drop-in shelter's doors in January 1990, around 20–5 used to attend and the numbers doubled over the following two or three years. When the parish stressed that they would have to ensure their own insurance cover and that if they 'get into problems, don't look to the Church to bail you out!', they raised their own finances. Because a lot of the men had had 'bad experiences with religion in some form or other', they decided that they would not evangelize. Rather, if the men 'want to see God, they'll see it in our actions' (Group interview, 15 Oct. 1992).

It is undoubtedly the case that there was heightened public concern about increasing homelessness in Britain in the late-1980s. The United Nations had declared 1987 to be the International Year of the Homeless and to mark this the Pontifical Commission 'Iustitia et Pax' submitted a major study to Pope John Paul II (1988). In the Diocese of Downlands the Justice and Peace Commission had arranged a study day on it in March 1988, seven months before the start of RENEW. Concerns about homelessness were, before RENEW, very much on the agenda of justice and peace activists. Nevertheless, it also seems clear that at least in the case of the drop-in centre in Riverton, and possibly also in other similar initiatives throughout the diocese, the catalyst for the commitment to such an on-going project was the action-response requirements of the weekly RENEW small groups, taken seriously by some. In 1990 the bishops of England and Wales published a highly critical statement *Homelessness: A Fact and a Scandal*. A survey of justice and peace activists (N = 120) in the summer of 1990 resulted in the selection of housing and homelessness as the issue to which most attention should be paid in the following two or three years. By May 1991 a *Homelessness Pack* had been prepared by the diocesan Justice and Peace Commission. All over the diocese groups were initiating a wide range of responses to the perceived injustice of homelessness and a process of networking was encouraged by a conference on 9 May 1991 attended by the bishop. Activists in St Matthew's parish were regularly involved as volunteers at the overnight shelter in Riverton and had formed a local branch of the Churches' National Housing Coalition which lobbied Parliament on 1 December 1992. In this respect, social concern was being supplemented by the further step of political action, an indication that at least some minority groups were developing a type 2 spirituality.

7.5   The Battle over Resources

In January 1990, shortly after the end of Season 3 of RENEW, the diocesan representative of the NLC reported:

Season III of the RENEW process . . . attempted to deal with the issues of social justice. There are some encouraging signs, coupled with dramatic changes in the world scene they may combine to shift attitudes that tend to be rooted in the past. Follow-up talks and workshops however have not been so well resourced as after previous [seasons], but this may be due to major changes in the diocesan J & P structure earlier in the year. However, the support from pulpit and parish has been patchy. In one deanery at least 5 parishes out of 12 were not displaying the appropriate notices or mentioning the events in parish newsletters, though full notice was given and material circulated in early December. The Diocesan J & P Commission has been further hampered by the resignation of Fr. Tim Langley, the coordinator . . . The knock-on effect of the reduction of the Commission from 12+ members and the excluding of an ecumenical dimension has been unhelpful and has reduced instant access to valuable networks . . . [T]he appointment of a Vicar for Social Responsibility from outside the J & P Movement would suggest a shift in Diocesan policy toward 'Social Concerns' . . . No part-time worker has yet been found to assist the commission.   (NLC Minutes, 13 Jan. 1990)

In this section we will briefly outline the struggle over many years which the diocesan Justice and Peace Commission had had in trying to persuade the bishop that in order to carry out its remit, more resources, in particular in the form of a field worker, were necessary. Resistance to this was seen by members of the Commission as evidence of the low priority which the pursuit of justice and peace issues had in the agenda of the diocese and of the marginalization of the J & P movement, in spite of all the rhetoric before Season 3. The long-time absence of representatives of the Commission from meetings of diocesan agencies appeared to provide further support for this interpretation.

The Commission which was formally constituted in 1979 had a part-time field worker in 1982/3 and a full-time worker in 1983/5. The latter, a Sister of St Joseph of Peace, had been gaoled after protesting about nuclear weapons outside the Ministry of Defence at Easter 1984. The chairman of the Commission wrote to inform the bishop (Letter, 18 June 1984) that although they were not all called to the same form of witness she had their full support. There are good reasons to believe, however, that her non-violent direct action and her overt feminism did not endear her to many in the diocese, including members of the diocesan Adult Education Centre with whom relations were always difficult. When she left the Commission in 1985 she was not replaced though Fr. Tim Langley, a busy parish priest, was appointed as co-ordinator.

This situation did not allow time for him to respond to invitations to speak to groups and inevitably the Commission began to discuss resource needs if it was 'to facilitate the work of J & P in the diocese, including the possibility of appointing a part-time J & P worker' (Minutes, 16 May 1987). Following discussion of the report of a working party and the expression of concern that any new appointment should not be marginalized as the previous worker had been (Minutes, 10 Oct. 1987), the chairman wrote to the bishop stating that the tasks which the Commission had been given of promoting justice and peace in the diocese were being compromised by the 'slender existing resources' available to the Commission. He identified six main ways in which a full-time worker could help the work of the Commission and concluded:

We are convinced that the job you have given us is important and that it justifies a substantial investment of money and resources, if we intend the gospel message of justice and peace—our response to such things as racialism, aggression, sexism, the lure of riches and the rejection of the poor and disadvantaged—really to penetrate our lives, our liturgies and the sacramental programmes of the Diocese.   (Letter, 22 Dec. 1987)

Interestingly, the letter also drew attention to 'the time of development' which it was hoped would follow the RENEW programme. It seems, though, that

the bishop had indicated that there would not be the financial resources to find a Justice and Peace worker because of RENEW. However members felt that if Justice and Peace was a priority in the Diocese this should be reflected in proper support for the work of the Commission.   (Minutes, 23 Apr. 1988)

A new chairman of the Commission was appointed in April 1988. Six months later and just before the start of RENEW, in an examination of its work, it was reported that

The parish and deanery reps had found the days the Commission organized helpful. However we were ineffective both in helping the Bishop in his task of teaching and as an effective pressure group. There was a great task to be done in raising consciousness amongst Catholics. A sense of frustration was expressed at attending seemingly fruitless meetings.   (Minutes, 1 Oct. 1988)

Six months later Fr. Langley reported in his newsletter (5 Apr. 1989) that the bishop had 'suggested a "slimmed down and more effective" commission' and that 'there is also the possibility of the Diocese once more employing a Justice and Peace worker'. The negotiations between the Commission chairman and the diocesan authorities about funding the post at a salary level which approximated to those paid to workers in aid agencies lasted over a year only for an 'appointment [to be] held up, at the last minute, by the Diocesan Personnel Committee which handles finances' at a difficult time of financial cutbacks for the diocese (Letter from chairman of Commission to J & P representatives, 1 May 1990). Eventually a part-time worker was appointed on a one-year contract from July 1990 and located in an office in the diocesan seminary. The fruits of the worker were soon apparent in the thorough researching necessary to produce the *Homelessness Pack*, plan the regular study days with parish representatives, improve ecumenical collaboration, and other projects.

Early in 1990 the bishop appointed a priest with little previous experience in the justice and peace movement to join the Commission. When the third lay chairman to have headed the Commission since its inauguration in 1979 retired in December 1991, this priest took over as the new chairman. After the frustrations of previous negotiations it was a surprise when proposals to extend the contract of the part-time worker, in the first place by six months but subsequently for three years from August 1992 (Minutes, 2 Sept. 1992), were accepted. Even then there were some extremely vague and untidy uncertainties and failures to complete contracts on time and which led 'commission members [to say they] were concerned at the unjust treatment of [the fieldworker]' (Minutes, 18 Nov. 1992). While it is probable that the extended contract was a consequence of an improving financial state in the diocese following the ending of the RENEW programme and some success in raising funds in a public appeal in 1991, it is not beyond the bounds of possibilities that the key factor in suddenly and unexpectedly making funds available was having a priest to negotiate on behalf of the Commission. The suspicion remains that with a shift to a clerical leadership, the Commission which in the mid-1980s had taken a prophetic stance alongside its field worker over defence strategies (type 2 in Figure 7.1), had become less threatening and been co-opted into a more domesticated role in the diocese (type 1). Just as RENEW argued for a softly-softly approach to social concerns, so it seemed that the justice and peace movement had become more respectable to many in the diocese and hence more worthy of financial support.

7.6   *The Domestication of Social Justice*

In this chapter we have analysed the controversial matter of the promotion of social justice and its place in the RENEW programme. We have again drawn on a wide range of research data. In the first place we interviewed a large number of informants, including the diocesan bishop and key priests in his diocese and members of both the international and diocesan RENEW teams. Secondly, one of us was a member of the diocesan Justice and Peace Commission for most of the period of our research and also a member of its working party which produced a resource booklet for use in the diocese during Season 3. We have drawn on the available minutes of the Commission. Thirdly, we have quoted from extensive field notes taken during our participant observation studies in two parishes and at various deanery and diocesan meetings. These various data sources have confirmed our earlier analyses of the top-down nature of control employed by RENEW and the willingness to tolerate a very limited emphasis on social action.

Three years after the end of the RENEW programme, the Justice and Peace Commission continued to struggle in its efforts to raise the consciousness of people in the diocese to the importance of justice issues. The work of the field worker on homelessness was recognized by his appointment as area co-ordinator for the Churches' National Housing Coalition (CNHC) and the bishop emphasized the importance of homelessness in an *Ad Clerum* to the clergy and agreed 'that Commission members speak to the deans or assembled priests in a deanery' (Minutes, 27 Apr. 1993). The bishop was still uncertain as to whether the field worker should be represented on the diocesan Pastoral Management Committee though the field worker had attended Heads of Agencies meetings (Minutes, 5 Feb. 1993 and 22 July 1993). The Commission's uncertainties were reflected in its decision to 'ask the bishop why J & P issues fall on stoney ground' (Minutes, 22 July 1993). Following the identification of social concerns as a diocesan priority area after RENEW (as will be indicated in the following chapter), a co-ordinator for Christian Responsibility and Social Justice, whose task would be 'to research into the formation of Catholics in Social Teaching of the Church' (Minutes of meeting attended by the bishop, 2 Nov. 1993), was appointed in the diocese. But the field worker was not shortlisted for the post and the relationship between the two posts had still not been clarified by the end of 1993. There remains the possibility, implicit in the description of the task noted above, that while the new post and the resources implied by it, might appear to indicate a strengthening of the commitment to justice in the diocese, it will in practice serve further to domesticate and make respectable the work of justice and peace in the diocese. Finally, however, the process of the clericalization of the Commission with the appointment of two further priest members in addition to the new priest chairman (Minutes, 7 Apr. 1992), seems subsequently to have been diluted with the expansion of the membership of the Commission in 1993 (Minutes, 2 Nov. 1993).

In this chapter we have attempted to extend our analysis of RENEW by considering, as a case study, the treatment of the issues of social justice and its relevance for the living out of the religious faith of the Catholics in the Diocese of Downlands. Such issues were frequently 'political' and so generated controversy and conflict and a 'switching off' of those who held that religion and politics should be clearly differentiated. Some people claimed scriptural warrant for an overtly prophetic and challenging approach to such issues. Others, notably the proponents of the RENEW package, argued that such an approach was ineffective because it alienated people, and in consequence they urged a more softly-softly approach to social concerns. In this chapter we have examined some aspects of the treatment of such issues in the diocese.

In the first instance we found it necessary to focus on one aspect of the typology of spiritualities developed in Chapter 2 and in Figure 5.1. By distinguishing between communal and privatized forms of spiritual culture and whether or not the spirituality aimed to promote a social project, we were able to distinguish between four types of spiritualities. In Season 3 of RENEW, in particular, the ways in which the Christian ought to respond to social injustices were explored and prompted, especially in the action-response section of the weekly small group meetings. We reported on our survey findings in the previous chapter. These showed that a much heightened awareness of social concerns in Season 3 substantially dissolved in the remaining two seasons. The evidence we reviewed in this chapter suggests that for some, at least, some embryonic form of 'social Catholicism' (type 2 in Figure 7.1) was successfully promoted. Some people were prompted to take part in a parliamentary lobby. Others responded by becoming volunteers at drop-in or overnight shelters for the homeless. Arguably this form of ameliorative social concern is best interpreted as an instance of post-Vatican piety (i.e. type 1).

Drawing heavily on our field notes and interview data, we next outlined the debate about the appropriate methodology which should be employed by the Catholic community to promote the issues of justice and peace and establish its importance in the way believers live their lives. This debate focused around the clash between the discourses of 'justice' and 'concern'. Active members of the justice and peace movement in the diocese and most, if not all, members of the diocesan J & P Commission, felt that the promotion of the concept of 'concern' by RENEW was a 'wishy-washy cop-out' from the explicit prophetic challenges to seek 'justice'. The request by the diocesan authorities for the Commission to change its name, in the hope that it could be presented as more respectable and acceptable in the diocese, was strongly resisted by the members of the Commission. But after fierce debate, they came to the pragmatic conclusion that the chances of raising the awareness of significant numbers of people in the diocese would be greatly enhanced by their active participation in the RENEW programme and particularly by their involvement in Season 3. But even here the resources made available, for example for the distribution of the Commission's *Justice Resource Book*, were limited and the mutual suspicions and distrust between the diocesan RENEW team and the Justice and Peace Commission persisted. Furthermore, they were not dispelled by the long-drawn-out negotiations about and seemingly reluctant appointment of a part-time field worker for justice and peace after the end of RENEW. Suspicions about the domestication of justice and peace in the diocese were fuelled by the seeming clericalization of the Commission and the appointment of a priest as chairman, and later, as a result of ambiguities over the relationship between the Commission and the newly appointed diocesan Co-ordinator for Christian Responsibility and Social Justice. In sum, the evidence we have reviewed in this case study of the treatment of the issues of social justice in the RENEW programme has reinforced our interpretation that RENEW was very much a top-down programme of religious renewal. Although it strongly emphasized faith-sharing and other communal expressions of faith, and to that extent warranted a location as much in Cell A as Cell C in our typology of spiritualities (Figure 5.1), the RENEW version of spirituality had only a weakly developed social project, which located it firmly in Cell 1 (Figure 7.1).

This interpretation was clearly reflected by a parish co-ordinator and justice and peace activist interviewed two years after the end of RENEW:

I didn't want [RENEW] to do more harm than good. I also, you know, felt that . . . it was a great opportunity to get to grips with what religious activity is all about: living a life of integrity . . . both in the personal and in the public [spheres], and this was a real opportunity... Justice and Peace has always been [seen] in terms of talking to the converted. It's very difficult to reach people who don't feel that they're political, ... just never been turned on by the issues. And it was one way of reaching people... Some of the material was good, and certainly the material was about relating faith to everyday life. I suppose I think it needs a more radical, more profound rethinking of everything by the Church to enable people to relate their everyday life and their political decisions. It takes more than a course [*sic*!] like this. (Interview, 16 Dec. 1992)

The co-ordinator went on to express anger at the attitude of a senior priest who had criticized the justice and peace movement for its 'failure' to address the people in the pews.

It's the life style of the clergy and of Catholics... It should be so basic to the way that Catholics order their lives that they don't even think of it being a separate issue being addressed by a separate ... commission ... J & P should be implicit in being a Catholic. If the Church isn't getting that message across, it isn't the Commission['s fault], it's the hierarchy, it's all of us who are failing. That failure has to be owned.

After criticizing 'bland, waffly, pastoral letters ... [which] bore no relation to anyone's life at all' and the failure to address 'the life style of a huge percentage of Catholics' or to 'help people love one another, whatever they are like', the co-ordinator concluded by saying, 'I see no evidence ... absolutely no difference' between the state of J & P now and four years previously, before RENEW. Perhaps people were better informed but there is no 'great social awareness' and after Mass 'still you get the doctors talk[ing] to doctors [and] nobody else' (Interview, 16 Dec. 1992).

In sum, even in the sphere of justice and peace, where a determined core of activists was committed to raising awareness during RENEW, the outcomes seemed to be rather minimal. As the official diocesan silver jubilee commemorative book observed:

there are probably a couple of hundred people (or around one or two per cent of Catholics in the diocese) keeping social issues, both national and international, before our minds as central to the Christian vocation to bring the Good News of salvation to the poor. Would that such matters were higher on our diocesan priority list! (Stapleton, 1990: 40).

8

The Outcomes of RENEW

8.1 Introduction

In this chapter we will be concerned with two main questions: what developments could be discerned in the diocese in the three years immediately after the end of RENEW, and what were the overall effects of the 2½-year RENEW programme. We start by outlining the attempts to articulate a diocesan pastoral strategy for the 1990s in the Diocese of Downlands and present an ethnographic account of the parallel attempt, in St Matthew's parish, to formulate a parish plan for mission. These were both attempts, at two different levels, to institutionalize the processes of action-response which it was hoped had been firmly established during the RENEW programme. Three years after the end of Season 5 it was reasonable to assume that a preliminary judgement might be made about the persisting effects of the RENEW programme. We therefore proceed to report the official evaluations of RENEW not only in the research diocese but also in a number of other dioceses, particularly in Scotland, which had followed the programme. In general the official evaluations were enthusiastic and congratulatory. The chapter concludes with a more critical appraisal of the RENEW programme in the light of the conceptual scheme which we developed in Chapter 2.

8.2 'Planning for the '90s'

Probably as a result of RENEW experiences in other dioceses, planning for the post-RENEW period started between Seasons 4 and 5. In April 1990 Bishop Patrick invited individuals and groups in the diocese to answer a questionnaire to identify the felt needs of the diocese and form the basis for the formulation of a pastoral plan for the 1990s. In total, 2,984 forms were submitted, including 2,075 individuals, 704 faith-sharing groups, 129 parish groups, and 76 societies. It was estimated that 8,616 people had been involved in the exercise, over one-fifth of adult Mass attenders in the diocese. Very few responses, however, came from those aged 35 or under.

Four-fifths of the respondents felt that their parishes were least well oriented towards mission, mainly because of shyness or reluctance or because they were inward-looking. Parishes in the main were liked for their friendliness and community spirit. Asked what other things they would like to see in their parishes, all were concerned with internal matters such as 'more support for youth' or 'improved liturgy'. The results of the exercise reflected the concerns of an introspective parochial life.

Asked to identify three or four major priorities which they would like to see the diocese supporting over the next decade, nearly two-thirds selected 'adult education and community', while over one-half selected both 'social concerns' and 'family/young people support'. Around three-quarters of respondents suggested that these priorities would require more training of lay leaders and also more clergy encouragement for the laity and co-operation with them. At the DPC meeting on 6 October 1990, just before the start of Season 5 of RENEW, and on the basis of the diocesan consultation, Bishop Patrick identified seven areas for pastoral action for the rest of the decade:

- *adult education*—especially the training of catechists and leaders.
- *social concerns*—an outward looking attitude to those who need the care of Christ.
- *marriage and family life*—seeking ways of preparing couples, supporting the early years of marriage, and sustaining the growth of partnership.
- *young people*—providing opportunities for them to hear the call of Christ.
- *ecumenism*—being with other Christians as we share the Good News.
- *prayer and liturgy*—the source of life and vitality.
- *small communities*—what has been discovered through RENEW to be built on and developed as a way of being Church. (Diocese of Downlands, *Planning for the '90s*, 1990)

For Ann Potter, a member of the diocesan RENEW team, RE-NEW had given the diocese 'a kick start' and had 'lit flames' and the 'whole diocese [had been] involved in a prioritization process of consultation'. There were open meetings in all twelve deaneries in June 1990 'and it was from that that certain priority areas were identified and from that and the need to address those, we came to the vision statement . . . The development of the vision was very much the bishop and inner core group who first promulgated it' and then invited various people to comment on it until it reached its final form. The next step 'has got to be using the vision as the complete umbrella for all that goes on in the diocese in the coming years up to the year 2000' (Interview, 2 Dec. 1992). The top-down organization of post-RENEW developments is evident in these remarks.

A diocesan Office for Small Communities under the direction of two former members of the diocesan RENEW team was established 'to help parishes maintain small groups, but also to foster the growth of these groups towards Small Christian Communities'. Nearly all parishes had named a contact person to be a link with the diocesan Office after their parish RENEW team had ceased to exist and about three-fifths of them had attended a weekend overnight stay for reflection on the distinguishing features of such Christian communities. Their immediate task was to recruit for and organize Lenten faith-sharing groups (*DT* Mar. 1991). They also revised and reproduced booklets *Called to be Faithful* and *Joyful Waiting* for the use of groups during Lent and Advent 1991 respectively. However, the former Director reported that while there were some thirteen thousand participants in the RENEW small groups in November 1990, only three months later, in Lent 1991, participation had 'drastically declined to 5,000 plus'. The reasons, he suggested, included: 'a back to "normal" attitude on the part of some parish leadership in the post-RENEW months; [and] the muddle caused by offering two options for Lent, namely the seasonal option for parish small groups and an ecumenical one' (*DT* Jan. 1992).

The dilemma was avoided in Lent 1992 because the Office for Small Communities recommended, as early as July 1991, that all parish contacts promote the nationwide course *Living the Good News*, material for which had been prepared on behalf of the Churches in Britain and Ireland. In a letter to parishes (8 July 1991) it was suggested that

the format will be very much along lines with which we are familiar and so we are recommending that ALL groups which meet in Lent 1992 use this material. This will mean that whether a group decides to continue to meet as a parish based group or whether some people wish to join Ecumenical groups in the local area, EVERYONE will be involved in the same study and reflection.

Meanwhile, the Director of RENEW 'came to believe that one would go nowhere [after RENEW] without a common vision' (Interview, 17 Nov. 1992). While there is some uncertainty about the sequence of events, it appears that Bishop Patrick set up a small working party which prepared preliminary drafts of a diocesan 'vision'. Later he chaired a Pastoral Management Team and a management consultant was recruited to facilitate the process. It seems that the original plan for a two-day consultation was reduced to a single day as a result of pressure from some clergy. In April 1991 some 150 priests in the diocese met to discuss the emerging vision of the bishop.

The diocesan newspaper blandly reported that 'the priests have taken back to their parishes the insights they shared on that day, to share them in turn with their people'. It seems that in the early post-RENEW period it was proposed that there would continue to be a very strong element of control from the diocesan centre and that parishes would be expected to follow the diocesan pastoral strategy. In the event, by all accounts, it did not quite work out like that. One senior priest referred to 'this terrible meeting' at which 'blood on the floor erupted' over whether the vision should proclaim, 'We, the people of Downlands' or 'We, the priests and people of Downlands'. The acceptance of the former was interpreted as of major symbolic significance by some, drawing on notions of taking ownership of a sharing Church. Some rebellious priests considered their existing programmes to be all that was needed and asked: 'who wants a vision? We've got the First Communion programme' (Interview, 17 Nov. 1992).

On 15 June 1991, seven months after the end of RENEW, the bishop attended a meeting of 300 people, representing most parishes, agencies, and organizations in the diocese. A deacon in the diocese with management experience explained that in order to draw up effective plans for where the diocese ought to be going over the next decade, it was necessary to specify a common vision. Bishop Patrick then presented a draft Vision Statement and stressed how it indicated 'a new way forward—together as the people of God' (*DT* Aug. 1991: 4). The original papers for this meeting on *Pastoral Planning for the 90's*, circulated to members of parish pastoral councils in May 1991, stated that 'After all the consultation a systematic planning process is being followed. This will involve parishes, groups and departments making their own, the steps which are to be taken.' This seems clearly to suggest that at this stage it was still envisaged that a diocesan pastoral plan would be dutifully implemented by the parishes—very obviously centrally controlled from the 'top'.

Although our evidence is not as complete as we would have liked, it seems that this earlier notion of a diocesan pastoral plan aroused considerable opposition and became subtly transformed. Thus after two days with the priests of the diocese in February 1992, it was reported that the bishop had set himself three aims: 'that the priests would own the common aims for the diocese and its parishes; that there would be a strong support for the clergy in their parishes; and that there would be diocesan support for everyone involved in parish ministry' (*DT* Apr. 1992). In the light of the bishop's diocesan vision, parishes would be required to prepare their own pastoral plan for the 1990s, adapted to their local circumstances and needs. Diocesan help for the parishes would be the responsibility of a reconstructed Department for Christian Formation. Meanwhile the Office for Small Communities hoped that all types of groups within parishes would *'encourage a gradual shift from "task-orientated" groups to small communities'* (*DT* May 1992; emphasis added).

This comment is perhaps of particular significance. It suggests an unwarranted dichotomy between 'task-orientated' groups and 'small communities' which would seem to conflict with the ideology and practice of basic Christian communities, for example in Latin America. Clearly there was to be a certain conscious downgrading of task-orientated groups, such as justice and peace groups and related groups seeking either to ameliorate the effects of social injustice (such as providing shelter for the homeless), or to lobby actively for the removal of the causes of injustice (for example by involvement in pressure group politics). The diocese appeared to be domesticating and marginalizing social concerns and reinforcing a more pietistic form of Catholicism.

The two alternative booklets recommended for use by parish groups in Lent 1993 provided some support for this interpretation. *Sticking Points* was designed for ecumenical groups and encouraged them to reflect on differences of opinion between different Christian traditions. The alternative source material, *Lent Prepares Easter Today*, was prepared by the Department of Christian Formation of the Diocese of Downlands as 'part of a series to help develop the "Vision" of the Diocese . . . To be Christ in Our World.' Each week the members of the group were invited to read and reflect on passages of scripture, pray together, and conclude by pondering on some appropriate action. But a close inspection of these suggested a pietistic response rather than any concrete action. For example, in Week 4 the suggested action was: 'each one could make a personal decision on one way in which to resist darkness and encourage light in each *today* of the coming week.' Similar pietistic themes were reflected in a subsequent booklet prepared for groups in the diocese for Advent 1993. They were also apparent in the early parish plans prepared in response to the bishop's 'vision'. Thus the *Downlands Times* reported in May 1993 that three-quarters of parishes has been visited by a facilitator but the first three plans reported were for 'prayer and youth programmes', 'the need to develop prayer', and 'youth, prayer, taking ownership, religious formation and making better use of the parish facilities'.

At the annual meeting of the DPC in May 1992 the bishop presented the final version of the Vision Statement for the diocese:

Looking towards the year 2000, we the people of Downlands pledge ourselves to deepen our understanding, our celebration and our witness of what it means to be Christ in our world: a community of love, partners in service, a source of hope for all, through God's power working in us. (*DT* July 1992)

The DPC then heard that there was an expectation that each parish would draw up its own plan in the light of the diocesan vision. This would be the responsibility of a parish team which 'would have a close relationship with the co-ordinators for the seven areas of need'. Parishes would be assisted to establish their plans by trained facilitators and the bishop presented a proposed timetable to work towards becoming a community of love (1993–4), partners in service (1995–6) and a source of hope (1997–8) (*DT* July 1992). The Office of Small Communities, under the direction of two former members of the RENEW team, prepared faith-sharing material, *To Be Christ in Our World*, on themes based on the diocesan vision for five sessions in the Autumn of 1992. This was intended for all parishioners and not just those already in groups of one sort or another.

It might be noted that two years after the end of RENEW, a strong and directive central thrust to pastoral developments in the parishes was still regarded as essential. The empowerment of people in the parishes, which had been a hoped for fruit of the RENEW experience, had clearly not happened to any significant extent and the diocesan authorities clearly felt they could not rely on parishes spontaneously promoting renewal and a more missionary orientation on their own. Bishop Patrick, like a number of bishops throughout the world, had taken the line that the development of pastoral strategic planning was obligatory even if parishes had the right to do it in their own way.

Some of the Bishop Patrick's strategic thinking was expressed in an interview two years after the end of RENEW (7 Oct. 1992). In this he strongly affirmed the task of the bishop to set the agenda ['vision'] for the diocese and for the parishes, while allowing each parish to determine its own route to the vision in the light of its own particular needs and circumstances. The way this effected the process of pastoral planning in one parish will be examined in the following section.

8.3 St Matthew's Parish Strategy Group

Shortly before the final season of RENEW a new parish priest was appointed to the parish of St Matthew's. Around this time the PPC began to 'take stock of the way our Parish is working' and a survey of the effectiveness of existing parish committees and patterns of activities was undertaken. In a letter to members of the PPC (17 May 1991), before an extraordinary meeting to consider the results of the survey, the parish priest informed them of developments in the diocese 'which may well have some bearing on these present discussions in the parish'. This was a month before the Bishop Patrick presented his vision statement to representatives of all parishes.

Unaware of these developments and quite independently of the diocese, two members of the PPC secured its agreement to present a draft Parish Plan for Mission to the Annual General Meeting of the parish on 19 June 1991. This acknowledged the role of the PPC and committed it to prepare, in consultation with all parishioners, parish groups, and other Christian communities in the area, a Parish Plan for Mission. This would respond to the vision statement of the diocese, identify parish priorities, and commit resources to realizing those priorities. At the meeting, two other members of the parish who had attended the diocesan meeting at which the bishop had presented his vision, summarized the thinking of those who had outlined the diocesan framework. The meeting agreed that the PPC should proceed with the specification of a plan within eighteen months and after the summer break set up a Parish Strategy Group (PSG) to do this.

The PSG attempted to 'start where [people] are at' and to *listen* especially to the under-25s. It sent a letter to every known group in the parish inviting comments on what it felt like to be a Catholic, especially from the 'lapsed' children of active parishioners. This approach elicited very few responses. A second approach to parish committees, groups, and organizations in March 1992 invited them to specify their activities and perceived strengths and weaknesses, and the reasons for them. It also asked them to indicate what they regarded to be priorities or strategies in each of the five areas of understanding, celebrating, sharing, acting out, and spreading the

Good News. The exercise yielded a comprehensive profile of twenty-seven responding groups including a parish maintenance and gardening team, a 'post-RENEW' group, several neighbourhood groups, the Prayer Team, Liturgy Committee, Justice and Peace group, visitors to a local prison, and a working party on homelessness. A recurring need was for more leaders, especially in the younger age groups. Existing participants were often involved in multiple activities and were experiencing increasing pressures at work during the recession. Among the priorities repeatedly stressed were the need for adult education, a greater variety of liturgy, a strong ecumenical emphasis, practical help for neighbours, and generating confidence and improved communications.

At the parish AGM in June 1992 the chairman of the PSG reported on the results obtained from the surveys of individual and group opinions, the diocesan developments, and the formalization of the bishop's vision for the diocese. General approval was given to proposals for the next stage of the process and the selection of priorities and ideas for practical implementation. Later in the summer the chairman of the PSG drafted the first outline of what was to become the parish's pastoral plan. It was around this time that the PSG began to feel that it was time for the PPC to take ownership of the plan as the Parish Pastoral Team covering the seven areas identified by the diocese (PSG Minutes, 10 Sept. 1992). In the absence of a sufficient number of volunteers, however, this matter still remained substantially unresolved at the end of our data collection early in 1994.

After consideration by the PPC, the revised plan was finally presented to an open meeting of the parish in February 1993. Well under 10 per cent of adult Mass attenders were present. There was much criticism of the plan. An elderly parishioner felt that it paid too little attention to 'what the bishop had in mind'. Other parishioners thought the plan was 'too timid' or not specific enough to this parish, or placed too little emphasis on prayer or ecumenism. When it was noted that it was difficult to find new people to be involved in parish activities, one parishioner suggested that the parish 'can only attract people if what we offer is relevant for their lives', for example redundancy, the stress of family life, and other problems commonly faced. Finally, one of the youngest parishioners asked who the plans were intended *for*, adding that involvement in a project for the homeless 'might not add any new members to the parish but at least the Church would still be relevant' (Field Notes, 2 Feb. 1993).

The PSG amended the draft in the light of such comments and the final version of the plan was approved by the PPC in April 1993 and sent to Bishop Patrick. It was inaugurated at the Parish AGM on 20 June 1993. The plan envisaged three phases and priorities built around the diocesan vision statement:

(1) 'Deepening our understanding of what it means to be Christ in our world . . . Developing our Parish communications.'
(2) 'Deepening our celebration and prayer . . . Broadening our individual perspectives of the full range of Parish activities.'
(3) 'Deepening our witness . . . Developing or expanding two Parish projects related to care and social responsibility.'

In November 1993 Bishop Patrick made a pastoral visitation in recognition of the fortieth anniversary of the first Mass in one part of the parish. At each Mass he was given a presentation copy of the Parish Plan for Mission during the offering of gifts. Following the visitation, the presentation copies of the Parish Plan were hung in both churches in the parish as a reminder of the Act of Dedication made in the presence of the bishop. When he met members of the PPC and the PSG he congratulated them on their plan and observed that only 40 per cent of parishes in the diocese had so far submitted their plans. He said that sometimes in other dioceses, consultations had not led to any developments in the parishes. This is why he had offered a diocesan vision and requested each parish to develop its own plans and so lead to an emergent diocesan strategy with help from the diocesan agencies (Field Notes, 13 Nov. 1993).

Two observations can be made in the light of this brief report of the attempt made in one parish to develop its own pastoral plan as an appropriate follow-up to the whole RENEW programme. First, although the plan emerged from the bottom up in this parish, it seems clear that its final articulation and future implementation are likely to be constrained by the strong diocesan framework which was being put in place. This included *Initial Guidelines on the Nature and Work of Parish Pastoral Planning Teams and Parish Pastoral Councils* which gave 'some initial assistance on the process of *selecting* such a team' and indicated that 'it would be *up to the Parish Priest to decide*' whether the parish co-ordinators in the seven pastoral areas (selected as a result of the *Planning for the '90s* exercise) would form part of the Parish Pastoral Team (*Ad Clerum*, Apr. 1992; emphases added). This example in one parish lends support to our interpretation of a top-down pastoral strategy.

Secondly, there is no evidence in this parish that the small core of dedicated activists and leaders in the parish had been increased as a result of the RENEW experience. If anything, it seemed as if in the more unsettled and insecure world of the 1990s, parishioners were willing to participate in short-term commitments but not take on the onerous tasks of leadership. To that extent and in this respect, in St Matthew's parish, at any rate, RENEW did not appear to have had any significant pay-off. Indeed, numbers involved in small groups during Lent and completing volunteer forms or a 'skills register' have all declined since the end of RENEW. Concrete evidence of the lasting effects of RENEW were hard to find.

8.4 Official Evaluations

Two years after the end of RENEW, Bishop Patrick was asked what he regarded to be the main successes of RENEW. He replied:

The main successes, I think, are the fact that an appreciable number of people, . . . especially those who were in small groups, have found a new way of 'being Church', . . . a new love of scripture, . . . a new confidence and a sense of support in their living out of their faith in their daily lives . . . That is number one. Number two, . . . I think that a diocesan process, whatever it is, if it's carried through thoroughly, . . . enables people to experience diocese perhaps in a new way. And some of the events of RENEW I think helped that . . . It gave them a sense that we're not alone. I think that was another success of RENEW. Third success would be, I'd have to say, an increased awareness of scripture touching their daily life, the Word of God. (Interview, 7 Oct. 1992)

Bishop Patrick continued and suggested that, although he would need more evidence of it, a fourth possible success had been the extent to which social action responses, which had been demanded in faith-sharing groups, had been promoted.

Members of the diocesan and international RENEW teams suggested a number of other ways in which RENEW had contributed to the revitalization, however embryonic, of the diocese. Mgr. Bob Reilly, now a member of the International RENEW team, saw RENEW as a 'long-term retreat' and appreciated the need for a 'breather' between the six-week seasons. RENEW was 'gentle, . . . orderly, . . . disciplined' (Interview, 21 Sept. 1992). He was fond of quoting Archbishop Hurley of Durban, South Africa, who saw RENEW as lighting 'the fire of the Second Vatican Council' with the need 'to fan the fire and build it' afterwards. Mgr. Reilly also robustly defended the highly structured nature of RENEW which he saw as the Americans' 'know-how . . . [and] gift to the Church at this time' (Interview, 21 July 1992). Similar remarks were made by Jane Morris, a member of the diocesan team:

I think what I liked about RENEW was that there was a happy blend of professionalism, drawn from the best of the secular world, which quite rightly was applied to [the] management of people within the Church, but done in a prayerful way . . . making way for the Holy Spirit to work . . . but realizing that they were good tools to use, [and] not being afraid to use them.   (Interview, 25 Nov. 1992)

Thus one of the successes of RENEW was 'probably ways of planning, the whole thing, having a vision, having confidence to build your own parish plan, . . . to target various aspects of parish life.' Finally, 'RENEW was a healer' for priests who previously had been alienated in some way in the diocese. It 'gave them the chance to get back on board without losing face and a lot of them took that opportunity' (Interview, 17 Dec. 1992).

Two years after the end of RENEW, a member of the diocesan RENEW team was asked 'where do you actually see the evidence for a revitalized diocese?' The response to the question and the subsequent conversation was revealing in a number of respects.

That, I think, is an extremely difficult question to answer. I'm not sure I can put my finger on any one particular [thing] . . . You have parishes where people talk to each other where they didn't talk to each other before. It's a nebulous thing, terribly difficult to itemize, which is why I hesitate over numbers and figures . . . because I'm not sure how you quantify . . . something which is nebulous . . . My own experience of talking to priests in another diocese is that there is an acceptance that . . . something has gone on in Downlands which has woken people up, which has changed the focus . . . [They say] when you say Mass in a church . . . there is more life, more involvement, . . . more feeling of community. How do you quantify that? . . . It's revitalized individuals which become revitalized in the parishes . . . Numbers, facts, and figures? I don't know . . . I accept the bias of only looking for the positive, but . . . the main idea of the evaluations was not so much to evaluate what had happened, but to point people in the direction of what might happen . . . Yes, RENEW was top-down [in] so far as it was a structure which was laid [out], if you like, and people were encouraged, invited, cajoled, into participating within a structure. And I firmly believe that from participating in that structure, people were given confidence, then, to walk on their own feet in carrying the parishes forward . . . People who'd never done anything before suddenly said 'yes'. It was empowering. Wonderful!   (Interview, 2 Dec. 1992)

First, the informant indicated revealingly a heavy reliance on subjective impressions based on a few selective examples of changes and little or no quantifiable evidence. Any requests for evidence of changes as a result of RENEW were almost invariably met with the response that such changes were not really measurable, were 'nebulous'. As social scientists we have no difficulty in admitting that we cannot measure the depth of faith but we do insist that manifestations of that faith or claims of religious revitalization, for example, in greater institutional involvement, financial contributions, social concerns activities, and so on, are empirically available as concrete evidence.

Secondly, the admission that there was a certain bias in the diocesan evaluation procedures and that their purpose was not an objective assessment of the effectiveness of the RENEW programme but encouragement to do more or better, is welcome, even if belated. We believe that the diocesan claims about the success of RENEW must be regarded as exaggerated and subject to revision in the light of better data than the diocesan team collected. In contrast to the diocese, we collected a more comprehensive range of different types of data (including quantitative survey data, interviews with a wide range of informants, and more systematic participant observation) in ways which substantially reduced the chances of bias (such as the attempt to assess both positive and negative outcomes).

Thirdly, the admission from a member of the RENEW team that RENEW was a 'top-down' programme is also welcome and supports the whole thrust of this study. Whether it did or did not empower people in the parishes is an empirical issue for which some objective assessment of evidence is again intrinsically possible. Three years after the end of the RENEW programme in the Diocese of Downlands we see few, if any, signs of revitalization or empowerment. Consider three obvious examples at the level of the diocese. Mass attendances in the diocese in 1992 were 3,800 (7 per cent) lower than in 1987, though receptions (conversions) into the Church were up by 60 (31 per cent). The latter might indicate a more mission-oriented Church but this would need to be checked out with other data. An indicator of lay empowerment might be the number of lay people listed in the annual diocesan directories as officials in the various diocesan structures. A comparison between the 1989 and 1994 directories indicates a large increase in the number of identified lay people. However, a large proportion of them were in secretarial roles. There does not seem to have been any significant increase in the number of lay people in major policy-making roles so that by this criterion, there has been no noticeable process of

lay empowerment in the diocese. We offer some evidence from participants at the parish level in Section 8.6.

8.5 Evaluations from Other Dioceses

We have made it clear throughout that this book does not purport
to be an evaluation, or a judicious weighing up of advantages and
disadvantages in the light of available resources and alternative
possibilities, in the sense that social scientists might use the term.
Rather, we have reported a case study of RENEW in a single diocese and within that diocese, a case study of one particular parish.
Wherever possible we have indicated where there is evidence which
suggests that our findings are not peculiar to our research parish or
diocese.

The Associate Director of RENEW in a Scottish diocese, speaking
in the Diocese of Downlands before Season 1, identified a number
of 'positive contributions of RENEW to Church Life':

- emergence of new leaders in the parish
- tremendous sense of community
- gifts, previously unknown, discovered among parishioners
- social barriers crossed, especially in small groups
- change in attitude
- return of many lapsed
- converts
- growth in ecumenism
- sense of belonging to a diocese
- co-operation between parishes
- increased interest in retreats, scripture, adult education
- more seeking spiritual direction
- daily Mass attendance well up
- Justice and Peace groups established
- good liturgy in most parishes
  (*DT* Aug./Sept.: 1988)

The social scientist seeking independent confirmation of these
claims is in some difficulty. Pastoral statistics for Scottish dioceses
published in the annual *Catholic Directory for Scotland* are extremely limited, but what there are provide no support for the view
that the downward trends found in Scotland generally had been
stemmed or reversed in those dioceses which had experienced the
RENEW programme. Unfortunately, unlike England and Wales, no
published statistics for Mass attendance or conversions are published

for Scotland. However, for the four Scottish dioceses which followed the RENEW programme between 1986 and 1990, the overall declines over the period 1984–91, in the estimated Catholic population, the number of baptisms, and the number of priests, were about twice as great as the declines in other Scottish dioceses. While such results might reflect demographic and urban changes, they do indicate that there is no *prima facie* evidence, in the relatively short-term at any rate, that RENEW had had a significant impact. Statistics of more relevant indicators of religious vitality are not available.

The Director of RENEW in the Scottish Diocese of Dunkeld has written glowingly about RENEW in his diocese and how it aimed to encourage planning for mission through the building of parish faith-communities with a model of ministry which was collaborative rather than monarchical. He asked 'how do we measure success' (Creegan, 1993: 134) but fails to identify measurable indicators. Rather, he stressed that RENEW

is not a renewal course nor a programme, but a process. The distinction is important. A programme . . . is something which you follow over a period of time and it leads to predetermined conclusions. A process like RENEW is really a growth cycle; the end results depend on the Spirit of God and how far we enter into the process. (Creegan, 1992)

We would point out that a form of reductionism is set in train by this general outlook. The explanation that the outcomes of RENEW depend on the Spirit of God is taken to justify a failure to measure that which is measurable. Examples of potential indicators include the numbers of continuing faith-sharing groups, parish activists and justice and peace groups, instances of greater social or political involvement, and increased weekly offerings and charitable giving. The appeal that RENEW is really a process which takes time, however true, does not invalidate attempts to measure appropriate indicators over both the short- and long-terms.

In an attempt to give due weight to the generally enthusiastic evaluations of those who had sponsored RENEW in their dioceses, we wrote in February 1994, towards the end of our study, to nine people who were known to have been important actors in the promotion of RENEW in four Scottish dioceses and/or had had a briefing about RENEW at Newark in 1985. We invited them to give us their assessment of RENEW in retrospect and sent them a checklist of suggested questions (see Appendix 4) in order to achieve as comprehensive a coverage as possible of the issues we wished to raise. We did not have the resources (or the necessary permissions) to undertake a proper analysis of RENEW in these other dioceses.

Our purpose, then, was to take account of the outcomes of RENEW as perceived by those who were institutionally involved in having promoted it. Apart from the nine contacts from the four Scottish dioceses, we had previously received a long memorandum from the bishop of an African diocese about its impact there.

In general those who replied about the effects of RENEW in their own dioceses were enthusiastic about its outcomes. One bishop regarded RENEW as 'the single most important pastoral initiative' with which he had been associated in his years as a bishop (Letter, 2 Mar. 1994). Another bishop wrote that he was

deeply impressed with what RENEW had to offer in itself as well as what it does in regard to opening the diocesan awareness to the need to meet in a particular kind of way and plan pastorally for the future in a distinctive kind of way. In a sense . . . we are living off RENEW and its benefits four years after the experience ended here. That was and is its real and greatest benefit.   (Letter, 5 Mar. 1994)

A third bishop observed that although around 90 per cent of the parishes in his diocese had agreed to follow RENEW, 'the level of commitment and skilful implementation varied a lot'. He was also critical of the quality of some of the post-RENEW follow-ups. Nevertheless:

The good effects of RENEW have been manifold: the development of small faith sharing groups, the increased use of scripture, the sense of community and involvement of lay people, enhanced liturgy and a much greater willingness to be involved in justice issues are perhaps the principal ones.   (Letter, 8 Mar. 1994)

Two important initiatives, the RCIA and PPCs, 'both have taken root in nearly all the parishes' as a result of RENEW. He did not think the extra cost of RENEW constituted 'a heavy burden on either the diocese or the parishes' and the continued involvement of 'many of the leaders who emerged before and during RENEW' was 'a very important and valuable result'. He considered RENEW to have been 'a great grace for this diocese' and 'would certainly embark upon RENEW if I had to make the choice again'.

Finally, his observations about the extent to which decision-making came primarily from the diocese showed interesting similarities with the Diocese of Downlands:

During RENEW there was a certain amount of resistance to the necessary structures and programming involved. The impression sometimes was that the diocese was dictating what had to be done in the parishes. So, as a basic post-RENEW principle, I decided that the diocese would only serve parishes and that the parishes themselves should take responsibility for the follow-up and for identifying their needs to the diocese. In practice, however, the diocese has continued to offer suggestions and guidance to parishes.

There is in this statement a revealingly frank admission that decision-making was essentially top down, that this provoked a certain amount of resistance, and that in consequence there was a shift to defining the role of the diocese from one of direction to one of service. Of course we do not have any direct evidence of the outcome but it is noticeable that the diocese continued to offer suggestions and guidance to parishes. In terms of our model of spirituality, there is no evidence here of a predominantly 'organic' organizational style.

Our request for information was not appreciated by everyone. One busy former Director of RENEW replied that he did not have the time to respond in the time-scale we envisaged and wrote 'most significantly, I do not share your understanding of the criteria for the evaluation of a process such as RENEW, as outlined in your check list' (Letter, 19 Feb. 1994). One of the bishops similarly suggested that our check-list made him 'quite anxious about the nature of your assessment of a process of spiritual and pastoral renewal'. These reservations surprised us as it seemed to us that the criteria we suggested were implicit in the aims of RENEW and were attempts to operationalize and measure in some objective way the fruits of the 2½-year-long programme. Thus one might have expected revitalized parishes to have attracted higher numbers of Mass attenders and hence offering commitments as well as increased contributions to the official Catholic aid agencies. Such increases would have been evidence of behavioural shifts which would have been recognized by the social scientist.

In a letter to *The Tablet* (21 Mar. 1992), Archbishop Hurley of Durban, South Africa, emphasized the importance of the parish as a 'community of communities' approach to Christian formation and evangelization. He argued that 'we have tried the three basics, preaching, catechesis and liturgy, but these have proved inadequate. We need the fourth dimension of conscious cultivation of community.' There were two ways of introducing small Christian communities: RENEW and an approach originating from a missiological institute in South Africa.

In sum, the testimonies of the sponsors of RENEW in other dioceses were, like those of Bishop Patrick and his senior clergy in our main research diocese, almost uniformly positive about the programme. These testimonies by the diocesan leaders are important social facts which have significant social consequences for the members of the institutional Church. For example, small basic communities are being promoted, methods of incorporating lay people are being developed, and different spiritual emphases are being encouraged. We do not wish to denigrate the social and religious effects of RENEW. But as social scientists we do wish to place some of the claims about RENEW in a proper perspective. It is, we suggest, relevant to the assessment of RENEW that, on several key indicators where claims had been made before the start of RENEW, there was no clear evidence to support those claims. We have a bias in expecting that claims for a revitalized religious institution would have measurable consequences in a variety of types of social action on the part of the participants.

8.6   The View from the Grass Roots

In Chapter 6 we reported our findings on the experiences of RENEW in the parishes. There is little doubt that for many small group participants, RENEW provided opportunities to meet and befriend people whom otherwise they might have known only by sight. Sometimes the faith-sharing experiences were rich and rewarding. Scripture-reading was encouraged among a wider range of Catholics. Communal forms of encouragement were given to the development of individual piety and tentative steps were taken to encourage a greater openness to action-responses to and concerns for one's neighbour which went beyond formal weekly attendance at Mass.

A number of our interviewees had noticed useful effects of RENEW, particularly in terms of social support and a more outward-looking orientation. A former chairman of St Matthew's PPC observed that a few talented individuals had been discovered, one of whom had volunteered to serve on the PPC. More people were helping with the parish liturgies and there was generally a greater sense of community in the parish (Interview, 15 Sept. 1989). A number of respondents referred fondly to their small groups, some of which had persisted after RENEW. They expressed a sense of sadness and spiritual loss when unable to attend the regular meeting. Such groups were seen as 'not far off' being 'small Christian communities'. Other deep-seated changes were perceived

in a way of working as parish. We've found a different way of doing things as a result [of RENEW]. It's not the promised land ... [but] people are . . . just beginning to realize, perhaps, we need to create the right kind of . . . prayerful spaces in our current pastoral planning that will allow us to move on and not spend all our time in parish meetings getting bogged down with drains and sewers and redecorating the parish hall . . . (Interview, 25 Nov. 1992)

Such encouraging assessments of RENEW were adequately reflected in the official evaluations which, as we have noted, were heavily biased in favour of positive outcomes. In order to provide a more balanced judgement it is necessary to note some of the criticisms which were also voiced at the parish level. One small group leader added a spontaneous comment at the end of the Season 5 questionnaire, that it appeared ironic that since RENEW and being a facilitator, his/her adult children had stopped attending Mass and the sacraments (Field Notes). This draws attention to the relative failure of RENEW to appeal to the younger age groups. Interestingly, the parish priest in St Matthew's parish drew attention to the fact that in March 1994, just over three years after RENEW, no one under 25 had completed a voluntary survey of parishioner skills (seen as an opportunity to volunteer for some of the parish social, liturgical, and caring activities).

A parish co-ordinator, while admitting that some good did come out of RENEW 'in as much as people got to know each other, and I'm sure a lot of faith-sharing groups did help each other', nevertheless pointed out that 'it can become a jolly, closed, smug little club, where everything's fine for the members'. But as for empowering people, 'this, honestly, didn't seem to happen'. With a new parish priest who did not seem able to inspire people, and within two years of the end of RENEW,

things are . . . really dying in our parish already . . . Now it's all as dead as a dodo . . . We're almost going back to square one . . . For all the lip service [the Church] gives to the laity being given responsibility, . . . in my experience . . . even the bidding prayers have to be censored . . . I think laity involvement means the priest telling them what to do and then they do all of it. (Interview, 16 Dec. 1992)

The informant concluded by suggesting that there needed to be 'a questioning [of] the way in which structures have grown up historically and how they are maintained', less emphasis on hierarchy ('Jesus hated hierarchies'), more accountability and more emphasis on the choices of local communities. Sadly, 'the Church doesn't nurture my spirituality; it's elsewhere. I find it in the everyday nature of my friends, relationships, some Christians, some elsewhere, some in my work.'

A parishioner from the Sacred Heart parish was 'extremely suspicious' of the plans for the post-RENEW period which were 'now
being foisted on the parishes'. He was particularly incensed by the
nurturing of the 'base communities' and was 'appalled by these
political activities' (Field Notes, 4 July 1990). An active participant
in the same parish sadly remarked that 'someone younger, with new
ideas' was required to attend deanery meetings but

no one was coming forward [and] all ideas [were] clergy-led. [There was]
nothing original; the same old faces [were] everywhere and those lay people
who turn up do so because of a sense of duty or because they like an
outing with congenial people. [There was] no real feeling of commitment
to change or progress.   (Field Notes, Jan. 1992)

Two years after the end of RENEW, the same informant observed
that before RENEW there had been enthusiasm and competition in
the elections for membership of the Parish Council but that 'democracy has now vanished'. It was said that the new parish priest
insisted that people must be 'action-centred', and 'chosen' so that a
core committee of dedicated RENEW types now ran the parish with
'guidance'. Most people, however, had lost interest, the very committed felt guilty that they were not doing enough, and others were
apathetic. RENEW had been great in increasing social relationships
between people and encouraging scripture reading but not much
else (Field Notes, 3 Dec. 1992).
   Such testimonies bear on one of the central concerns of our
study: the question of 'who controls spirituality within the Church?'
The accumulated evidence from our study was that it was predominantly top down, in spite of much talk about lay 'empowerment'
and 'taking ownership' of the 'process'.
   We have indicated that RENEW required a highly committed
core team in each parish to promote the 2½-year-long programme.
Inevitably this provided opportunities for some activists to promote
their own version of religious revitalization with the legitimation
provided by the diocesan-wide adoption of RENEW. We have no
evidence that this was widespread but an informant did indicate
that in St Thomas's parish there had been 'a surge of charismatics,
very powerful people in the parish'. RENEW had opened up the
parish to their influence and this had been 'very, very divisive'.
While it had been extremely therapeutic for some people, it 'had
obviously caused hurtful divisions amongst parishioners' and some
resentment at the élite-like pretensions of the 'elect' group in the
parish (Conversation, 10 Apr. 1992).
   Some committed participants in RENEW were critical that some of

the implicit aims of RENEW were not taken on board by the diocesan decision-makers. At the level of the diocese, decision-making remained the prerogative of the bishop and his close advisers and at that level, there was no faith-sharing in the way that was being encouraged at the parish level. Such criticisms were made by several senior actors in diocesan affairs. One informant also complained of the 'ambivalence', for example, over whether to continue to promote the small communities or groups which had emerged during RENEW, or allow a return to the pre-RENEW ecumenical Lenten house groups. More generally, 'I find muddle in the diocese; something radically wrong' (Interview, 17 Nov. 1992). Similar concerns were expressed by another key participant who observed that there had never been 'proper heads of department meetings' at the diocesan level in order to give the diocesan agencies 'a sense of ownership' as a team moving forward with RENEW.

The quality management approach that underpinned the RENEW organization was not part of the central diocesan way of working . . . My perception [is] that at the heart of the diocese there's a muddle and I think there's a lack of professionalism . . . [But it] either was not ready for [the new management tools] or was not prepared to alter . . . There's a sort of amateurism at the heart of the diocese . . . There's a laity issue there as well . . . (Interview, 25 Nov. 1992)

This informant proceeded to suggest that the diocesan structures and clergy in some cases felt threatened by the very competent lay people who had been applying their professional skills during RENEW in managing parish affairs. The implication was that in spite of rhetoric about collaborative ministry, lay empowerment, and shared ownership, the reality was that the clerical leadership in the diocese strongly resisted any shift from a 'mechanistic' to an 'organic' management structure, at least at the diocesan level.

Before concluding this section, it is important to acknowledge the importance of contingencies such as a sudden change in parish priest or the sudden illness of key committee members in the parishes. In order to illustrate the possible implications of such unforeseen contingencies we will draw on some of our ethnographic data from St Cyril's parish. The parish priest in this parish was a much-loved man who became ill and died before the end of Season 4 of RENEW. During the critical period before the appointment of a new parish priest, a small cadre of three or four lay activists was able to replace the priest in all but sacramental and preaching functions. Although the former priest had regarded them very much as part of the ministerial team, their empowerment and the delegation of powers it entailed came only with RENEW and the later illness and death of the priest. The new parish priest was seen more as a traditional fund-raiser than a pastor and he soon alienated parish activists over plans to build a new parish hall. Disaffection was reflected in sudden changes in the offertory collections and the migration of some activists to neighbouring parishes. The RENEW team kept the programme 'on track' but without the inspiration of the former priest, there was no expansion of the agenda of RENEW.

As a result of RENEW, a number of activities in St Cyril's parish, such as a range of secretarial work and liturgical planning, were now performed by lay people. Other activities which pre-dated RENEW, such as sacramental catechesis, appeared to be better organized. Such developments are probably fairly general throughout the diocese. It is interesting to note that several key members of St Cyril's parish were only able to contribute substantial proportions of their time and energies to parish work because they were not in full-time employment. There was still an absence of any notion of full-time paid lay ministries in the parish, a situation almost certainly true of nearly all the parishes in the diocese. The 'gatekeeper' role of the parish priest cannot be underestimated. In all the parishes for which we have some data, the priest was a key actor who could inspire and empower lay people, on the one hand, or alienate them, on the other.

8.7   An Evaluation of RENEW

In 1985 James Kelly evaluated the RENEW programme for the Lilly Foundation in the United States and concluded that 'RENEW "works", but not quite as dramatically as its sponsors claimed'. He commented on the avoidance of controversial issues with 'many men and women seek[ing] mostly to deepen their attachment to the core elements of the average Christian life: the Scriptures, the Mass, prayer, uncomplicated fellowship and support' but expressed 'some unease about RENEW's avoidance of doctrinal disputes'. He suggested fears of 'an unhealthy parish pietism' might have been exaggerated and that while 'RENEW does not push too hard . . . the distinction between charity and justice . . . receives more attention than the materials themselves might suggest' and in the United States was reflected in an increase in the number of parishes with Social Concerns Committees. He pointed out that RENEW involved large numbers of lay leaders, especially women, and that these were likely to be essential as the Church faced a major decline in the number of priests, and encouraged small group discussion on controversial issues such as those raised by the American bishops in their pastoral letters on peace and economic justice. In sum, Kelly concluded that RENEW sought 'to provoke piety not passion' (1987: 197–9).

At the end of Season 2 in St Matthew's parish we similarly concluded that parishioners 'were primarily socially constructing a revitalized personal piety and devotionalism and also promoting and welcoming the development of more friendships and community-building occasions in the parish' (Hornsby-Smith *et al.*, 1991: 110). None of the data we collected in the remaining three seasons of RENEW or in the three years after the end of the programme itself dented that judgement. Indeed, the special study of 'the politics of social concern', which we reported in the previous chapter, served to reinforce the judgement that RENEW was a top-down programme of renewal with a strong emphasis on traditional forms of piety. In spite of some rhetoric about lay empowerment, we observed few examples of any departure from the formal guidelines laid down. It is true that there was evidence of independence and sometimes authoritarianism on the part of some small group leaders but this was almost always in the direction of traditional forms of Catholicism. We came across no instances where there was serious innovation in a non-traditional direction.

In this chapter we have traced the follow-up of the RENEW programme in the Diocese of Downlands for a period of three years. We have reviewed some of the claims made for RENEW both in the research diocese and in a number of other dioceses. Drawing heavily on our focused interviews and ethnographies we have suggested that the official account was biased and systematically selected out positive features of RENEW. The reality was not so tidy but was contingent on a large number of contextual variables. For all its much-vaunted community-building capabilities, we have found little evidence of any significant, measurable, or long-lasting consequences. The suspicion remains that the research diocese has changed little from 1988 when it embarked on the RENEW programme. We suggest that there is little evidence yet that a significant *process* of pastoral renewal has been set in train.

We have examined some of the outcomes of RENEW. First, we reviewed the way in which the Diocese of Downlands followed up the RENEW programme. Under the bishop's leadership, people in the diocese were widely consulted in *Planning for the '90s* about their needs and priorities for the future. From these emerged the seven priorities for diocesan pastoral action. It is interesting that these were all institutional or 'churchy' concerns. Even the matter of social concerns appeared to have been domesticated and the matter which was particularly addressed during the period under review, viz. homelessness, was a relatively 'safe' and non-controversial matter. RENEW did not encourage the addressing of any of the major social issues of the late 1980s or early 1990s, such as Christian responses to contraception, abortion, marital breakdown, child abuse, homosexuality, embryo experimentation, redundancy and unemployment, the widening gap between rich and poor, the rise of racism, global warming and environmental concerns, and stewardship. RENEW failed to offer any form of action-response other than in the parish context. The form of spirituality promoted tended to be personal, individual, and pietistic rather than communal and justice-orientated. It was parochial and inward-looking rather than ecumenical and outward-looking. The post-RENEW developments in the diocese seem likely to reinforce these trends with a continuation of a strong diocesan agenda, timetable, and expectations of the parishes.

Secondly, in this chapter we considered the attempt in St Matthew's parish to follow up RENEW and develop its own parish plan for the next few years. In the event, although a coherent plan was devised by the PSG, it was strongly constrained by the proposals emerging from the diocese and in particular by the bishop's vision (a fact that the PSG was largely unaware of at the time). In spite of the attempt to respond to expressions of priorities within the parish, there was a great deal of scepticism about the plan. In spite of its traditions of caring and small group activities pre-dating RENEW, a certain weariness seemed to have set in as the older activists despaired of recruiting significant numbers of new leaders.

Thirdly, in this chapter we attempted to provide an overview of official evaluations of RENEW both within the Diocese of Downlands and, somewhat briefly, from the four Scottish dioceses which had used the RENEW programme in the late 1980s or early 1990s. Without exception, all regarded RENEW as having been a great success in terms of small group faith-sharing experiences and more scripture reading for large numbers of Catholics, greater sense of parish community and diocese, more active leaders, and a greater social concern. Only one bishop admitted that the evidence was not always strong. But hard evidence in support of RENEW's success, in terms of a significant return of 'lapsed' Catholics to Mass or material evidence of a greater parish commitment or social concern, was not forthcoming. There is no convincing evidence that RENEW was a better bet than indigenous programmes might have been or that its effects would be long-lasting.

Fourthly, we offered a broader perspective on RENEW from the grass roots than the diocesan evaluation process allowed. We demonstrated that a number of highly committed participants in the RENEW programme were extremely sceptical about its consequences. Issues such as lay empowerment were seen as instances of 'controlled participation' and criticisms were made that the centre of the diocese itself had failed to follow the process which was being sold to the parishes. Some of our respondents suggested that the theme of lay empowerment was a device which helped the bishop bypass clerical intransigence. We pointed out that in spite of a great deal of lay input into the programme over three years or more, parish developments could be very dependent on contingencies, such as the collaboration in shared ministry with a supportive priest. In spite of the rhetoric about lay empowerment, the legitimacy accorded to lay activists remains heavily dependent upon their clerical leaders and hence vulnerable to idiosyncratic exercises in clerical authoritarianism. On this, RENEW offered no obvious help but rather tended to reinforce existing hierarchical structures.

At one stage in the analysis of our data we sensed that there might indeed be strong evidence of a process of clericalization in the diocese in the period since the end of RENEW. This seemed to be the experience of the Justice and Peace Commission at that time, as we noted in the previous chapter. However, we are not certain that that hypothesis can be sustained when taking a broader view of diocesan developments. The comparison of the entries in the annual diocesan directories does not provide convincing evidence either way. The case for a process of clericalization may be 'not proven', but by the same token, that for the contrary process of lay empowerment is also weak and unconvincing.

A lay person who had been very deeply involved in RENEW expressed the view that there needed to be a shift of diocesan resources to lay facilitators:

If you think about it, the amount of money spent on the upkeep of the cathedral is equivalent to the employment of three lay people . . . The Church these days is not bricks and mortar . . . The Church actually, out there, . . . is people, living and breathing. And people need people to sustain them. They do not need bricks and mortar . . . Honestly, that's my personal experience . . . [Y]ou get more value out of one person going into a parish to talk to the people concerned and you're likely to get more involvement if you've got a human being who's contacting a human being. We still plough vast quantities of money into bricks and mortar when, in fact, we should be putting it into the real expense of the Church, which is people. (Interview, 2 Dec. 1992)

Finally, it would be an omission if we made no comment about the financial costs of RENEW. The inadequacy of the specification of the resource implications of RENEW was one of the three main concerns we had at the start of our study in September 1988 (see also Hornsby-Smith *et al.*, 1991: 102–4). In the event we did not pursue this matter in any depth. For the record, the Diocesan Financial Secretary reported in 1990 that the gross cost of RENEW in the period 1987–90 had been £352,310. Allowing for small charitable grants, the cost to central diocesan funds was £104,551 and the proportion allocated to parishes, mainly through their purchase of materials, was £225,759. But this latter figure related only to income received by the RENEW office for supplying materials to the parishes and was undoubtedly boosted by other expenditure, such as photocopying, telephones, printing, stationary, and other incidental expenses which were not quantified (Letter, 25 July 1990). The total cost, therefore, is unlikely to have been less than £500,000, or £10 per Mass attender.

While these figures seem modest, the diocese appeared to be in financial crisis at the end of the RENEW programme (*DT* Aug. and Sep. 1991) and two long-service lay people in major diocesan agencies left to obtain alternative employment. Informants have suggested that the financial crisis would have happened anyway and was due to other factors. They also denied that the loss of senior lay employees was primarily a consequence of the expense of RENEW. Whatever the causes, before the end of the RENEW programme in 1990, the bishop appealed for £2 million in interest-free loans from the laity to help reduce the financial problems in the diocese (*DT* Feb. 1991). The appeal had reached £811,000 by Easter 1991 (*DT* Apr. 1991).

9

The Politics of Spirituality

9.1 From Opportunistic Case Study to Model of Spirituality

This study of the process by which RENEW came to be adopted, implemented, and followed up in the Diocese of Downlands arose as a piece of opportunistic research. We, as Roman Catholic sociologists in the diocese, felt that it was such an important pastoral initiative in Britain that it ought to be the subject of serious investigation. It would consume a very large proportion of the diocesan resources, staff, and both clerical and lay energies over a period of several years, and we seemed to be best placed to undertake such a study.

We had no particular axe to grind though before RENEW started we did have a number of reservations about the initial lack of specification of the goals of the programme and the seemingly excessive concern with setting up appropriate structures. This, on the face of it, appeared to be a classic case of goal displacement (Merton, 1957) with a bureaucratic obsession with *means* replacing a concern to clarify the essential *goals* of the whole exercise. A third area of initial concern was a failure to specify clearly the resource implications. The sponsors of RENEW seemed remarkably touchy about the costs of RENEW and questions about the beneficiaries of copyright payments and fees for the facilitators from the International RENEW Office. In the event, apart from some initial reflections in an early paper (Hornsby-Smith et al., 1991: 102–3), we did not pursue this aspect of the programme or examine the financial advantages for the publishers of the RENEW literature. It seems that the Archdiocese of Newark did not benefit to any extent and the cost estimates we made for the Diocese of Downlands before the start of the programme were reasonably accurate, as we noted in the previous chapter.

The fact that our study was almost entirely unfunded meant that we were constrained in the range of research we could pursue. As

CULTURAL AGENDA	SOURCE OF STRATEGY	
	Leadership	Grass roots
Modern	Renewal	Re-formation
Traditional	Restoration	Revitalization

FIG. 9.1   A Typology of Religious Change Strategies

we indicated in Chapter 1, by substantially adopting an ethnographic approach, involving a great deal of participant observation and focused interviews with a wide range of informants, we were able to concentrate on the interpretation of the RENEW process. The literature we read on renewal and revitalization movements, resource mobilization, on power and social control, and on community development research, all provided valuable insights. These supplemented our own previous understandings of the religious transformations in the Roman Catholic Church in the period after the Second Vatican Council (Hornsby-Smith, 1987; 1989; 1991), and of community development projects (Norris, 1977). In our study we were able to make use of soft data analysis, a technique developed in the context of an investigation of a community development project (Norris, 1981).

We began to interpret our investigation as a study of the promotion of a specific kind of spirituality. In our attempts to conceptualize our research problem, we came to focus on two key dimensions: the organizational dimension, including the matter of who it was who controlled the spirituality, and the cultural dimension of what type of spirituality was being promoted. The former dimension gave us few problems and we distinguished 'top-down' and 'bottom-up' forms of control. The cultural dimension posed far more problems because the potential elements of culture: this-worldly or other-worldly, communal or individual, mission-orientated or individual salvation-orientated, rules subject to reinterpretation or unchanging, and so on, did not all seem to stack up in the same direction. We attempted to resolve these difficulties in Chapter 2 by focusing on responses to modernity but found it necessary to elaborate the distinction between communal and individual forms of spirituality by taking into account the extent to which a social project was pursued (Chapter 7).

In the light of our analysis, we suggest it would be helpful to make the following conceptual distinctions (Figure 9.1):

Renewal is a form of spirituality promoted by the clerical leadership in the Church which aims to respond to perceptions of modernity and the same leadership's understanding of contemporary needs. In this type of spirituality, the leadership retains control and aims to update the cultural agenda. In the Catholic Church the conciliar process of *aggiornamento* seems best to fit here.

Re-formation is a form of spirituality which emerges from the perceived needs of the laity and, in addition, presents a wider agenda for the religious quest while remaining under the direct control of the laity. In the Catholic Church this seems to be illustrated most clearly in some types of liberation spiritualities.

Restoration is that form of spirituality which has the express purpose of restoring traditional forms of piety and devotionalism under the explicit guidance and control of the clerical leadership in the Church. The spirituality of Opus Dei seems to fit well into this category.

Revitalization is a form of spirituality emerging from the grass roots and remaining under the control of the laity which aims to reinvigorate traditional forms of religious piety and devotionalism. Popular forms of indigenous Catholicism, such as local pilgrimages and some Marian devotions, fit well into this category.

It is our contention that this typology, in terms of the two dimensions of social control and culture, provides a useful framework for the comparison of a wide range of spiritualities. On the one hand it draws attention to the power and influence of the controllers of spirituality and their particular religious and institutional interests. We suggest that in view of its political importance, too little sociological attention has hitherto been paid to this dimension. On the other hand, the typology addresses the question of cultural content and what the controllers define as really 'religious'. It also considers the extent to which the content aims to respond to the agenda of modernity and, in particular, the degree to which a social project is defined as religious. The sociological analysis of this dimension draws attention to the extent to which cultural definitions of what counts as religious are socially determined and historically contexted.

Taken together we argued in Chapter 2 that these two dimensions offer a fruitful basis for the comparative analysis of spiritualities, not only within Catholicism, but also in other Christian traditions and possibly also the traditions of other faiths. Furthermore, our study of RENEW and review of the historical structuring of spiritualities, point to the possibilities for diachronic forms of investigation of the different paths taken by spiritualities over time. (Obvious examples here might be the gradual control of Franciscan spirituality by the medieval Church, and the way in which the charismatic movement has become domesticated and incorporated by institutional Catholicism in recent years.) Thus, what originated as an exploratory case study of a religious programme to reinvigorate Catholics and their parishes in a single diocese, led us to propose a general framework for the comparative analysis of different types of spiritualities.

9.2 The RENEW Case Study

We commenced our study of RENEW because it appeared to be a significant attempt within the Roman Catholic Church to reinvigorate its members and its institutional life. It aimed to halt the steady decline in membership, enhance the religious vitality of its members, and rejuvenate its institutional life in the parishes, particularly by co-opting the laity more fully into the Church's mission. It also sought to clarify and strengthen its response to the new problems emerging in the 'modern' world.

One sign that these issues might be addressed by RENEW was the very strong insistence that RENEW was a process rather than a programme. Clergy and laity were encouraged to 'take ownership' of the mission of the Church and to undertake a journey with unpredictable outcomes, but with faith in the guidance of the Spirit who would empower them. Optimistic promises of radical trans-formations in the community of believers softened the blow of the breadth of organization which activists were required to set up in order to get the whole programme up and running. A review of the literature on revitalization movements and community development projects, however, led us to suspect that, given its basic organizational structure, RENEW was not likely to promote a new transformative process of the kind suggested at the outset.

Our fieldwork experiences were vital to our developing understand-ing. It was only when we became participants in RENEW that we began to see it in reality not so much as an unpredictable process but as a programme to invigorate both individuals and parishes. We then formulated our perception—one which did seem alive in a number of historians' analyses of previous revivalist movements in Christianity—that the development of religious consciousness, be-lief, and action were bound up with both internal Church politics and the politics of Church members' activity in society generally. We realized that sociologically, whatever the Church's ultimate source of inspiration, the nature of spirituality and what people become in religious terms, was intimately bound up with the nature of the Church as an organization, a community of people collaborating out of a sense of religious commitment and for religious purposes within a specific social and historical context. This realization led us to face up to the realities of Church history and the experiences of past spiritualities and religious movements. We came to the view that the two key variables for understanding their rise and decline were those of the organization itself, and the encounter of the institution and its members with a specific historical world, and the culture within which those members had to work out their own salvation and in which they were called to testify as God's witnesses.

While RENEW was clearly an attempt to respond to the call of the Second Vatican Council for genuine renewal at all levels in the Church, it soon became clear that structural renewal in the Church—questioning the location of power and redesigning ministry both from the top down and from the bottom up—was not part of the agenda. For all the claims made for the process, not only was the real focus on bringing back to life the existing structure of the parish but, as we documented in Chapters 3 and 4, the power to initiate change was primarily exerted by the bishop from the top. Two types of change were to be encouraged. First, within the parish it was hoped to bypass priests who were set in their ways and galvanize those who had become despondent or passive in the face of the inactivity of parish life, and to activate laity to take on 'ministerial' roles, modernizing the liturgy, becoming special ministers, and setting up voluntary social concern activities, largely within the parish boundaries. Secondly, the attempt was also made to modify the 'piety' structure of English Roman Catholics. To the traditional dimension of individual conversion was added the dimension of group support for evangelization. The specific nature of these changes and the detailed instructions embedded in the programme meant that the empowerment of both clergy and laity was limited.

In Chapters 5, 6, and 7 we reported on our surveys of parishioners and small group members in a number of parishes and drew heavily on fieldnotes and interviews with a wide range of informants to present an account of the RENEW experience and its follow-up in the Diocese of Downlands. We analysed our findings in terms of our basic typology of spiritualities and showed that the effect of RENEW was to reinforce traditional bureaucratic and hierarchical styles of diocesan organization. The evidence presented in Chapter 6 demonstrated that although loyal participants felt that their efforts during RENEW had been rewarded, relatively little change among most participants took place on dimensions regarded as important by the sponsors. We noted, in particular, that the raising of consciousness about justice issues in Season 3 was not sustained and there was a collapse of concern in the remaining seasons.

This was explored further in Chapter 7 where we examined the participation in RENEW of activists in the diocesan Justice and Peace movement. We showed how they were initially suspicious that the promotion of social concern would dilute and domesticate a more challenging and prophetic stress on justice themes. After much debate, activists opted for a pragmatic participation in RENEW and were particularly prominent in preparations for Season 3, 'empowerment by the Holy Spirit', which dealt with justice themes in scripture and the recent teaching of the Church. These efforts appeared to have borne fruit in Season 3 but unexpectedly did not survive at the same level in the remaining two seasons. Some responses to a growing problem of homelessness in the diocese could be attributed to the action of RENEW small groups. At the diocesan level, however, there remained difficulties of resourcing and a measure of clericalization did not indicate that lay people had been empowered as a result of RENEW.

Finally, in Chapter 8 we reviewed some of the developments in the diocese since the end of the RENEW programme in November 1990. We interpret these as continuing the process of strong central initiatives and directives, in spite of some resistance in the parishes, and several exercises over the past decade or so to consult the laity. Our point is that there was very little evidence in fact to support the unwarranted claims of RENEW to have empowered the laity. The power of the priest as a gatekeeper was demonstrated most obviously where there was a change of priest in a parish.

Given the evidence we have reviewed, then, where does RENEW 'fit' in terms of the four-fold typology of religious change strategies? It is intrinsic to the Weberian concept of 'ideal-type' that they are rarely, if ever, found in their entirety in any empirical situation. Thus we cannot say that RENEW lies clearly and unambiguously in any one of the four cells in Figure 9.1. In reality it falls somewhere in the middle of all four cells, though in the case of individual participants the identification with one particular cell might be quite strong. We have produced a great deal of evidence, notably from our soft data analysis and our analysis of the process of selecting the option of RENEW, implementing it and following it up, to demonstrate clearly that in the Diocese of Downlands (but also, as far as we can judge the evidence we have been given, in other dioceses, too) that RENEW was very much a top-down pastoral initiative. Even so, part of its rhetoric stressed lay empowerment and indeed, we did come across a few instances of lay initiative. When we consider the cultural dimension, again much of the rhetoric stressed the modernization of religious cultures and an emphasis on small Christian communities. Here again, though, the empirical reality was not that clear-cut, especially when we extended the analysis to include a consideration of the social project.

In practice there was much talk about 'opening up' to new forms of religious culture but most activity was directed to reinforcing traditional forms of piety and devotionalism. We would suggest that the overwhelming bulk of the data we have reviewed in this study indicate that RENEW was primarily concerned with renewal and restoration. While there might have been some scope for the revitalization of traditional piety and devotionalism, there was practically no evidence of the spontaneous emergence of re-formation.

9.3 Church Renewal or Social Movement?

In the light of the findings from our case study, we concluded that RENEW was primarily a strategy of Church renewal and restoration, initiated, directed, and led from the top down. It did not, and cannot in RENEW's present form, stimulate social movement from the grass roots in response to perceived religious and social needs, and did not seek either to revitalize traditional and popular Catholicism or to generate emergent forms of religious commitment. Among the findings which we have briefly outlined above we would draw particular attention to five which have implications for the future of the Church in the research diocese.

First, RENEW was more of a fixed and highly structured programme than a process which allowed, or indeed encouraged, initiative and spontaneity. In practice there was considerable hierarchical control in initiating it, and near total control over the content. The major themes, season-by-season and week-by-week, the agenda to be followed by the small groups, and the liturgical contents to be followed by the parishes, were all prescribed.

Secondly, the consequence of the top-down strategy of social control was that there was little scope for the development of a sense of religious responsibility for the individual, for the group or parish, and for the modern world generally, despite the empowerment of some activists. While some agenda-setting is inevitable, the level of control and its emphatically top-down directionality were such that it was almost impossible to convert the programme to a processual experience. Not surprisingly, therefore, there was little evidence that large numbers of Catholics took control of their own and their groups' socio-religious circumstances.

Thirdly, from the outset the focus of the small groups was scriptural and abstract rather than concrete and experiential. It did not originate from the everyday experiences of the modern world in which the believers lived and on which they would then have based their scriptural reflections. We believe that such a groundedness in everyday reality is an essential ingredient in any genuine process of generating popular commitment to Catholicism. Only when this happens can one talk about a genuine social movement of religious change. Such themes are at the centre of Freire's pedagogy (1972) which, in opposition to the 'banking' system of education, stresses the pursuit of conscientization, the raising of a Christian reflexivity about the everyday experienced reality, and the striving for liberation, all of which are themes which lie at the heart of radical contemporary Catholic theology (Gutierrez, 1974).

Fourthly, opportunities for prophetic challenges in RENEW were very deliberately limited on the pragmatic grounds that such challenges were counter-productive. RENEW tried hard to replace the concept of 'social justice' with the less threatening concept of 'social concern'. Thus there was encouragement for 'caring' in the local community and the amelioration of deprivations, such as homelessness, but a failure to address issues of injustice in the modern world, war, ethnic cleansing and racism, the trade in arms, international debt and trade restrictions, famine, unemployment, poverty, and the distribution of resources in modern society. Such charitable responses as RENEW encouraged did nothing to challenge the underlying causes of injustice. We concluded that the whole style of RENEW precluded the development of a Christian basis for justice consciousness. The generally conservative character of the Catholic population in the Diocese of Downlands was undisturbed by the gentleness of the RENEW approach.

A fifth finding, to which more attention needs to be paid, is the relative underinvolvement of men and the substantial lack of involvement of young Catholics. The former demonstrates that 'the degree of involvement in the work processes of modern industrial society correlates negatively with the degree of involvement in church-oriented religion' (Luckmann, 1967: 30). The failure to enthuse the young in significant numbers is likely to have particularly serious implications in that it suggests that the attempt to renew institutional Catholicism will stumble because of the continuing alienation of the younger cohorts from orthodox religious practice.

In the light of the above conclusions we would speculate that movements of revitalization and re-formation are likely to develop in only two areas, and even these are likely to be extremely precarious. First of all, it is possible that there could be a movement of social concern. This might take the form of either sporadic (e.g. on behalf of miners threatened with pit closures in 1991) or more sustained, ameliorative assistance on behalf of those elements of the underclass deemed to be deserving. Thus there is evidence of a generalized concern over homelessness and a rash of projects to provide drop-in centres or night shelters throughout the diocese. Such charitable responses, 'corporal acts of mercy', are entirely worthy. It seems unlikely, however, that such responses will ever develop into a movement providing comprehensive cover either in the diocese or in the nation. Nor do they tackle the task of analysis of the causes of the disadvantage or injustice, so that charity rather than justice is the only possible outcome. Three years after RENEW in the Diocese of Downlands, even in the area of homelessness, there is no evidence of a significant diocesan-wide movement on their behalf.

A second possible movement relates to the maturing of the RENEW small groups into small Christian communities, regularly meeting together for prayer, scripture reflection, and action-responses to some of the concrete issues faced in the everyday lives of the members and in the wider society. The emergence of such groups was undoubtedly one of the hopes of the bishop in the post-RENEW period and some diocesan resources were put into the encouragement of such developments. But again, three years after RENEW, relatively few of the former RENEW faith-sharing groups continue to meet or show signs of developing into significant communities such as envisaged by the originators of RENEW (Kleissler *et al.*, 1991). We would speculate that where such groups do continue they would tend to emerge on the border between cells C and D in Figure 5.1, i.e. promoting a traditional religious culture whether under direct or loose hierarchical control. Such groups might form around devotional projects and have some kind of 'chaplain' arrangement or they might develop pentecostal-type programmes and even absorb religious influences from outside Catholicism. Such developments might become an irritant for the clerical leadership but their continuity is likely to be problematic and their social impact negligible. Other groups might remain within the ambit of traditional devotionalism: Marian or rosary groups, First Friday groups, pilgrimage and miracle-oriented thaumaturgical groups, etc.

But the main model coming out of the RENEW experience is the continuation of a slowly declining, parish-centred Church, with higher

Types of Religious Culture	Types of Organization		
	Traditional	Modified	Modern
Modern	1	2	3
Modified	4	5	6
Traditional	7	8	9

Fig. 9.2   An Extended Typology of Spiritualities

levels of involvement among the middle classes and the more highly educated than among the working classes. The middle classes are still able to develop 'God-speak' and a sufficiently coherent individual spirituality from contact with prayer groups and parish liturgies to enable them to cope with their everyday lives. However, they continue to face the problem of transmitting their faith to their children. Far from stemming the steady haemorrhage of members, the likelihood is of ever-decreasing numbers of church attenders and the continuing tension between the 'cultural mobilization of memory' promoted by the institutional authorities, and what has been called the 'ethical prophecy and emotional mobilization of memory' favoured by young people (Hervieu-Léger, 1994: 137).

9.4   Church and Spirituality in the Modern Era

What kind of Church and spirituality, then, can we expect to emerge in the future? We can use Weberian ideal-type constructs to hypothesize a range of possibilities although that range is likely to be restricted by the concrete circumstances of today, including the type of society within which the Roman Catholic Church finds itself. In Figure 9.2 we have proposed an extended typology of spiritualities in terms of our two key variables: type of organization and type of religious culture. We have elaborated our previous model to include intermediate categories of both organization and culture. This generates nine theoretically possible types of spirituality. In practice, however, the range of empirical instances is likely to be restricted.

Thus traditional Church spirituality, based on the medieval or post-Reformation model, is not going to be a practical alternative because of developments which have taken place in the modern consciousness. Even those who might sympathize with such a model would almost certainly shrink from the denial of freedom of thought found in the medieval Church and the role of the Inquisition and use of coercive sanctions. A simplistic, fundamentalist approach would be precluded by the teaching authorities of the Church today. In other words, there is no going back and type 7 is unlikely to be a viable option. As far as the other possible combinations are concerned, we would suggest that there is likely to be a tendency to align organization with religious culture and hence shift to the two remaining congruent types (Etzioni, 1961: 12–13) in cells 5 and 3. We conclude our study by describing these two alternative types of spirituality in ideal-typical terms. (It will be recalled that an ideal-type is not a description of empirical reality but a model to facilitate the comparison and analysis of actual cases.)

A   A Modified Spirituality

A modified traditional Church with a modified traditional spirituality appears the most likely to emerge and dominate, particularly in Europe. In its pure form it has the following characteristics:

(1) The modified traditional Church would continue to be highly centralized and have a substantial and ever-growing Roman *Curia*, as bureaucracy in the modern period threatens to get out of control. In the absence of radical decentralization, regional bodies, such as the Conference of European Bishops, are likely to increase in importance.

(2) There is likely to be an increasing stress on the primacy of the papacy which will attempt to exercise direct control over cultural developments within the institutional Church world-wide, and strive for the imposition of Catholic values in societies where Catholics remain a dominant majority. In other words it will seek to retain 'monopoly Catholicism' wherever it can (Martin, 1978; Inglis, 1987; Fulton, 1991). In situations of religious and cultural pluralism, the Church is more likely to adopt a strategy of accommodation, 'play the pluralist game of religious free enterprise, and come to terms as best [it] can with the plausibility problem by modifying [its] product in accordance with consumer demands' (Berger, 1973: 156). In such a situation rigid battle lines over sexual and family morality and the sacrality of life will be renewed.

(3) Current organizational patterns of male clerical dominance would be reinforced, and female sensitivities (e.g. over the failure to use inclusive language in the new Catechism) would be over-ridden. Such dominance would require lay deference, and this, in turn, might be thought to justify the suppression of open discussion of institutional limitations and weaknesses. The maintenance of a clerically-

dominated Church would be promoted with compulsory celibacy for the priesthood.

(4) This type of Church would be pleased, though probably not contented, with the development of an inward-looking group spirituality, one in which the laity found comfort and support within the religious community for their individually-oriented spirituality. A locally-oriented social concern would be promoted. But this level of social consciousness would not be seen as a bad achievement in countries where Catholics were in a minority and monopoly religious politics were not possible. Under these conditions a denominational, pluralistically tolerant but inwardly looking Church would be regarded by Rome as the only practical alternative.

(5) The modified traditional Church would be happy to concentrate on the growth of the holiness of the individual in the belief that an appropriate social consciousness would emerge from it. The emphasis would be on fasting and self-denial, the life of individual prayer, and the development of a personal consciousness of God. There would be strong emphases on personal conversion, good works, and the vocation to the religious life. The modified traditional Church would retain a narrow definition of what constitutes the social project of the Church. Issues of family, sexual, and life moralities would remain prominent while some distance would be retained from social issues, such as those of war and peace, the legitimacy of nuclear deterrence strategies, and the whole range of socio-economic issues from unemployment to aid and development. While lay people are clearly expected to act on the former matters on the assumption of a unanimity of moral values, there is a pragmatic accommodation to primarily class-based differences of socio-economic values.

(6) This type of Church, under the impact of modernity, would tend to be isolated from mainstream social life, absorbed with the promotion of relationships among its members, the mutual aid and support they offer each other, and the quality of its own inner life, highly conservative, but unable to address the problems of the world outside; a Church without a social message or social significance in the state or civic society. Its entire social project would then be reduced to the effort to maintain a balance between sect-like intransigence and the accommodation to secular values.

B   Modern Spirituality

In looking at the issue of a modern Church spirituality, there are difficulties in applying a Weberian ideal-type analysis since a form of critical and futuristic sociology is required. (Weber's sociology was essentially historical.) Critical theory makes judgements about what type of change could be tolerated without the dynamism of a religious community's experience of its symbols being radically impaired. In the case of Christianity and the Catholic tradition, one would be defining whether or not its religious reality was disappearing and something else taking its place. It may be that theological aspects are filtering through. Even so, we would maintain that Christianity as a project, and for that matter all world religions, can be sustained in conditions of modernity, but only through dramatic transformations of both structure and culture. We point out that such transformations have occurred before: in Christianity, for example, with its transformation from a subordinate religion to that of the religion of the Roman Empire; and in Judaism, in the passage from a Torah-only based religion to one dominated by Torah and Talmud. What might be at issue is the extent to which a papal-dominated Catholic Church might be transformed if the role of the papacy was radically altered. We suggest the following ideal-type of a modern Church spirituality for Roman Catholicism:

(1) In a modern Church with a modern spirituality the Church would radically decentralize its organizational structures. Resort to papal primacy would be a final port of call, a reference point for the world-wide unity of the Church. It would only intervene when such unity was threatened or when there were internal squabbles in local Churches or when the rights of individuals were under threat. The Vatican as a state would be dissolved and the pope would revert to activities as a special bishop, though still with some role in raising Catholic consciousness. He would still retain a superior's role in bringing to task individual bishops, but this would be an occasional rather than a routine feature of his role. Ecumenical Councils would be frequent occurrences and would be the main vehicle for recognizing the consciousness of the whole Church. Both Councils and the Bishop of Rome would develop their consciousness-raising role and seek to mobilize the Church world-wide to address the issues facing the modern world as well as seeking to rejuvenate individual and group religious consciousness at the same time.

(2) Bishops would be appointed locally following wide consultations among priests and lay people in the dioceses. The local diocesan Church would have a great deal of autonomy both in the development of its own response to and relations with the local society and in the ordering of its ministry. Issues such as the celibacy of the priests, the distribution of the leadership roles of priest, prophet, and teacher, and women's role in the Church would be solved

locally in the light of local, national, or ethnic needs. Bishops' Conferences would have decision-making responsibilities at national and regional levels.

(3) The modern Church at all levels would recognize its mission to the wider society and the modern world. It would be concerned to address the crises which it faces and put its physical and spiritual resources into addressing the issues facing the contemporary world. Thus, while the spiritual life would continue to have concern for the inner relationship of the individual with God, conscientization would also aim to raise a group awareness and response to the world-wide mission of universal love through the following: the search for justice and human rights for all; stewardship for the globe and its resources; and an equitable distribution of wealth, enabling others to achieve sustainable development. Preaching the Good News of salvation through Christ would then exist both in word and in deed and, in addition, would require tolerance and respect for the beliefs of others. By pursuing its mission in this way, the community of the faithful would articulate the relevance of their mission for the modern world (McSweeney, 1980).

(4) In this Church the development of communal forms of spirituality, particularly in small basic Christian communities, clustered together in 'communities of communities', would be actively promoted. This would release energy for, and an openness to, the mission to the modern world; it would articulate an awareness of the continuing closeness of God and the need to turn outwards and express in concrete terms a love of one's neighbour. This task would require its own forms of asceticism, but would still require traditional self-discipline and dedication in order to develop and sustain the necessary strategies and appropriate activities.

(5) This modern type of Church would mobilize its members to seek the reform of the structures of injustice in their own society. It would encourage its members to engage in political, economic, and productive life. It would cultivate a respect for the sacrality of life, and address the problems of the distribution of wealth, the restructuring of the global economy, the promotion of sustainable and environmentally safe development around the world.

(6) In the pursuit of these goals, the modern Church would risk its own safety in hostile environments, and also disunity and conflict among its membership. It would commit itself to recover any lost unity, including that between Churches separated by past conflicts. It would seek dialogue with and respect the beliefs of those in other faiths and, in seeking both to receive from their wisdom and to give of its own, would encourage the recognition of the one creator, redeemer, sustainer God throughout the whole world.

9.5 Present Direction of Roman Catholic Spirituality

Our findings on the RENEW programme give credence to views of
what is happening generally in the Church in Britain and throughout the world three decades after the Second Vatican Council, namely
a firming-up of traditional rather than modern spiritualities. In other
words, there is at the moment a modified traditional politics of
spirituality being pursued by the Church authorities from the top.
This is reflected in those pastoral initiatives which are encouraged
(such as RENEW), and the exercise of control over significant renewal initiatives (such as the charismatic movement). Among the
many signs that a modified traditional strategy is being pursued are
the following:

(1) There are no obvious moves to expand the diaconate in the
greater part of Europe or even to debate its desirability in the Church.
The issue was not part of the RENEW materials or even fielded to
parish laity for discussion. This appears to confirm that what RE-
NEW was about excluded matters of Church order and organization, while the type of spirituality promoted was in the main confined
to forms of piety and paternal charity.

(2) Other issues are banned from discussion and serious consideration. The most obvious example, in terms of the inner organization of the Roman Catholic Church (although highly topical in sister
Churches), is the ordination of women. Other examples relevant to
the social project, include the matter of 'over-population' in Third
World countries and its relationship to sustainable development.

(3) There has been an attempt during the present papacy to re-
new.youth and culture in Europe by redeveloping the pilgrimage on
a European scale. The hope appears to be to re-create a Christian
culture in Europe, with a strong devotional base. But this has been
based on a highly selective view of past European history (the
importance of Saints Cyril and Methodius, the Marian shrines, etc.,
rather than the religious wars of the Reformation, the two World
Wars, and the Holocaust). This 'politico-utopian project', presented
on formal pilgrimages, represents 'a cultural mobilization of memory'.
What has been found by Hervieu-Léger (1994), however, is that
contemporary youth in France (and probably elsewhere in Europe),
base their spirituality on their contemporary experiences of modern
society. The world of the past, however selectively presented, is not
salient for them. This suggests that with modernity, religious growth
comes not from a collective memory of a past 'golden age' embedded
in the world of traditional society, but from their experiences in the
modern world of today, within which they are challenged to reread

the root symbols, myths, and rituals of Christianity, in order to mobilize their religious response to that modern world in an appropriate life-long, ethical-religious commitment.

(4) The attempt to reassert a Christian culture in Europe has something of the flavour of 'monopoly Catholicism'. It appears to exclude any genuine inter-faith and inter-Church ecumenical consciousness in the construction of a new Europe, or any attempt to engage with the emerging issues in the world of today, or any development of a shared social consciousness for that world which goes beyond the expression of solidarity with the group of believers.

A modern spirituality, as we conceive of it, can only develop fully when the issues with which modernity confronts us are seen as generating the social agenda of a religious faith. Among the most important issues are the need for a sense of vocation for and a spirituality of both politics and economics, and the development of a spirituality of ecumenism.

(a) Issues which concern the form of the civil society and state point to the importance of developing a sense of the vocation of and spirituality for public life. The agenda is vast and includes such matters as the membership of political parties, and pursuing a religio-political career in politics, economics, or business. Such matters can only be addressed adequately by the Church if there is a genuine encounter with modern society.

(b) In the same way there needs to be a religiously motivated conscientization of economics, taking into account such experiences as the development of a co-operative consciousness in business, a global development consciousness, and the reconciliation of growth strategies with distributive justice. The rights of labour in the global capitalist economy need to be constantly redefined.

(c) There is a need to develop a spirituality of ecumenism at the level of both inter-Church and inter-faith dialogue (see e.g. Hooker and Sargant, n.d.). This is crucial for several reasons. It can be a main vehicle for religious people to overcome ethnic prejudice and racism, and is vital to solving problems of religious strife itself. Also, by allowing joint witness of religion to the secular-minded, it permits the secular-minded themselves to recognize that religious consciousness is not necessarily tainted with such racism and ethnocentrism, and cannot be consigned to the status of the residual baggage of a traditional world.

(d) Finally, there is a need to nurture the signs of development towards a modern spirituality which are to be found amongst activists in the Justice and Peace movement, and those involved, for example, in Third World issues, poverty, or homelessness. There are two dangers which such groups have to negotiate. The first is domestication. Should the nascent spirituality of such groups be swallowed up in cell C (in Figure 5.1, i.e. mechanistic organization and traditional culture), and they become sect-like cults of either pentecostal or devotional bent, and with spiritual growth individualized, we would predict that they would decline in social relevance and influence. There is also a second danger for such groups, that of their marginalization within a modified traditional Church. Here the danger would be centrifugal, with the consequence that such people might withdraw altogether from close contact with institutional Catholicism and seek a non-Church oriented 'religious' legitimation for their action in solidarity with other like-minded people. The consequence might be the emergence of another type of 'ethical prophecy and an emotional mobilization of memory' (Hervieu-Léger, 1994), breaking away from Catholicism as such.

9.6 Religion, Research, and Ethics

We will conclude this study by reflecting briefly on some of the problems we faced as Catholic researchers investigating a major pastoral innovation in the Catholic Church. At the very beginning of our study we noted that the third element in Stoecker's treatment of the case study was 'an involved rather than a distanced researcher' (1991: 108). In our own case we could not have been more involved; all of us were active members of one of the RENEW committees in our own parishes. We participated in the full range of parish activities, such as the small groups, attended deanery and diocesan events associated with RENEW, and undertook a considerable amount of ethnographic work. This invites a consideration of our objectivity and biases, questions of reliability and validity, ethical issues relating to the use of covert and overt research methods, and the matter of confidentiality and anonymity which arose in the course of our six-year study.

Towards the end of our data collection, a number of senior clergy, on the basis of conference papers we had read (Hornsby-Smith *et al.*, 1989, 1990, 1991, 1992), expressed concern at what they saw as our lack of objectivity and detachment, and a bias in favour of critical evaluations of RENEW. These clergy who had been involved in the decision to initiate RENEW in the Diocese of Downlands or who were currently actively involved in its promotion, were 'appalled' at what they regarded as 'distortions', untruths, and inaccuracies, and feared they would do 'great harm', presumably to the International RENEW effort. The implication was that our analysis could not be considered to be of an appropriate professional calibre.

We cannot deny that we were somewhat shaken by the strong reaction of senior clergy with whom we had previously had friendly relationships. We believe we can offer a reasonable defence against these criticisms and we are happy to be judged by our professional peers. In the first place, explicit invitations 'to put on record what your reservations are, if you feel there is serious distortion, if you think there are untruths . . . [because we had] no interest in peddling untruths' (Interview, 7 Oct. 1992), were not taken up.

Secondly, there was a misunderstanding on the part of our respondents about the nature of the research enterprise. They failed to distinguish between our research *hypotheses* at the commencement of our study, and our reported *findings*. One example of this is a sense of grievance which several clergy expressed at our initial consideration of the forthright views of several informants that RENEW might be a very profitable enterprise for the Archdiocese of Newark. In the event it seems that the evidence does not support this hypothesis but, as social scientists, we would insist that it was a perfectly proper question to have posed. Also, because we decided not to pursue the matter, we are not in a position to evaluate the advantages accruing to the publishers of the RENEW materials.

Thirdly, it was claimed that our selection of parishes was unrepresentative and that we had given undue weight to the critics of RENEW. At the end of Season 1 every parish was required by the diocesan authorities to complete an evaluation form. Particular attention was paid by the diocesan RENEW team to claimed small group membership as a proportion of reported Mass attendance figures. In Table 1.2 we reported the distribution of responses for the 113 parishes for which data were publicly available. We have emphasized that our own research should be regarded as a series of case studies and that we are not making any claims about the representativeness of the Diocese of Downlands, as one of around 200 which have followed the RENEW programme. Nor do we claim that St Matthew's parish is necessarily representative of all the parishes in the diocese. But it is noticeable in Table 1.2 that our main research parish was in fact ranked thirteenth out of the 113 parishes in terms of small group participation. It can hardly be claimed, therefore, that our main research parish failed adequately to reflect parishes where RENEW had 'gone well'. Apart from St Matthew's parish, we also obtained some comparative data from six other parishes. The distribution of these parishes clearly does not support the view that we were biased in favour of reluctant parishes.

Fourthly, we suggest that the evidence we have given convincingly demonstrates that the official diocesan evaluation process at the end of each season was explicitly biased in favour of positive outcomes. Parish evaluators were instructed to encourage participants by emphasizing the strong points. In contrast, we have attempted to report the actual experiences of a wide range of both participants and non-participants, of both those who were involved at the diocesan level or in parish RENEW committees and small groups, and ordinary parishioners. We can reasonably claim, therefore, to have given a more complete account of the actual experience of RENEW than have our critics.

It goes without saying that they have invested a considerable commitment of time, effort, and emotional involvement in the RENEW programme. In this respect they are no different from any social group, especially those like community workers or those concerned to help others who have done their best for a client group. We do not doubt that at all. But like other committed workers, their personal involvement and optimism, so necessary for them to continue in a difficult task, are obstacles to any neutral critical assessment of their own work. This is a well-known factor in evaluation, and social scientists are prepared for pained reactions to any suggestion that hard work and dedication have not achieved intended ends. Therefore, we should not have been surprised at the strong reaction to a main finding of our study which was that a major variable in the promotion of different types of spiritualities is organizational power. Accusations of researcher bias, or of disloyalty to an organization to which one claims an allegiance, can be seen in part as resources used by the powerful to control the interpretation of research findings, in this case relating to the outcomes of pastoral programmes.

This leads us to address the question of our own loyalties and commitments. We believe that we have a vocation or 'calling' as social researchers. Following Weber we acknowledge 'the duty of searching for the truth . . . of bringing about self-clarification and a sense of responsibility . . . [and] the plain duty of intellectual integrity' (Weber, 1948: 146, 152, 155). We make no claims to be 'value-free'. We are committed to a 'dialectical' sociological approach which both recognizes that social actors are largely constrained in their actions by external constraints, earlier socializing processes, dominant cultural norms, and the like, but that they also, to a considerable extent, socially construct their own social reality through struggle. Thus we agree with Wallis and Bruce who observe that:

No-one will adequately explain social action who does not understand how individuals interpret their world. But no-one will understand how individuals interpret their world who is not aware of the social and historical context within which they do it. (1983: 109)

What we have offered in this study is our account, which we acknowledge is only one among many possible accounts, and which clearly differs from the accounts of a number of senior clergy. Nevertheless we have sought to be 'objective' in the sense that we have endeavoured to provide evidence for our interpretation throughout. We have attempted to do this systematically and in a way which has led us to conceptualize different types of spiritualities and so encourage both historical and comparative analysis of religious movements.

We believe that sociological propositions should be subject to empirical testing and the canons of measurement reliability (i.e. a concern to ensure that what we have recorded would also have been recorded by others), and validity (i.e. that what we have measured have been valid indicators of the concepts we have developed). We recognize that the task of the social researcher is often one of 'demythologization' and of challenging the accepted wisdom. We are committed to the goal of extending certifiable knowledge. In this particular study this means that we have been concerned not only to describe and interpret the RENEW experience in the Diocese of Downlands during the years in 1988–90 and its subsequent follow-up, but also to develop general propositions about renewal processes in mainstream religion and to indicate the significance of the power dimension and the question of who controls the paths taken by emergent spiritualities.

As is often the case, social research is often controversial and raises ethical issues which need to be addressed seriously (Homan, 1991). In particular there are problems with covert research and, in practice, with the principle of informed consent. We take the view that social institutions, such as the Catholic Church or the Diocese of Downlands or RENEW, do not necessarily have the same rights as individual actors in those institutions. In practice

Some form of compromise solution seems inevitable . . . as the researcher endeavours to balance his or her obligations to extend certified knowledge while at the same time respecting the rights of others. In seeking this balance the researcher has the ultimate responsibility of judging between the competing claims. He or she will have significant resources, not only of accounts of earlier researchers and the debates about their methods in the professional literature, but also a number of ethical codes or guidelines which are the product of decades of reflection by the research community. (Hornsby-Smith, 1993: 66).

The research reported in this book was conducted relatively openly. Very early in our study, in August 1988, we were advised by a priest of the diocese to 'be cunning as serpents' (Matthew 10 : 16) and use covert methods in order to gain access to and co-operation from informants. In the event, we decided that this would be un-ethical in circumstances where other methods were available, and unnecessary because the evaluation process built into the RENEW programme was an open invitation to use lay skills. When two of us joined the Evaluation Committee in St Matthew's parish, we explicitly indicated our interest as sociologists in researching RE-NEW. Similarly, each of our interviewees was also made aware of our research. In this sense we used overt methods. But it is inevit-able, in situations where participant observation is being under-taken, that not all participants are aware of the researcher's concerns. To this extent, the actions of the participants remain uncontaminated by researcher reactivity. We decided, however, to inform the bishop of our professional interest only when we had accumulated suffi-cient data and had resolved sufficient emergent research problems to be persuaded that we should proceed to produce a more scientific analysis than the in-built evaluation alone could possibly generate. At an intermediate stage in our research we showed some senior clergy copies of some of our conference papers, with the reaction we have noted above.

In the course of our research a number of matters were reported to us in confidence. In our judgement such matters often substan-tially supported the general thrust of our argument. We have not disclosed them because we promised our informants that we would not. Even where we have quoted directly from the diocesan news-paper, parish newsletters, or other public sources, or where a key informant had not requested anonymity, we have endeavoured to disguise the source as far as possible. On other occasions we have aimed to preserve anonymity by simply indicating the category of respondent or informant. All our interviewees gave us their informed consent and we have endeavoured to ensure appropriate levels of confidentiality and have protected the anonymity of informants, parishes, and the diocese by the use of pseudonyms throughout.

We decided to call this book *The Politics of Spirituality* because we wished to stress the salience of the hitherto under-researched question of the social control element entering into all spiritualities. Our first major criticism of RENEW was that it was a top-down process and was not designed to facilitate the emergence of an appropriate grass roots spirituality. Yet we are mindful of two observations made to us in the course of our study. Dean Hoge, the American sociologist, challenged us: 'If you were bishop, would you have adopted RENEW?' This is a fair question. A member of the diocesan RENEW team had no doubts at all: the diocese 'might have to wait for ever' (Interview, 21 Jan. 1991) for such an emergent spirituality. Fortunately for us, our vocation is not that of episcopal leadership but that of analysis. It is our sincere hope that our analysis might be helpful for the Church. Our second major criticism of RENEW was that it failed adequately to address the challenges of modernity and, in particular, to grapple with the task of identifying a social project appropriate for the needs of people at the end of the twentieth century. We are committed to such a project and offer our analysis as a contribution to its formulation.

Appendix 1

Coding Framework for Soft Data Analysis

Concepts grouped in six categories, each with seventeen subcategories.

Statements expressing preference for/orientation to traditional ideas (TS):

TS1 (A + C) Orientation to predetermined programme of change, defined tasks, RENEW programme takes precedence over other initiatives for Christian action.

'RENEW ... is a basic plan ... a primer ...'

'Nothing (other than RENEW activities) is to be set up unless it goes through the RENEW office.'

TS2 (A + C) Reliance on experts, in this study almost always clergy.

'pastoral needs ... these should be referred to the attention of the parish priest.'

'we are very reliant on our priests.'

TS3 (A + C) Hierarchical, bureaucratic procedures, delegation of tasks to selected personnel, Rome centred.

'This [RENEW] group is [to be] made up of the priest[s], the overall co-ordinator, and the chairpersons of the ten committees.'

'Select ... select and train ... persons to ...'

TS4 (A + C) Authority from above, loyalty to leaders, in this study almost always clerical.

'It is strongly recommended [by clerical authority] not to ...'

'If [x occurs] I'd stop it immediately.'

TS5 (C + D) Co-operation between participants and existing organizations assumed to be unproblematic e.g. organizations to be informed rather than invited to participate.

'Keep other Christian churches informed.'

'assume other organizations will work with ...'

TS6 (A + C) Clergy and leaders have duty to be responsible for others, sometimes justifying manipulatory actions.

'Ultimate responsibility rests with ...'

'It is the responsibility of ... to ...'

TS7 (C + D) Definition of 'rules' [moral, ethical, etc.] assumed to be unproblematic, 'obvious'.

'RENEW is about spiritual growth, not a discussion group.'

'Not intellectual . . . [but] concerned with spiritual development.'

TS8 (A + C) Resources (finance, materials, skills) administered from top of a pyramidal hierarchical structure.

'Select . . . distribute . . . materials [provided].'

TS9 (A + C) Edited, one-way communication or confidentiality, censorship.

'Receive reports . . .'

'Confidentiality is essential . . .'

TS10 (A + C) Benefits conferred by clergy, leaders, upon other participants.

'Welcome the group.'

'this will help them . . .'

TS11 (C + D) Maintenance of *status quo*, or gradualism.

'don't let's go flat out . . . just bumble along.'

'softly, softly . . .'

TS12 (A + C) Participant sphere of operation clearly, authoritatively defined.

'facilitator keeps focus of session on track . . . may need to go beyond group resources to gain answers . . .'

TS13 (C + D) Conflict suppressed, ignored.

'preplanning will avoid conflict . . .'

'mustn't give offence.'

TS14 (A + C) Evaluation to be conducted for the benefit of the diocese, RENEW organization.

'keep a record.' (coded both TS and MS)

TS15 (C + D) Private, individual piety/prayer, gradual spiritual growth.

'individual me-God relationship.'

'my Catholic compartment is personal and private.'

TS16 (C + D) Proselytism, conversion from other religions or none.

'bring people in to Church.'

TS17 (C + D) Apolitical charity, other-worldly orientation.

'RENEW a way to explore life through religion, not through political ideas.'

Statements expressing preference for/orientation to modern ideas (MS):

MS1 (B + D) Orientated to 'process', change resulting from participant decisions, not predetermined by powerful agencies, higher authorities.

'RENEW is truly a process . . . not a programme which begins and ends.'

MS2 (B + D) Confidence in 'all participants' ('all' includes clergy and laity).

'RENEW is for everybody at whatever stage they are at.'

'structures won't renew us, the people will.'

MS3 (B + D) Participation by all in deciding and executing policy.

'Core team not a task force but a growing cell, modelling for rest of parish.'

'Image of parish and church as hierarchical, pyramidal is not appropriate for RENEW.'

MS4 (B + D) Participants should negotiate authority and its limits.
  'Be prepared to offer some suggestions for future planning.'
  'If majority want it and (priest) doesn't, he must face it ...'
MS5 (B + D) Co-operation, particularly with existing organizations, but sometimes perceived to be problematic; ecumenical.
  'importance of ecumenism.'
  'imperfectly, we already experience a real unity [with fellow Christians].'
MS6 (B + D) Mutual responsibility of 'all', 'all' sinners, 'all' holy.
  'prepare the liturgy in liaison with the priest ... give special attention to ... the homily.'
  'no-one is solely responsible for what happens in any given session.'
  'we help each other to become Christians.'
MS7 (B + D) Definitions of ethical or moral 'rules' regarded as problematic, efforts to reinterpret.
  'change one's image of God from a God of power and threat.'
  'get to grips with what Vatican II is saying.'
MS8 (B + D) Resources, materials, finance, skills, raised by all, redistributed by mutual agreement.
  'encourage local creativity.'
  'people are to do tremendous things.'
MS9 (B + D) Undistorted, complete information, freely communicated amongst participants.
  'maintain good communication with (colleagues).'
MS10 (B + D) Mutual benefits expected/perceived to accrue to all participants.
  'clergy ... please join small groups—taste what could be.'
  'many benefits [from participation by clergy and laity].'
MS11 (A + B) Ideas challenge *status quo*, radical changes anticipated.
  'renew the face of the earth.'
  'things relevant for the new age.'
MS12 (B + D) Participants to negotiate spheres of operation.
  '[RENEW provides] a [new] function for the Church.'
  'opening to others depends on circumstances and leadings of Grace.'
MS13 (A + B) Conflict welcomed as a potential means of effecting change.
  'people are able to challenge each other without causing offence—leading to spiritual growth ...'
  'expect some opposition.'
MS14 (B + D) Evaluation to be conducted for the benefit of all participants.
  'Evaluate entire process and offer ... suggestions for adaptation or change.'
MS15 (A + B) Sense of community, active sharing in worship, prayer as fuel for mission, justice.
  '[RENEW has a] sense of mission and evangelism.'
  'the hope is to foster ... vibrant faith communities.'
MS16 (A + B) Open evangelism, personal witness, invitation, dialogue.
  'not just knocking on doors but screwing up courage to [gives examples].'

MS17 (A + B) Political, this-worldly orientation.
> 'suffered riots ... left people rattled, but got people saying perhaps [their views were] right ...'
> 'promote social justice action.'

Activities which help to further more traditional ideas (TA):

TA1 (A + C) Clear definition of aims, goals, detailed plans.
> '[committee] ... to select team of home visitors.'
> 'Prepare a card index ...'

TA2 (A + C) Competence demonstrated by leaders, reliance on leaders' advice.
> 'X is extremely efficient, the committee works hard.'
> 'Highly professional presentation by X at public meeting.'

TA3 (A + C) Efficient bureaucratic procedures, hierarchy, clear delegation of tasks to compliant participants, delegation accepted.
> 'after ... outline of process ... priests invited to reply to question ... should RENEW ... be offered to the parishes?'
> 'many tasks reported to have been undertaken in accordance with RENEW instructions ...'

TA4 (A + C) Affirmation of authority, acceptance of authority, loyalty stressed, authority defined or acknowledged.
> '[Leader] to ask Fr. X for permission.'
> '[Priest] will tell us what to do.'
> '[Programme] went forward on basis of affectionate loyalty to [Bishop].'

TA5 (C + D) Efficient, unproblematic, liaison with/information to existing organizations.
> 'all the parishes ... have used the diocesan formula.'
> 'X organized [an ecumenical meeting] ... took RENEW prayer cards and promised to pray for us.'

TA6 (A + C) Higher echelon accept, assume, responsibility, even if manipulative.
> 'core team undertake tasks [the responsibility of other committees] as they thought this too much for [others] to undertake ...'
> 'Fr. X thinks he can persuade ... use personal suasion [to participate] ...'

TA7 (C + D) Traditional 'rules' affirmed.
> 'it is necessary to go to personal confession before communion.'
> 'criteria for marriage in Catholic Church reaffirmed ...'

TA8 (A + C) Adequate resources efficiently distributed from above, financial benefits given.
> 'The meeting was mainly concerned with practical aspects of getting RENEW material to ...'
> '[debts] ... diocese is writing these off ...'

TA9 (A + C) Adequate, if incomplete, factual information flows up and down, confidentiality safeguarded.
> 'All this has to be in confidence ...'

TA10 (A + C) Expert advice given/accepted, benefits conferred by leaders/clergy/nuns.

> '[Nun]: My immediate reaction was to offer to record the Scripture reflections [for benefit of diocese]—no great effort as I worked a fair amount with recordings.'
> 'details of group dynamics and strategies were given [during RENEW training].'

TA11 (C + D) Expedient, step by step policy decisions, cumulative, not radical. (No examples.)

TA12 (A + C) Participants' spheres of influence, responsibilities, defined or limited authoritatively.

> 'The duties of this Committee are ...'
> 'Your role is ...'

TA13 (C + D) Conflict contained, unanimity affirmed.

> 'evangelical groups less potentially disturbing than lay theological interest.'
> 'X is most conciliatory.'
> 'kept our tongue and mind to ourselves.'

TA14 (A + C) Evaluation pursued for benefit of organization (e.g. RENEW, diocese).

> 'It's them evaluating us ... no help to parish ...'

TA15 (C + D) Activities include private individual/prayer/conversion, striving for spirituality.

> 'More communions, more confessions, reported [possibly more frequent, not necessarily more people involved].'
> 'Pray personally ...'

TA16 (C + D) Proselytizing, converting from other religions or none. (No examples.)

TA17 (C + D) Apolitical charitable activities, other-worldly orientation.

> 'helping other people by putting hand in pocket.'

Activities which help to further more modern ideas (MA):

MA1 (B + D) Clarification of 'process'—aims unspecific until participants decide them.

> 'Renewal is an ongoing process.'

MA2 (B + D) Commitment by individual participants, self-development and initiative encouraged.

> 'marvellous [members of] laity working out a different model of RENEW from that projected ...'
> 'shared preparation in advance.'

MA3 (B + D) High level of active (not passive) participation by many laity, shared responsibility for activities.

> 'Majority of laity really trying to breathe life into the structure.'

MA4 (B + D) Participants make decisions, propose new initiatives.

> 'Laity crying out for concrete action.'
> 'request for healing service.'

MA5 (B + D) If liaison with existing organizations incompatible with RENEW process, reasons clearly stated and understood; or liaison organized by participants.

'X explained why RENEW was not launched as an ecumenical effort (reasons clearly stated) . . .'

MA6 (B + D) Mutual responsibility affirmed.

'we [Nuns] took part in the small group faith sharing which we really appreciated.'

MA7 (B + D) Reinterpretation of 'rules', conventions questioned (rightly or wrongly).

'better not to perpetuate old practices.'

'not right to say children [of currently non-practising parents] not members of Church . . . problems of rejection.'

'contribution to break-up of rigid forms.'

MA8 (B + D) Adequate resources distributed according to mutual agreement amongst participants. (No examples.)

MA9 (B + D) Adequate, complete information freely exchanged, freely flowing in organization.

'[Parish] costs of RENEW [announced].'

MA10 (B + D) Expertise recruited from amongst lay participants to facilitate RENEW process.

No specific examples, lay experts generally selected rather than elected by peers.

MA11 (A + B) Conscious policy decisions made on basis of progressive ideas.

'Administrative structures growing . . . [to produce] . . . highly trained and motivated people.'

MA12 (B + D) Participants' spheres of influence, responsibilities, negotiated.

'How is this [existing activity] to be incorporated into RENEW?'

MA13 (A + B) Conflict used creatively.

'Call a spade a spade.'

'Fr. X really made people stop and think, was threatening.'

'Quite a lot of argument . . . peaceful conclusion.'

MA14 (B + D) Evaluation pursued for benefit of participants, action taken to further mutually agreed changes.

Some examples of both strengths and weaknesses reported in newsletters, though no action known to be taken at other than parish level.

MA15 (A + B) Activities promote sense of community, active sharing in worship, prayers as fuel for mission, justice, inner-directed striving for spirituality.

'Leeway for every kind of prayer, like prayerful meetings.'

'Prayer the foundation.'

'Those who came [to large group events] felt a greater sense of the parish family.'

MA16 (A + B) Open evangelism, personal witness, invitation, dialogue.

'I mentioned [contacts in churches], they know I think and act, if they want they can contact me.'

'Saying how you think in normal conversation, that's my idea of evangelization.'

MA17 (A + B) Political activity (other than shifting power relationships within Church).

'we invite those of our parish who hold the same views . . . to write to the Prime Minister . . .'

Activities and occasionally statements which hinder achievement of more traditional ideas (HT):

HT1 (A + C) Unsuccessful attempts to define tasks and goals, language obscure, fudges issues, or e.g. USA and not UK oriented.

'the fundamental purpose of RENEW is the personal metanoia of those taking part.'

'unclear, not really aims at all.'

'nebulous concepts . . . foreign language.'

HT2 (A + C) Leaders demonstrate incompetence.

'insufficient thought given to practicalities of doorstep calling.'

'(financing RENEW) I'm not sure about this . . . every year it's a colossal crisis . . . it's very loose.'

HT3 (A + C) Bureaucratic procedures omitted, disloyalty, private lobbying, manipulation, delegated tasks not completed.

'numerous examples of tasks not undertaken or completed . . .'

'it's the biggest committee—but nobody turns up.'

HT4 (A + C) Authority, including delegated authority, not legitimated.

'[Lay] authority is not recognized by either priests or laity.'

HT5 (C + D) Inept liaison with existing organizations.

'This will clash with [current ecumenical or other] programmes.'

'[Pre-RENEW, existing activity] now automatically called [RENEW activity].'

HT6 (A + C) Higher echelons neglect responsibilities.

'RENEW team not assisting in any inter-parochial administration.'

'RENEW team did not want to know [re other enquiries] . . .'

HT7 (C + D) Moral, ethical, 'rules' not confirmed by action, or broken. (No examples.)

HT8 (A + C) Inadequate resources, materials, skills, incompetent distribution.

'kindergarten stuff.'

'lack of preparation, naïvete [if not duplicity] about costs.'

'inadequate funds for materials, etc.'

'no one knows how much to order until . . . does not allow time . . . anticipating high response may be expensive, underestimating may wreck programme.'

HT9 (A + C) Inadequate, partial information amongst peers; lack of confidentiality downwards, or selective confidentiality amongst peers.

'Not a good idea, nobody thought it was going to cost individuals anything when it was voted for.'

'Communication absolutely appalling.'

HT10 (A + C) RENEW team/Leaders' advice resisted, disputed, ignored, neglected.

'Priests did not mention RENEW.'

'Following [RENEW] instructions produced disastrous results, threw away advice, did own thing.'

HT11 (C + D) Rapid changes disturb *status quo*, when gradual change planned or anticipated.

'Will alienate moderates, lead to drop in Mass attendance similar to drop in confessions in response to new form of reconciliation.'

'Lay role constitutes a threat . . .'

HT12 (A + C) Participants exceed boundaries of delegated tasks.

'[Determined questioner at public meeting addressed as] that [person described] . . . AGAIN?' [Questioner felt embarrassed]

'[Leader] was autocratic . . . against development of sharing in groups.'

HT13 (C + D) Conflicts of opinion expressed within organization, personalized conflicts.

'Divisions in some parishes . . .'

'Resent people who publicly parade piety, Holy Joes.'

HT14 (A + C) Evaluation for organizational purposes resisted, neglected, unbalanced evaluations (success only reported or subjective opinions offered).

'[RENEW team member] suggests use of random sampling [method described not random sampling, inferior, opportunistic].'

'No one else [apart from one independent 'very opinionated' commentator] has ever done a study.'

'Under great pressure from X to produce . . . favourable evaluation . . . not allowed to be independent.'

HT15 (C + D) Liturgical novelties imposed.

'What is the significance of that dead tree?'

'American razzmatazz, like selling soap powder.'

'Like a fairground.'

HT16 (C + D) Inept proselytism, inept attempts to convert from other religions.

'Knocking at doors can do harm, it cuts people off.'

'Some non-Catholic spouses are distressed.'

HT17 (C + D) Apolitical or charitable activities inadvertently politicized.

'They fear Season 3 . . . not ready to take (political) steps . . .'

Activities and occasionally statements which hinder achievement of more modern ideas (HM):

HM1 (B + D) RENEW process not fully, clearly understood/explained.

'Average parishioner will be heartily sick of RENEW if current muddle and uncertainties about aim of programme continue.'

'What's it [RENEW] supposed to do?'

HM2 (B + D) Lack of confidence in any participants demonstrated.
  'Some priests took exception to presence of laity.'
  'a lot of clerical rumblings against [lay initiatives].'
HM3 (B + D) Apathy, agreed tasks not fulfilled by any participants.
  'Lack of involvement by youth, men.'
  'Some do not want to be involved, have been put off.'
  'Some leaders decide to opt out, too time consuming.'
HM4 (B + D) No agreement on action amongst participants before it is
  initiated, imposed activities other than liturgical.
    'More stress on getting people to agree to do something rather than
      much discussion of what should be done.'
    'Like national curriculum, can't vote with feet, choose church where
      worshipper feels comfortable, only acquiesce reluctantly or aban-
      don practice.'
    'I'm here under false pretences; not my idea of what groups are for . . .
      I find this alarming.'
HM5 (B + D) Inept liaison with existing organizations.
    'non-Catholics should not have been invited to a Mass and told not
      to communicate.'
    'no agreement over sign-up days by adjoining parishes—people can
      avoid commitment by commuting.'
HM6 (B + D) Mutual responsibility ignored, usurped, or neglected.
  'X was away, I was left holding the baby [issue of some importance].'
HM7 (B + D) 'Rules' imposed, conventional norms assumed.
  'Some forms of behaviour establish who are the élite.'
HM8 (B + D) Inadequate resources, or handling or distribution imposed
  by authority.
    'If [another organization] could have had 5 or 10 per cent of the
      finance and attention [which RENEW had] the sky would have
      been the limit.'
    'Parishes are getting into debt through [RENEW] . . .'
    'overwork . . . fatigue . . . exhaustion . . .'
HM9 (B + D) Inadequate, partial, distorted information.
    'I was recorded as being [in a lay post] but didn't do anything at
      all.'
    'really a bit naughty . . . hadn't come clean.'
HM10 (B + D) Expert advice not available when requested; or imposed.
  'When asked, organizers would not clarify.'
HM11 (C + D) Agreed radical changes resisted, neglected.
  'Some people cross diocesan borders to avoid it.'
  'It's a joke, refuse to participate.'
HM12 (A + C) Inflexible tasks allocated or delegated without expected
  negotiated agreement.
    'Resent arm twisting, pressurizing . . . did feel coerced.'
    'If pressure is applied, it is justifiable to adopt stratagems which will
      make you inconspicuous; some priests are doing the same.'

HM13 (A + B) Repression of, or flight from, conflict. Conformity, unanimity imposed or stressed.

    'tried to let X off hook.'

    'wrote a letter, didn't send it.'

HM14 (B + D) Evaluation for participants' purposes resisted, neglected, unbalanced evaluations (success only reported or subjective opinions offered).

    Examples as for HT14, rarely clear which orientation.

HM15 (A + B) Agreed liturgical or other spiritual innovation resisted.

    'Why say "Good morning, Father" like crowd of schoolkids when Mass begins with an opening greeting?'

    'worried by general absolution.'

    'distracting lack of dignity and reverence.'

HM16 (A + B) Inept open evangelism, witness, invitation, dialogue.

    'Here they [Roman Catholics] are again in a little enclave.'

HM17 (A + B) Inept political activity.

    'Typically myopic American identification of communism and socialism.'

Appendix 2

Parishioner Questionnaire

Season Four of RENEW ended recently. The Parish Renew Team would be grateful if you would answer this questionnaire to help us look at progress and see if improvements can be made before Season Five in October. Please tick the appropriate boxes. We apologize again for interrupting Mass, but this is the most efficient way of collecting information for Renew.

1. Did you go to small group meetings?   Yes ☐ No ☐

2. Did you pray more than usual this season?   Yes ☐ No ☐

2a. Please tick the prayer commitments you fulfilled:

> Said Renew prayer daily?
> Prayed before the Blessed Sacrament weekly?
> Read and prayed over Scripture daily?
> Said Rosary daily?
> Said Rosary weekly?
> Offered a day of prayer and fasting?
> Attended a weekday Mass?
> Prayed as a family?
> Prayerfully prepared Sunday readings?

3. Did you read the daily scripture reflections?   Yes, daily ☐
         Yes, most days
         Yes, sometimes
         No

4. Was any one theme this Season especially memorable?

                                      Yes ☐ No ☐

If 'Yes', which theme was it? ....

what helped you to remember it? ....

5. Which of the following most helped you to take part more fully in the Mass during this Season (only one tick, please):

    The homily
    The rest of the congregation
    The singing
    The symbols
    The exchange of peace and friendship

6. Which two of the following things most helped you to take part in Renew this Season (only two ticks, please)?

    Belonging to a small group
    Attending Sunday Mass
    Attending other Masses
    The altar posters
    The scripture reading booklet
    The weekly take-home leaflets
    Attending a large group event

7. What aspect of RENEW made the greatest impact on you this Season?

8. Have you done anything different as a result of Season Four?

                                                    Yes ☐ No ☐

    If yes, what did you do?

9. When RENEW ends, would you like to:

    Build on the work in small group meetings?   Yes ☐ No ☐
    Strengthen the liturgy committee?   Yes ☐ No ☐
    Strengthen the work of social concern groups?   Yes ☐ No ☐
    Take part in another programme like Renew in
        a year or two?   Yes ☐ No ☐
    Any other suggestions—please explain?

10. If you did not take part in Renew this Season was this because you:

    Actively dislike the idea?
    Feel uncomfortable with 'sharing'?
    Think Renew is for the holy?
    Do not like the material supplied?
    Did not like the previous Seasons?
    Were simply not interested?
    Did not have time?
    Some other reason (please say why)

I am: Male   ☐   Aged 12–15 ☐   Married   ☐
         Female ☐   16–20 ☐   Single   ☐
                            21–35 ☐   Divorced or Separated ☐
                            36–50 ☐   Widowed   ☐
                            51–65 ☐
                            Over 65 ☐

And have pre-school age children   Yes ☐ No ☐

Appendix 3

Questionnaire for Small Group Members

Assessing Renew (Small Groups—Season 3) Members

To members of small groups: Will you please help us again this Season to examine the impact of RENEW and to try to improve our efforts? We have tried to simplify the form this time. Please circle round your replies.

1. How many RENEW small group meetings did you attend?

    1 .... 2 .... 3 ..... 4 .... 5 6

2. Did you belong to a small group in Season 2?   Yes .... No

    If yes, were people in your group in both Seasons:

    The same people .... Mostly the same .... Mostly different ......
    All different? ....

3. How good was the material provided for use?

    Very good .... Fairly good .... Not very good ....

    How did it compare with the material for last Season, if you attended?

    Better .... About the same .... Less good ....

4. Which TWO of the following things were most important to you personally this Season? (Please put a tick in two of the left hand boxes, below).

Two Most   Two Least

Two Most		Two Least
☐	.... Prayed more or better	☐
☐	.... More self-aware, confident, personal development	☐
☐	.... More awareness of worldwide community	☐
☐	.... Better communication with family, friends	☐
☐	.... Stimulated discussion	☐
☐	.... Made new friends	☐
☐	.... More interest in scripture	☐
☐	... Stimulated to take part in parish, or local community...	☐
☐	... More open to sharing feelings about faith with others...	☐
☐	.... Other, please explain	☐

(....)

5. Which two were least important to you? (Please put a cross against them in two of the right hand boxes, above.)

6. To which of the following would you like your group to pay more attention during next Season? (Put a tick in the box—you can tick more than one box, if you like).

    ☐ Prayer
    ☐ Personal and group spiritual growth
    ☐ Scripture reading
    ☐ Discussion
    ☐ Action, related to weekly themes, in the home
    ☐ Action, related to weekly themes, in the parish
    ☐ Action, related to weekly themes, in the wider community

7. Would you like to offer any other comment (overleaf if there is not enough room here)?

Appendix 4

Assessment of RENEW in Retrospect

Some Suggested Questions

I *Reasons for Taking Up RENEW*
 – What led you to think of RENEW in the first place?
 – Why did you choose it rather than develop your own diocesan programme?
 – What were your main goals and hopes in adopting RENEW?

II *The Experience of RENEW*
 – How committed to RENEW were your priests? lay people?
 – What were the main fruits of RENEW?
 – What disappointments were there?

III *Follow-Up After RENEW*
 – What provisions did you make for following up RENEW?
 – What long-term developments in your diocese originated in RENEW?
 – What elements of RENEW failed to take root and last after RENEW?

IV *Evaluation of RENEW*
 – What do you regard as the lasting advantages of RENEW? Would other programmes have had the same effect?
 – What disappointed you most about the RENEW experience?
 – What difference has RENEW made to the religious vitality of the people in your diocese?
 – How serious were the extra costs of RENEW? Was it worth it? If the same resources had been allocated in other ways, would they have had the same effect?
 – How many of the small faith-sharing groups continue in existence now?
 – What effect, if any, did RENEW have on Mass attendance rates in your diocese?
 – How many new parish leaders continue to be actively involved? Did lay leaders experience serious 'burn out'?
 – What 'social concern' initiatives can be attributed to RENEW? Can you give some examples?
 – How many more justice and peace groups are there now in your diocese as a result of RENEW? How effective are they? In what ways?
 – Have the Sunday/weekly offerings increased? And contributions to SCIAF/CAFOD?

- What evidence is there of a deeper faith? lay spirituality? self-confidence in faith-sharing? ecumenism? scripture reading/study? action-response? political commitment?
- In your own words and in retrospect, what lasting difference did RENEW make?
- If you had a chance to do it again, would you make the same decision to follow RENEW or would you develop your own programme?

THANK YOU VERY MUCH INDEED FOR ANY HELP YOU CAN GIVE US. PLEASE LET ME KNOW WHETHER I CAN QUOTE YOU OR WHETHER YOU WOULD PREFER YOUR RESPONSE TO BE ANONYMOUS

Bibliography

ABBOTT, W. M. (ed.) (1966), *The Documents of Vatican II*, London.

ARMSTRONG, R. (1971), 'Community Development and Community Organization: Allies or Rivals', *Community Development Journal*, 2 : 103–9.

BACHRACH, P., and BARATZ, M. S. (1970), *Power and Poverty: Theory and Practice*, Oxford.

BERGER, P. L. (1973), *The Social Reality of Religion*, Harmondsworth.

BIDDLE, W., and BIDDLE, L. J. (1965), *The Community Development Process: The Rediscovery of Local Initiative*, New York.

BURNS, T., and STALKER, G. M. (1966), *The Management of Innovation*, London.

BUTLER, C. (1981), *The Theology of Vatican II*, London.

CARY, L. J. (1970), *Community Development as a Process*, University of Missouri.

COLEMAN, J. S. (1957), *Community Conflict*, Glencoe, Ill.

CONGAR, Y. (1965), *Lay People in the Church: A Study For a Theology of Laity*, London.

CREEGAN, J. (1992), '"RENEW": A Pastoral Approach', *Intercom* (May 1992).

—— 'How Do We Renew Our People?' (1993), *Priests and People*, 7 : 134–137.

DENZIN, N. K. (1970), *The Research Act in Sociology: A Theoretical Introduction to Sociological Methods*, London.

Department for Christian Responsibility and Citizenship of the Bishops' Conference of England and Wales (1990), *Homelessness: A Fact and a Scandal*, London.

DOOHAN, L. (1984), *The Lay-Centered Church: Theology and Spirituality*, Minneapolis.

DULLES, A. (1976), *Models of the Church: A Critical Assessment of the Church in All Its Aspects*, Dublin.

EBAUGH, H. R. (1991), 'The Revitalization Movement in the Catholic Church: The Institutional Dilemma of Power', *Sociological Analysis*, 52 : 1–12.

EDGINTON, J. (1974), 'Society at Work: The Batley Battle', *New Society*, 29 : 622.

ETZIONI, A. (1961), *A Comparative Analysis of Complex Organizations: On Power, Involvement, and Their Correlates*, New York.

FIELDING, N. G., and FIELDING, J. L. (1986), *Linking Data*, Beverly Hills, Calif.

FIELDS, E. E. (1991), 'Understanding Activist Fundamentalism: Capitalist Crisis and the "Colonization of the Lifeworld"', *Sociological Analysis*, 52 : 175–190.

FREIRE, P. (1972), *Pedagogy of the Oppressed*, Harmondsworth.

FULTON, J. (1987), 'Religion as Politics in Gramsci', *Sociological Analysis*, 48 : 197–216.

—— (1991), *The Tragedy of Belief: Division, Politics, and Religion in Ireland*, Oxford.

GIDDENS, A. (1990), *The Consequences of Modernity*, Cambridge.

GLASER, B. G., and STRAUSS, A. L. (1973), *The Discovery of Grounded Theory: Strategies For Qualitative Research*, Chicago.

GURVITCH, G. (1971), *The Social Frameworks of Knowledge*, London.

GUSKIN, A. E. (1971), 'Advocacy and Democracy: The Long View', *American Journal of Orthopsychiatry*, 41.

GUTIERREZ, G. (1974), *A Theology of Liberation: History, Politics and Salvation*, London.

HANNIGAN, J. A. (1991), 'Social Movement Theory and the Sociology of Religion: Toward a New Synthesis', *Sociological Analysis*, 52 : 311–331.

HERVIEU-LÉGER, D. (1994), 'Religion, Memory and Catholic Identity: Young People in France and the "New Evangelization of Europe"' in *Religion and the New Europe*, eds. J. Fulton and P. Gee, Lampeter, 125–38.

HILL, M. J. (1972), 'Community Concepts and Applications', *New Community*, 1 : 279–88.

HOMAN, R. (1991), *The Ethics of Social Research*, London.

HOOKER, R., and SARGANT, J. (eds.) (n.d.), *Belonging to Britain: Christian Perspectives on Religion and Identity in a Plural Society*, London.

HORNSBY-SMITH, M. P. (1987), *Roman Catholics in England: Studies in Social Structure Since the Second World War*, Cambridge.

—— (1989), *The Changing Parish: A Study of Parishes, Priests, and Parishioners After Vatican II*, London.

—— (1991), *Roman Catholic Beliefs in England: Customary Catholicism and Transformations of Religious Authority*, Cambridge.

—— (1993), 'Gaining Access' in *Researching Social Life*, ed. N. Gilbert, London, 52–67.

—— and LEE, R. M. (1979), *Roman Catholic Opinion: A Study of Roman Catholics in England and Wales in the 1970s*, Guildford.

—— FULTON, J., and NORRIS, M. (1989), 'Assessing RENEW: A Study of a Renewal Movement in a Roman Catholic Diocese in England'. Paper read at the SISR Conference, Helsinki.

—— FULTON, J., and NORRIS, M. (1990), 'Renewing the Face of the Earth? RENEW in an English Diocese'. Paper read at the Conference on '25 Years After Vatican II', Washington, DC.

—— FULTON, J., and NORRIS, M. (1991), 'Assessing RENEW: A Study of a Renewal Movement in a Roman Catholic Diocese in England' in

Power in Religion: Decline and Growth, ed. P. Gee and J. Fulton, London, 101–14.

—— NORRIS, M., and FULTON, J. (1992), 'Revitalizing Mainstream Religion: A Study of the RENEW Process in an English Catholic Diocese'. Paper presented at the Urban Faith Conference, Helsinki.

INGLIS, T. (1987), *Moral Monopoly: The Catholic Church in Modern Irish Society*, Dublin.

JENKINS, J. C. (1983), 'Resource Mobilization Theory and the Study of Social Movements', *Annual Review of Sociology*, 9 : 527–53.

KELLY, J. R. (c1986), *A Study of the 'RENEW' Program and Some of Its Impacts: Report to the Lilly Endowment Inc.*, New York.

—— (1987), 'Does the RENEW Program Renew?', *America*, 156 (7 March 1987): 197–9.

KLEISSLER, T. A., LeBERT, M. A., and McGUINNESS, M. C. (1991), *Small Christian Communities: A Vision of Hope*, New York.

LEES, R. (1973), 'Action Research in Community Development', *Journal of Social Policy*, 2 : 239–48.

LUCKMANN, T. (1970), *The Invisible Religion: The Problem of Religion in Modern Society*, New York.

LUKES, S. (1974), *Power: A Radical View*, London.

McCARTHY, J. D., and ZALD, M. N. (1977), 'Resource Mobilization and Social Movements: A Partial Theory', *American Journal of Sociology*, 82 : 1212–41.

McGUIRE, M. B. (1982), *Pentecostal Catholics: Power, Charisma, and Order in a Religious Movement*, Philadelphia.

McLOUGHLIN, W. G. (1978), *Revivals, Awakenings, and Reform: An Essay on Religion and Social Change in America, 1607–1977*, Chicago.

McSWEENEY, B. (1980), *Roman Catholicism: The Search for Relevance*, Oxford.

MARTIN, C. (1982), *Leadership Book (RENEW)*, New York.

MARTIN, D. (1978), *A General Theory of Secularization*, Oxford.

MERTON, R. K. (1957), *Social Theory and Social Structure*, New York.

—— and KENDALL, P. L. (1956), *The Focused Interview*, Glencoe, Ill.

MILLER, S. M., and REIN, M. (1975), 'Community Participation: Past and Future' in *Community Work Two*, eds. D. Jones and M. Mayo, London, 3–23.

MOYNIHAN, D. P. (1969), *Maximum Feasible Misunderstanding*, New York.

National Office of RENEW (NOR) (1988), *RENEW: An Overview*, Mahwah, NJ.

NEITZ, M. J. (1987), *Charisma and Community: A Study of Religious Commitment Within Charismatic Renewal*, New Brunswick, NJ.

NORRIS, M. (1977), 'A Formula for Identifying Styles of Community Work', *Community Development Journal*, 12 : 22–9.

—— (1979), 'Offenders in Residential Communities: Measuring and Understanding Change', *Howard Journal*, 18 : 29–43.

—— (1981), 'Problems in the Analysis of Soft Data and Some Suggested Solutions', *Sociology*, 15 : 337–51.

—— (1982), 'Developing Communities—An Analysis of Failures and Successes During a Five Year Study of a Voluntary Organization', *International Journal of Therapeutic Communities*, 3 : 33–43.

—— HORNSBY-SMITH, M. P., and FULTON, J. (1995), 'Styles of Religious Renewal in an English Roman Catholic Diocese: Qualitative Data Analysis from a Community Development Perspective', Studies in English Catholicism No. 3, University of Surrey.

Pontifical Commission 'Iustitia et Pax' (1988), *What Have You Done To Your Homeless Brother? The Church and the Housing Problem*, London.

REIN, M., and MILLER, S. M. (1967), 'The Demonstration Project As a Strategy of Change' in *Organizing for Community Welfare*, ed. M. N. Zald, Chicago, 200–19.

ROSE, H., and HANMER, J. (1975), 'Community Participation and Social Change' in *Community Work Two*, eds. D. Jones and M. Mayo, London, 25–45.

ROSE, J. (1982), *Outbreaks: The Sociology of Collective Behavior*, New York.

SCHUTZ, A. (1962), 'Concept and Theory Formation in the Social Sciences', in *Collected Papers*, The Hague.

SCRIVEN, M. (1967), 'The Methodology of Evaluation' in *Perspectives of Curriculum Evaluation*, ed. R. W. Tyler, R. M. Gagne, and M. Scriven, Chicago, 39–83.

SELZNICK, P. (1966), *T.V.A. and the Grass Roots: A Study in the Sociology of Formal Organization*, New York.

SHELDRAKE, P. (1991), *Spirituality and History: Questions of Interpretation and Method*, London.

SMITH, C. (1991), *The Emergence of Liberation Theology: Radical Religion and Social Movement Theory*, Chicago.

STAPLETON, J. (ed.) (1990), *The Downlands Story: 1965–1990: The First Twenty Five Years*, Hove.

SUCHMAN, E. A. (1967), 'Principles and Practice of Evaluation Research' in *An Introduction to Social Research*, ed. D. Doby, New York, 327–51.

STOECKER, R. (1991), 'Evaluating and Rethinking the Case Study', *Sociological Review*, 39 : 88–112.

WALLACE, A. F. C. (1956), 'Revitalization Movements', *American Anthropology*, 58 : 264–81.

WALLIS, R., and BRUCE, S. (1983), 'Accounting for Action: Defending the Common Sense Heresy', *Sociology*, 17 : 97–111.

WALSH, M. (1989), *The Secret World of Opus Dei*, London.

WEBER, M. (1930), *The Protestant Ethic and the Spirit of Capitalism*, London.

—— (1948), 'Science as a Vocation' in *From Max Weber: Essays in Sociology*, ed. H. H. Gerth and C. W. Mills, London, 129–156.

—— (1968), *Economy and Society: An Outline of Interpretive Sociology*, New York.

Index